W9-CNQ-388

# Seven Roads to Hell

Don Burgett at age 19, taken in Mourmelon le Petit, France, after the Battle of Bastogne, his third campaign and third time wounded. He went on to fight many battles after this, all the way to Hitler's home in Berchtesgaden.

# Seven Roads to Hell

## A Screaming Eagle at Bastogne

Donald R. Burgett

★

PRESIDIO

Copyright © 1999 by Donald R. Burgett

Published by Presidio Press
505 B San Marin Drive, Suite 300
Novato, CA 94945-1340

**Library of Congress Cataloging-in-Publication Data**

Burgett, Donald R. (Donald Robert), 1925–
   Seven roads to hell / by Donald R. Burgett.
      p.    cm.
   ISBN 0-89141-680-3
   1. Burgett, Donald R. (Donald Robert), 1925– . 2. Ardennes, Battle of the, 1944–1945. 3. United States. Army. Airborne Division, 101st—History. 4. World War, 1939–1945—Personal narratives, American. 5. United States. Army—Biography. 6. Soldiers—United States—Biography. I. Title.
D756.5.A7B87   1999
940.54'21431—dc21            98-51693
                             CIP

Printed in the United States of America

*To all who served in all wars the world over in the cause of freedom. May those who survived honor those who did not by keeping the freedom they earned for our children and all generations to come. God bless and keep Renée Lemaire, the young Belgian nurse who lost her life while attempting to save wounded Americans in this Battle for Bastogne.*

# Contents

# Preface

It would be my fondest wish if, in writing this, I could name every paratrooper in the 101st Airborne Division by name and his acts of courage, but that is not feasible. I therefore offer an introduction to and a brief synopsis of the 101st Airborne Division's operations prior to the Battle of the Bulge, then go straight into describing combat as I and the men closest to me saw it.

Among the men who served with me in Company A, 506th Parachute Infantry Regiment, were Sherwood Trotter, one of the most fearless men I have ever known; Henry Boyd, a man among men; John, Joe, and Bob Powers, two brothers and their first cousin, all of whom were leaders; and Bob and Ray Teeter, identical twin brothers. They were joined by Amos West; Bill Rary, Justo Correa, Red Knight, Slick Hoenscheidt, Paul Carter, Speedy Snelgrove, and Prentice Hundley—to name only a few. All of these men were among the first to rise up and run forward in an attack. They were the backbone of the outfit, they were the leaders, they set the standards we all followed, which paratroopers the world over attempt to emulate today. I have never considered myself a leader, but I never hesitated to go where ordered and do whatever was required of me.

We were joined in the battle for Bastogne by men of the 9th and 10th Armored Divisions, the 609th and 705th Tank Destroyer Battalions, the 969th Field Artillery Battalion, and others who gave their all in that battle—including a rag-tag collection of stragglers, office workers, cooks, mechanics, truck drivers, and engineers who became known as "Team Snafu" (for Situation Normal All Fucked Up) and were gathered together in the center of Bastogne to be used in a last-ditch stand, if it came to that. Fortunately, they weren't needed in that role. Although the members of Team Snafu experienced artillery shellings and bombings within Bastogne's city limits, they were spared from frontline, one-on-one combat.

Please keep in mind that what you read in these pages is an account of what I and the men closest to me experienced during that fateful December of 1944. Multiply our experiences and actions by the fourteen thousand or so men in the 101st Airborne Division and you will have a better appreciation for what we, the defenders of Bastogne, the centerpiece and grand prize in the climactic Battle of the Bulge, went through.

Add to the sum of our collective experience that of the men in the twenty or more Allied divisions that eventually took part in the campaign, plus the men in our Air Corps, and then factor in the more than thirty-eight German divisions involved (nine of which were assigned solely to seizing Bastogne), and top it off with the large civilian population in the region. Only then will you begin to comprehend the enormity of the slaughter and destruction of the Battle of the Bulge. By way of comparison, the Battle of the Bulge covered more territory and involved more military personnel on both sides, plus civilians, than did the celebrated Battle of Stalingrad.

Raging within the Battle of the Bulge was our battle for Bastogne. It was a battle that centered on a small American force defending a fourteen-mile perimeter around the city of Bastogne with its all-important road network. The American troops there were completely surrounded by a sea of hostile, heavily armored German forces. This garrison consisted solely of the American 101st Airborne Division and the aforementioned meager battalions and platoons of American armored and artillery units. Together, "We Stood Alone."

It is of these defenders of the city of Bastogne—the "Battle-Battered Bastards of Bastogne"—that I write. At the onset, when others abandoned the front, we stood voluntarily in defense of Bastogne, just as our forefathers did at Bunker Hill and the Alamo. We stood against overwhelming enemy manpower, firepower, and armor—and we held.

I wrote this account shortly after World War II while it was still fresh in my mind. Then I set it aside in a cardboard box, where it remained until just recently. It is not the time-fogged memories of an old paratrooper, but rather the recollections of a young man just home from the war transferred to crisp, clean paper from the time-yellowed pages on which he first recorded them.

The 101st Airborne Division and Bastogne are synonymous, inseparable. History records that Bastogne was fought for and won by the 101st. I am very proud of this fact and bask in the credit bestowed upon us for our role in this battle of battles. But in telling history as I witnessed it, I want to make sure a rightful share of the honor and credit goes to those brave men who fought alongside us. Those who read this account will learn about the important role played by Maj. William R. Desobry and his collection of tanks and armored infantrymen from the 10th Armored Division, who absorbed the enemy's initial onslaught at Noville on the morning of 19 December 1944. Desobry and his men denied the massed German armor a free pass down the Houffalize road into the city of Bastogne. Their brave action allowed the 101st the precious hours it needed to get into battle position.

On entering Bastogne, the "Screaming Eagle" Division did not hesitate but immediately went into the attack, pushing outward on all sides, turning the war back onto the Nazi aggressors. Small elements of the 9th and 10th Armored Divisions, the 609th and 705th Tank Destroyer Battalions, and the 969th Field Artillery Battalion fought unwaveringly alongside the 101st from the first day to the last. It would have been all but impossible, even for an airborne division, to fight and win with M1 rifles against the German panzers, the finest armor in the world at that time. The battle at Arnhem in Holland proved that. The armored units mentioned above, our tenacious and dauntless comrades in arms, met their enemy counterparts not one-on-one but one against nine and held, while we in the 101st Airborne Division also met our counterparts one against nine and held.

Ragged, cold, hungry, battered, low on ammunition and short of weapons, the men of the 101st Airborne Division held as ordered. We held the enemy at bay until the rest of our forces and our British allies could rally themselves, reorganize, and come join our fight. We were never rescued, as some claim. We held as ordered, one against nine, until our forces could gather themselves to enter the fray.

Lieutenant Colonel Creighton W. Abrams, commander of the 37th Tank Battalion in Gen. George S. Patton Jr.'s spearhead 4th Armored Division, led his men in a fierce battle to break through the German forces surrounding us at Bastogne. They cleared the way for other units and for needed replacements, ammo, food, and clothing to be brought to us in our besieged city. Later, Lieutenant Colonel Abrams was rightfully promoted to general as proof of his combat capabilities and inspiring leadership. The formidable Abrams tank today bears his name.

Once rearmed, we in the 101st Airborne Division continued in the attack for twenty-two additional continuous days and nights, until the Germans were beaten back and our lines restored. Only then did we march out on our own.

I am proud to have served in combat with such heroic men as my brother paratroopers and the armored and artillery soldiers who shared our ordeal at Bastogne.

May all those who died in battle for world peace rest forever in honor.

Donald R. Burgett
2d Squad, 2d Platoon, Company A,
1st Battalion, 506th Parachute Infantry Regiment,
101st Airborne Division, 1943–1946

# Acknowledgments

My heartfelt thanks and love to my wife, Twyla, for standing by my side, giving love, comfort, and encouragement when I really needed it these past forty-five years. Thanks to my sons, Kenneth, Mark, Gary and Jeffrey, and to my daughter, René, for never losing their love or their faith in me.

I would also like to thank Mark Bando, military historian, writer, and a friend of many years for his knowledgeable support, and for just being a friend. Thanks to Jeff Reed, who was there when I needed help with the electronic maze and bewilderment of my computer, to fellow paratrooper, Edward Beneke, for the many photographs he took while in combat, some of which he allowed me to use in this book. To Richard Winters, captain, paratrooper, who took the extraordinary combat photo of the historic church in Noville, Belgium. To Zemper Studios for their time and extra effort in reproducing those time worn photographs within these pages. To Maj. Dale Wilson, ret., for the fine tuned editing of my manuscript. To the publisher, Presidio Press, for accepting the challenge. And last, but not least, to Rhonda Winchell, my agent, for her tireless and successful efforts in placing *Seven Roads to Hell.*

# 1 Breakthrough

Combat. We were going back into combat. The realization hit us like an 88mm shell slamming into our midst. We had only recently been relieved from action in Holland. Now we were going back in again—no advance notice, no time to get ready, no marshaling areas, no sand tables, no map reconnaissance, no briefings, nothing. Just saddle up and go. We were ordered to grab our weapons and head out into the dark of night, straight back into combat.

Less than three weeks earlier, on 28 November 1944, we were pulled out of Holland after seventy-two days of bitter, behind the lines fighting. Then, on 17 December, we got the word we were going in again.

We needed more rest. We needed new weapons issued and old, worn-out weapons repaired. We needed troop replacements. We needed clothing, boots, and medical treatment. There wasn't a man among us who didn't have old and new wounds, old and new scars. Most men had trench foot, some had trench mouth, and some had scabies, lice, or whatever.

I had had trench mouth so bad that puss oozed from my gums. My teeth became so loose that I could move them freely with my tongue, and blood would run out of my mouth from the light pressure of the razor when I shaved. Penicillin had all but cured that malady, but my teeth were still not totally firm.

Most scabies cases cleared up with benzol benzoate treatments. Scabies are contagious little critters that take up residence under your skin—tunneling, feeding, and reproducing there. Their tunneling causes an insatiable itch until they are killed by medication.

1

We sprinkled DDT powder liberally on our bare bodies and in our clothing to get rid of other unwanted vermin.

We were coming around, but what we needed more than anything else was plain and simple rest. We needed time away from killing and the smells of the battlefield: the smells of gunpowder, of the freshly killed, of raw iron in fresh blood, and of burnt human flesh. We needed to be free of the sweet, sickly smell of death and the sight of green flies laying maggots in the open mouths and gaping wounds of the rotting dead. We needed time to heal—but that was not to be.

On the night of 5–6 June 1944 we had flown through a fiery, tracer-laced, flak-torn sky as the spearhead of the Normandy invasion. Our plane was in the point of that spearhead and we were among the first Allied troops to land on D day. My stick parachuted from its C-47 at 1:14 in the morning to pave the way for the beach landings that began more than five hours later. We fought hellacious battles there, suffering a high casualty toll—both killed and wounded—among the hedgerows and in the villages, towns, and cities of coastal France. Paratroopers did not die quietly or easily. They died violently, bringing the war to the enemy on his own ground. The Germans learned about American paratroopers the hard way in that campaign. We killed them in great numbers, and they began to call us "the butchers with big pockets"—referring to our skill in combat and to our jumpsuits with oversized pockets.

We returned to England after the invasion, welcomed back our wounded who had recovered, and received replacements for those who would never return.

We had barely begun fitting replacements into the vacancies left by our casualties and training them to our way of fighting, when we again found ourselves in marshaling areas being briefed on a new mission. We were to spearhead another invasion, this time into the Netherlands.

Operation Market-Garden was the brainchild of British Field Marshal Bernard Law Montgomery. It was to be a carefully coordinated airborne/land attack designed to skirt around the end of the Siegfried Line, drive straight through Germany's industrial heart, the Ruhr Valley, and then on to Berlin. Field Marshal Montgomery was sure his plan would bring the war in Europe to an end in a matter of weeks.

Operation Market, the largest airborne assault in history, was to be executed by the First Allied Airborne Army, made up of the American 101st and 82d Airborne Divisions, the British 1st Parachute Division, and Poland's 1st Parachute Brigade. We were issued a shoulder patch identifying us as members of the First Allied Airborne Army with instructions to sew it on the right shoulder of our jumpsuits above the American flag we wore there. Many troopers refused to wear the new patch because of the strong loyalty they felt for the 101st Airborne Division and its "Screaming Eagle" patch. A few of them did sew the patch on, but they put it *below* the American flag.

The plan called for the newly formed First Allied Airborne Army to parachute into Holland and seize and hold bridges over the Wilhelmina and Willems Canals and the Dommel, Maas, Waal, and Rhine Rivers. The ground operation, code-named Garden, called for the British XXX Corps to break through the German line on the Dutch border and race forward to link up with the paratroopers holding the bridges, cross the Rhine, and then push straight on to Berlin.

It didn't work out that way.

Field Marshal Montgomery ordered the airborne divisions into action even though he knew in advance that they would be facing a formidable foe beyond their ability to subdue. Thanks to up-to-date intelligence reports and aerial reconnaissance photos, Montgomery was aware that the enemy had just pulled crack, battle-tested, elite SS panzer (armored) units outfitted with the newest, finest armor in the world into the Arnhem area. Operation Market-Garden, knowingly doomed to failure before it began, should have been aborted.

For seventy-two days and nights we fought constant battles pitting man against man and man against armor. The fighting raged all the way from our drop zone (DZ) in Zon to Eindhoven, up "Hell's Highway" through Veghel, Grave, and other towns to Nijmegen on the Waal River, where the 82d Airborne Division captured the bridge intact after a very bitter and costly battle. We fought our way from Nijmegen to Opheusden, located on a strip of land between the Waal and Lower Rhine Rivers known as "The Island," before finally moving into positions across from Arnhem. There, British paratroopers armed with little more than small arms and guts lost out to crack Nazi SS armor and SS panzer grenadiers.

Major General Maxwell D. Taylor and Brig. Gen. James M. Gavin, commanders of the 101st and 82d Airborne Divisions respectively, asked the British for permission to lead our two divisions across the river, kick German ass, and bring what was left of the British 1st Parachute Division back. Their requests were denied. The British paratroopers, who originally had been expected to hold the north end of their bridge for only two days, until their armor and ground troops could link up with and relieve them, were abandoned to their fate. The British armor and infantry finally arrived—eight days late—and set up static defensive positions on ground we Americans had liberated. Our British brother paratroopers were needlessly left to be slaughtered.

The Polish 1st Parachute Brigade, which jumped in at a later date, was ambushed while descending on its DZ. Germans waiting on the drop zone had a turkey shoot, killing and wounding nearly every Polish paratrooper. The Poles didn't stand a chance. Most of them were hit by small-arms fire before they reached the ground. Those not hit in the air were shot while trying to free themselves from their chutes on the DZ. The very few who made it off the DZ alive did so as prisoners of war. That ambush and slaughter was made possible because a map case containing detailed maps, charts, plans, schedules, and code names fell into German hands the day of the invasion when an English glider crashed, killing all of its occupants on impact.

It was a sad turn in the fortunes of war for the Allies. Why was such a detailed and complete package of the whole operation trusted to one map case and placed in a glider that was slated to land behind enemy lines? Airborne operations are risky enough without taking a chance on the entire operations plan falling into enemy hands. That mistake was paid for with Polish blood.

Operation Market-Garden was a dismal and costly failure, wasting many lives and much equipment and time. Airborne forces were originally designed to be used as a shock force, capturing and holding strategic targets for no more than a couple of days until they could be relieved by friendly ground troops. They were then to be pulled out, rested, refitted, rearmed, and made ready for another operation.

Because they were "bastard outfits" (the military term for a unit not permanently assigned or attached to a higher field headquarters), the airborne divisions could be assigned to any command that needed their expertise. So it was that the 101st and 82d Airborne Divisions became part of the First Allied Airborne Army and fell under Field Marshal Montgomery's operational control. "Monty" wore out both divisions in Holland before letting them go. The 82d was relieved from combat duty and sent to France two weeks before we were released from British control.

We had been used in the heaviest fighting as shock troops for Monty's XXX Corps. Boots stayed soggy on our feet and trench foot prevailed. Our jumpsuits were filthy, ragged, and torn. We didn't have a real bath in all the seventy-two days we were in action. The best we could do was take a very occasional "whore's bath"— washing our faces, armpits, and crotches with cold water from our helmets.

Our numbers were methodically decimated by battle. In the end, fewer than fifty of the two hundred–plus men who went into action with my unit—A Company, 506th Parachute Infantry Regiment (PIR)—remained. Second Platoon could muster just seventeen men in three squads of five men each, including the squad leader. Near the end of that campaign, we were led by Lt. Pat Sweeny, our platoon leader, and Sgt. Ted Vetland, our platoon sergeant. Normally we had four twelve-man rifle squads, plus a mortar squad, a machine-gun squad, some bazooka men, and the platoon headquarters. All together, 2d Platoon was barely more than a reinforced squad.

The First Allied Airborne Army's commander, Lt. Gen. Lewis H. Brereton, petitioned Field Marshal Montgomery for our release several times. However, his pleas fell on deaf ears. Finally, Gen. Dwight D. Eisenhower, the Supreme Allied Commander in Europe, issued "Monty" a direct order to release us posthaste. We were finally relieved by bagpipe-playing Scots, who strode noisily down the roads to our positions on 27 November. The 101st Airborne Division was transported that same day by Canadian trucks to a large monastery in the rear, where we had our first shower in nearly two and a half months. The next day we climbed aboard English lorries for the thirty-six-hour trip to Mourmelon-le-Grand, France.

Mourmelon-le-Grand was an ancient French town with houses and buildings haphazardly gathered and jumbled together, interlaced with narrow, spiderweb streets in an area that had been a battleground since man first took up weapon against man. Julius Caesar campaigned and bivouacked his legions there in 54 B.C. Countless other armies followed, camping and fighting throughout the region over the centuries. The region's history was steeped in battles. Warriors from the various armies passing through the area had been breeding with the local femmes for centuries, creating a potpourri of humanity. Eroded trenches and shell holes still scarred the old battlegrounds of Château-Thierry, the Argonne Forest, Saint-Mihiel, and Belleau Wood, where World War I had raged in all its fury.

Our barracks, located outside of town, were of a style that one associates with the French Foreign Legion out on some lonely desert outpost. The battle-scared stucco walls were pocked with occasional shell holes, and the concrete floors were cold and damp. The French occupied the barracks during and after World War I. They gave way to the Germans, who thundered across France with their blitzkrieg (lightning war) in June 1940. German panzer units occupied them until Americans liberated the area after the Normandy breakout. American troops were then rotated through, all of them moving on as the war ground inexorably eastward. Now it was our turn. This was to be our home during our R and R (rest and relaxation). We used the time to integrate troop replacements into our platoons and squads and to exchange our clothing and equipment. The goal was to be back to full strength and fully equipped when called on again for another mission.

One rainy day during a practice field problem I was digging a foxhole in one of the old abandoned trenches. My entrenching tool struck metal, and I dug up a rusty old French helmet with holes in the front and back through which a bullet had passed. I turned that rusted relic over and over, examining it inside and out. I thought of its previous owner. Was he a young man? Or was he an older man? Had he been drafted or did he volunteer? Had his body been transported back to a cemetery, or was he buried deeper in the trench? In those days it was customary to bury the dead under the floorboards and in the walls of the trenches. I wondered how many dead men might still be entombed in these abandoned trenches.

It was now December 1944. It was cold, damp, overcast, and foreboding. There was no cheery fire to warm us at night. There was only a single tiny, inadequate, coal-burning stove at one end of the barracks near the latrine. Our bunk beds were made of hastily nailed-together two-by-fours, which many times in the dead of night fell through or split apart, spilling startled troopers onto the cold concrete floor. Our mattresses were straw-filled cloth sacks. The straw, supplied by local French farmers, was amply laced with burdock and thistle. There was no comfort in this place, only misery. While we were there two 101st GIs, both veterans of Normandy and Holland, committed suicide, blowing out their brains with pistols. Our one ray of hope was in the knowledge that it was the holiday season. We had just celebrated the Thanksgiving dinner that we'd missed during the fighting in Holland, and Christmas was just around the corner. Every day, men went to mail call hoping for packages filled with goodies from home.

I usually received my share of mail, as did most of the other men, but there were a few troopers who received nothing at all. Time after time I would see these same men at mail call, standing at the outer fringes of the group, looking, listening, waiting, eyeing each letter as a name was called and the letter was passed back from hand to hand to the recipient. But these few troopers, good men all, never received a letter.

I knew one of those men pretty well and asked him one day if he ever received any mail. "Nope," he replied.

"Then why do you come to each mail call?" I asked.

"I don't know. It's just that someday, maybe . . ." His voice trailed away and he walked off with his hands in his pockets.

We had seen hard combat in Holland and we were tired. We also suffered from many physical maladies. During our extended stay in the rain-soaked, sodden lowlands many men developed severe cases of trench foot and other diseases. Many had cuts, sprains, minor wounds, and other injuries that weren't sufficient to justify a stay in the hospital but still hurt and were endured quietly by the troopers now in garrison. Some of our wounded had returned to us from hospitals with shrapnel and bullet scars still fresh on their bodies. Many weapons had been lost or destroyed in battle, and the ones we had left on hand were in a sad state of disrepair. Some troopers were without a weapon of any kind. Now, in this condition, we were being called on to go into combat again.

"We're goin' amongst 'em!" was how we put it. Even while in combat, as we prepared to make an attack, troopers repeated these phrases like mantras: "Yep, we're goin' amongst 'em. . . . We're gonna stack bodies. . . . Every time you pull the trigger, there's gotta be meat on the table."

This time it began just after some of the "old men" returned from a forty-eight-hour pass to Paris. They weren't old men in a physical sense; they earned the title out of deference to their seniority. They were the men who had been with the outfit the longest and had seen combat in our two missions. At the age of nineteen, I was one of the old men who had survived both operations, and I was one of those who had just returned from two days of hell raising in that wonderful French city. We sat or lay on our bunks in a small, huddled group near the center of the barracks, talking. A single bare electric bulb burned overhead, casting long shadows outside our little sphere of light. Most of the men had gone to bed to sleep, but we were young men who had just tasted life's wildest revelry in a city known throughout the world for its wine, women, and totally unrestricted love. We had tales to tell. Tomorrow, with its work details, drills, and drudgery could wait. We would suffer through it. But tonight we were alive. We had survived two major campaigns and we were alive. We had blitzed the city of London and drunk and brawled our way through Reims and Paris, and we were alive.

In forty-eight hours we had tried to drink Paris dry and make every pretty girl we saw. And the more we drank, the prettier they got. After a time there were no ugly girls, just a whole city filled with rare and willing beauties. We'd all had at least three months' back pay when we hit Paris. That was how long we had been in the marshaling area and in combat, and they had paid us in full when we got back to France. It's surprising just how fast one can go through three months' back pay when you're nineteen years old, in Paris, and fresh from seventy-two days of combat behind enemy lines.

I was sitting next to Siber Speer, one of my best buddies, along with Harold Phillips, Leonard Benson, Don Liddle, and John Bielski. I first met Speer in England, just after our return from Normandy. Speer was one of the replacements sent to fill in for our wounded and dead D-day comrades. I didn't like him when I first saw him. He was too short, he was too friendly, and he was homely. In fact, I remember wondering how a guy like him ever made it into the paratroops in the first place.

As time went by I found myself on work details with Speer. He never complained about work details, something that is not only every GI's right but duty. He was all too willing to do every task assigned to him. And he did it well. He was surprisingly muscular, and he did more than his share on any detail or chore to which he was assigned.

I made it clear to Speer on several occasions that I didn't care for him and would rather he was someplace else. He was always too willing to work. His heavy-featured face was deeply lined and tanned, and he had a big nose. But after studying him for a while I could see that if his nose were any smaller his face would be out of balance.

Speer never snuck out of camp with us to go to the Blue Boar or the Crown and drink up all the rationed English beer instead of work. But as time went on he kind of grew on me. He wasn't as bad looking as I'd first thought. In fact, he wasn't bad looking at all. In time, thanks to his good nature and forgiving ways, we became the best of friends—almost like brothers.

Phillips, who had been my good friend since before the Normandy invasion, was a little older than I. We were nearly identical in weight and build. He was Pennsylvania Dutch—blond, blue-eyed, and more than just a little superstitious. He told of good luck symbols and such painted on the outer walls of homes and barns back in Pennsylvania, and related stories of how those symbols had actually warded off evil and illness and worked to bring good fortune and health to the home or farm owner.

Bielski, another close buddy who came to us as a replacement after Normandy, was the same height as Phillips and me but stocky, broad, and heavier, with strong Polish features and fingers the size of small bananas. He had a joking answer for nearly every statement or situation. At times he would screw up his face, droop one eyelid, and act like a person who didn't quite have full command of his faculties.

Benson shipped over from the states aboard the *Empire Anvil* with Phillips, Jack Bram, me, and many other troopers. The *Empire Anvil* was a U.S.-built Liberty ship on lend-lease to England making its maiden voyage. We docked in Belfast, Ireland, after our eleven-day Atlantic crossing via Newfoundland. After a short stay at the Clandibouy estate, we moved on to England by way of Scotland. Our small group joined the 101st Airborne Division in Auldbourne, England, in the last part of February 1944 to help beef up that division for the Normandy invasion. We were placed in squads and platoons in A Company, 506th PIR. I ended up in the 2d Squad of 2d Platoon with Phillips, Benson, and Connie Bridges. Others were shotgunned throughout the company and the division.

Connie Bridges was built about the same as Phillips and me. He was from South Carolina and lacked a formal education. I used to write letters to his family and read his incoming mail aloud for him. He was nervous most of the time, and made more of a fuss about jumping from planes than did the rest of us. Connie Bridges was injured badly enough during our fighting in Normandy that he never returned to the outfit.

Benson was a little shorter than I and a lot slimmer. I don't believe he weighed more than 130 pounds, and he probably weighed a little less. He was dark-complected and had dark-brown eyes and straight, black hair. He was always keenly watching others and what was going on around him. He was mentally sharp and an avid craps player who won most of the time.

Then there was Donald B. Liddle (pronounced Le Dell), a Mormon from Myton, Utah. Liddle was one of the very first paratroopers in the U.S. Army. Known as the "Originals," they formed the nucleus of the 101st and 82d Airborne Divisions when they were activated at Camp Claiborne, Louisiana, back in 1942. He was a rock, a man seemingly without a nerve in his body. In Normandy I saw Liddle caring for wounded in the open with artillery and mortar shells bursting all around while others crouched in their holes. We called to him to take cover but he wouldn't even look up. He just kept at his grim work and shouted, "I'll take care of myself. You just take care of yourself."

Liddle was also about my height but more powerfully built. He was quiet and more of a loner than the rest of us. He had a large, square jaw; a straight, sharp nose; icy blue eyes that seemed to see right through a man; and short, curly hair that was thinning on top. A large burn scar showed around his lower neck when he wore an open collar. I never asked him what caused it, and he never told me. When he smiled, he showed what seemed to be about a yard of straight, white teeth. I felt a special closeness with Don, and he accepted me as a friend—at times confiding in me some of his innermost thoughts. Liddle never allowed anyone else to become a buddy or to get too close.

I turned nineteen just before the Normandy campaign. I was five feet nine inches tall, weighed in at 140 pounds without clothes, and had dark-brown hair and blue eyes. I hailed from Detroit, Michigan—born near the foot of the Ambassador Bridge, which spans the Detroit River between Detroit and Windsor, Canada. I quit Mackenzie High School in the tenth grade to join the army paratroops. They wouldn't take me because I was too young, so I worked as a carpenter and signed up again the day I turned eighteen in April 1943. It was a tough ordeal, but I was determined to make it and did.

My parents were originally from Alabama. They escaped from the slave-like conditions of the coal-mining camps in that state shortly after World War I to make a new start in a more prosperous north. It was the brave act of a young couple, for which I am eternally grateful. My father, after working at Ford Motor Company and in the shipyards, joined the Detroit Police Department in 1924. He retired after serving twenty-five years in the city's "Black Bottoms," one of the roughest neighborhoods in America.

I grew up during the Depression, when nearly everyone was poor. My father would regale us with the stories of John Dillinger, "Pretty Boy" Floyd, "Machine Gun" Kelly, Ma Barker, the Purple Gang, and other notorious gangsters. He also told us all about bootlegging during the era of Prohibition. Dad did not try to stop me from joining up. He was a firm believer in the idea that each man should do what he felt he had to do.

I was wounded twice on 13 June in Normandy during a bayonet attack in what we came to call "The Battle of Bloody Gulch." The 4th Infantry Division, which landed on Utah Beach on D day, had passed through our lines and relieved us so that we could return to England and get ready for another mission. The 4th Division then tried to break through a well-entrenched enemy just outside Carentan, a major city that we had just liberated. After the 4th Division's fourth unsuccessful try, we were ordered to take that ground.

We were successful but we paid a heavy, bloody price for that victory. A lot of our comrades were killed or wounded taking that small valley from the enemy. We had crawled on hands and knees to the edge of the hedgerow that the enemy was entrenched behind. We fixed bayonets and then, on command, charged headlong over the hedgerow into heavy enemy fire to do hand-to-hand battle with the Germans. We pushed forward into fierce enemy fire across grazed-over pastureland toward the next hedgerow—where the bulk of the enemy had withdrawn, leaving their dead behind. They cut us to ribbons as we ran over the open ground, charging after them. At least six enemy machine guns had us in a cross fire, and a mix of 81mm mortar, flat-trajectory 88mm cannon, high-angle 75mm howitzer fire exploded in our midst, filling the air with searing shards of shrapnel that tore through flesh and bone.

I made it over about seven hedgerows and fields, seeing a large number of my comrades wounded, maimed, and killed around me. Still we charged forward into the small-arms and artillery fire. I was slightly ahead of my squad when a German suddenly appeared out of a hedge a few feet away on my left front. He flipped a long-handled potato-masher grenade at me in a nonchalant manner before I could bring my rifle to bear, and then he disappeared back into the hedge.

The explosion knocked me out. My comrades left me where I lay, thinking I was dead, and continued on with the attack. It was the right thing to do. You should never stop an attack to look out for the wounded or the dead—if you do, you most likely will become one of them. You've got to keep pressing forward or you'll lose. After coming to, I discovered I was deaf but had no other apparent wounds. I tried to catch up with my attacking squad and was struck down by a shell fragment that tore through my right arm, cut through eight rounds of ammo in my cartridge belt, and entered my right side. That was the end of my fighting in Normandy. My buddies, meanwhile, had continued the attack, gained the enemy positions, and won our battle.

I was sent to recover in the American 216th General Hospital in Coventry, England. I made it out in time to make the Holland jump after undergoing artery and vein transplant surgery in my arm and receiving the best of care. The doctors gave me the piece of shrapnel they took out of my side and I kept it with me wherever I went as a lucky charm. I needed one. I was soon back in combat with my division, my scars still fresh and tender.

Now, three months later, we sat talking far into the night, each man telling of his Paris experiences. Our stories inspired laughter, awe, and envy in the replacements and a few of the older men. The new men in our outfit, all fresh from the States, were eager listeners and asked more questions about the wild life in Paris than they did about the combat skills that we, the older men, were supposed to be teaching them. Most of them asked if we thought they might get a chance to go to Paris while we were still in France.

"Sure," we assured them. "After all the old men have had their turn they'll let you guys go. You know, a few at a time until you all have a turn."

"Paris. God, I can't wait. The world's gonna know I've been there!" one of the new men burst out. Everyone laughed.

"Shut up you guys and go to sleep, for Christ's sake," said a voice from one of the bunks near the latrine end of the barracks.

"Yeah, we gotta keep it down. But I want to hear more," one of the new men said.

"Y'all just want to go to love city and get yer bean snapped," drawled a southerner.

"What the hell did you think I've been talking about?" asked the replacement. "Man, I hear they've even got rooms with mirrors all over the walls and ceiling. You can see yourself in every which way."

"Yeah, but did ya ever think of who might be sittin' on the other side o' them mirrors watchin' *you*?"

"I don't care. I just want to go."

The talk continued in a similar vein until about 1:30 A.M., when everyone, with unspoken agreement, turned in. We were all exhausted and knew reveille would come early.

Speer had the top bunk and I had the bottom. I waited until after he climbed up and settled into his before crawling into mine. A couple of nights before, his bunk—with him in it—had fallen through on top of me after we had gone to sleep. Now I lay there shivering. The blanket was cold and damp, and the straw mattress was getting thin. I could feel the board slats underneath. I made a mental note to get some fresh straw in the morning and refill the mattress cover. It was like trying to sleep on a picket fence lying flat on the ground. Nevertheless, I quickly drifted off into a deep, dark slumber.

The door flew open with a loud bang that made me sit bolt upright in my bunk. Other combat-wary men came immediately awake. Sergeant Vetland came blustering and shouting into the room, not bothering to shut the door behind him. A cold, damp December wind blasted into our already miserable room, adding to the chill and discomfort. A chorus of angry voices demanded that someone "Close that goddamned door!"

Sergeant Vetland was dressed in his jumpsuit and jump boots, but it was hard to tell if he had just gotten out of bed or not. He looked tired, and his loose hair hung down over one eye, as though he had just combed it with his fingers. But that was the way it always looked. Come to think of it, I don't think I ever saw him comb his hair with anything but his fingers.

"Awright you guys, let's hit it!" he bellowed. "Come on, off and on, let's hit it. Let's go, hubba-hubba one time. Off your ass and on your feet, start packing your seaborne rolls, we're moving out—now!"

Seaborne rolls? That could mean only one thing: combat. Up and down the barracks creaks and groans came from the double-tiered bunks as troopers began stirring from their sleep.

"Seaborne rolls?" a sleepy voice asked in disbelief.

"Yeah, seaborne rolls," Sergeant Vetland repeated. "Pack your seaborne rolls, we're moving out."

"When?" a man asked.

"Now. Just as soon as you men get ready and the old man gives the order. And you *will* be ready when he gives the order."

I checked my watch; it was 2:30 in the morning. I couldn't believe this was happening.

"Hell, you must be kidding, Sarge," someone else said from one end of the long barracks. "I just got to sleep."

"I don't know any more than you men do, but I'm not kidding," replied Sergeant Vetland. "The Germans have broken through our lines someplace and are running all over everybody—infantry, armored, everybody. Now it's up to us to stop them before they go all the way to the Channel."

"Jeezus Kee-rist," said another voice. "Why can't the infantry take care of themselves? We spearhead the invasion and liberate Holland for them, and the minute we turn our backs and try to have some fun, they go and foul up."

Most of us felt the same way. We were angry with the infantry for letting the Germans walk all over them. We were angry at the rear-echelon, noncombat commandos sitting on their fat asses back in 12th Army Group headquarters and at Supreme Headquarters Allied Expeditionary Forces (SHAEF), drinking wine and playing soldier with the local ladies while ordering us to do their fighting. I felt anger well within me. I was ready to explode but didn't know who to direct it at. We felt that a whole lot of people weren't pulling their weight and that we were carrying the load for them. How many times did we have to pull their irons out of the fire? We were tired and angry. Our seventy-two days in Holland under Monty had just about drained us.

All three of the overhead electric lights had been turned on, lighting up the entire room. Men cursed as they slid from under their covers and bare feet hit the cold concrete floor. Someone had closed the door but the frigid air hastened the men into getting fully dressed. We could see steam coming from our mouths as we breathed. Damn, that floor was so cold I thought my bare feet would freeze to it.

A few troopers—already dressed and wearing overcoats, wool caps, and gloves—gathered around the one small coal stove in the rear corner of the barracks. One of them poked an iron rod into the handful of feeble dying embers, trying to stir them to life and get a little heat out of them. His efforts were fruitless, but they stood around the damned thing anyway, staring wistfully at it like a bunch of kids staring at an empty candy box.

What was going through their minds? I wondered. Memories of home and loved ones? Grim thoughts about what lay ahead? What is really behind the vacant stare in the eyes of young men preparing to go into combat, knowing that many of them will die or be maimed?

The thought of death did not really bother me too much. Death is just the other end of being born. It is natural. We come into the world out of a dark, unknowing void and we return to it. What really bothered me was the thought of having my arms and legs torn from my body. Of lying there with my blood spurting out on a shell-ravaged field. Of seeing the jagged ends of splintered bone protruding from the torn, ragged stumps of flesh where my limbs used to be. Of smelling burnt powder and raw iron mixed with fresh human blood. I had experienced this with others in battle too many times. I didn't want it to happen to me. I would rather be killed. But I didn't have time to dwell on such things. I had a lot to do in order to be ready when we got the order to move out.

A flash of anger sparked somewhere deep inside my midsection. "Those goddamned Krauts," I muttered under my breath. "Those dirty, rotten, goddamned Krauts. They've lost the damned war and they know it. Why don't they give it up so we can all go home? The hardheaded bastards. We're going to have an ass-kicking party when we get up there, and they are going to supply the ass."

Listening to the talk going around among the troopers, each having his say, it was clear just why we were chosen for the job. If this breakthrough was as big as everyone hinted at, we would stand a good chance of being encircled by the flood of oncoming Germans and we would be fighting behind enemy lines again. That would not be anything new or alarming. Jumping into and fighting behind enemy lines was natural for us. It was what we had volunteered for, trained for, and what we were experienced at doing. But the limited supplies we were able to carry in with us were gone within seventy-two hours. It would be imperative that our infantry and armor break through to us within that time and resupply us with the needed ammunition and food, or that the Air Corps' Troop Carrier Command get the vital supplies to us by parachute. If they failed, we would have to make do and hold out using captured enemy weapons and whatever food we could scrounge until we were properly relieved.

We had learned from past missions, especially the last one, that thanks to our status as a bastard outfit we would be used and abused by whomever had control of us. Our prophecies proved all too true. Within the next two months we would earn the distinction of becoming the only division in American history to fight in three separate armies, in three separate army group sectors, under three different commanders. In Holland we were under Field Marshal Montgomery, Gen. Omar N. Bradley controlled our operations in Belguim, and Gen. Jacob L. Devers commanded us in Alsace—all within the space of sixty days!

We saw hard combat on many other European battlefields as part of several different armies and corps before the war ended. We had proven we were the elite of all combat troops and it seemed like everyone had need of our special talents whenever their part of the war got too hot for them to handle.

Now we, the experienced older men, began packing the small rolls that would normally follow us into combat after we had established static lines. This was normal procedure with us. When going into combat, a paratrooper can carry and jump with just so much, so each and every article he carries into combat must be of vital importance to fighting and survival. Weapons, ammo, explosives, first-aid gear, water, food, a mess kit, a blanket, a raincoat folded through the back of the cartridge belt, and a few luxury items such as socks, underwear, cigarettes, and chocolate all went with us. We always carried our weapons and ammo where they would be handy when needed. We stored food (K rations and D bars), different types of grenades, TNT, composition C (a plastic explosive), and other such items in the large pockets on the outer legs of our jump pants and tied them down on our upper thighs with strings attached to our pants legs. Other goods were distributed throughout the many other large pockets in the jumpsuit and jacket. Items ranging from mess kits to writing paper and toiletries were usually stowed in a musette bag that we fastened on the back of our shoulder harness. The balance of our gear went into the seaborne rolls we were making up now.

For shipping and handling purposes these rolls were not to be more than thirty inches long and not more than twelve inches in diameter. Into this small package we had to pack toilet articles, extra clothing, a second blanket, and everything else we might need in the following weeks of fighting.

The new men watched as each of us laid a shelter half on the floor and then spread a blanket on top of it. We then put whatever items we thought we'd need later on this mat, folded the long edges in toward the center, and rolled it up as tightly as possible. We then wrapped a piece of tent rope around it, leaving a long, loose loop that ran the full length of the roll and tied it to each end to serve as a shoulder strap.

We were required to stencil our last name and the last four digits of our army serial number on every article of clothing and belongings—including our socks, underwear, and handkerchiefs. If a foot or other body part was the only thing recovered of a man after a battle, a sock, or other piece of clothing with his name and last four numbers stenciled on it might be the only way to identify him.

We made sure our name and number showed clearly on the outside portion of the shelter half when the roll was completed. It made owner identification easy, even when it was in a pile with many other rolls.

Usually within a week after our lines became static, rear-echelon troops would bring our seaborne rolls up to an area near the front line. We would then go back a few at a time, pick our rolls out of the piles that had been dumped hastily on the ground, and return with them to our foxholes.

In wars and battles before paratroopers came into being, most troops went to war on ships or landing barges and fought their way inland. Their personal gear, wrapped and tied in blanket rolls, would be brought in by other ships at a much later date, thus the name seaborne rolls. We still called them that, even though troops now went into combat by sea, air, rail, truck, and on foot, and the rolls were, for the most part, delivered by truck.

Chow. The call so near and dear to all soldiers' hearts and stomachs was relayed from GI to GI throughout the camp as men echoed the cry loud and clear. Chow! In a matter of moments everyone in camp, no matter where, knew it was time to eat. We had been busy reevaluating the weight of our gear, weighing our packs and rolls by hefting them. If they felt too heavy, we would undo them, weed out the least important items, and repack the roll.

It's strange how some things may mean so much in garrison, but when you're getting ready to go into combat—where every ounce is carried on your back—many of these items suddenly lose value and are discarded. Some didn't even make it into the barracks bags that would be stored in some warehouse until our return. For the most part, when a man didn't want something and didn't want to put it back in his barracks bag, he would hold it aloft and call to all within hearing, offering it to whoever would take it. If there were no takers, the item was usually pitched into the center aisle that ran the full length of the barracks. There it would remain, walked over and kicked around, until the clean-up crews came in after we left. Members of the cleaning crews inherited some choice souvenirs, war trophies, and other articles in this manner.

What the hell? I wondered. Why should we bother putting *anything* back in our barracks bags? We couldn't carry everything we owned into battle with us, and every time we went in, the bags we left behind were invariably ripped open and looted by the rear-echelon troops. Almost everything we owned of any value would be stolen. War souvenirs, personal things, and desirable GI-issue items usually wound up in the hands of thieves. Photos of loved ones were ripped from their frames and the frames stolen. Nothing was sacred. The next time we saw our barracks bags it seemed like the only thing they contained was our dirty laundry—and sometimes not even that. All some guys got back was an empty bag with their name and serial number stenciled on the side.

Chow call interrupted my reverie. Men were scrambling all around, grabbing their mess kits and running like hell to the mess hall. The slower men always wound up at the ends of very long lines, with little chance of making it through in time for seconds. It paid to be a very fast runner or billeted close to the mess hall.

Wherever we went, even into combat, we always carried our mess kits. If you lost your mess kit and then by some miracle your unit happened to receive a hot meal down the line, you would go hungry—

unless you ate out of your helmet, using the steel shell for a bowl. There were also times when we ran into a "lost" chicken, pig, or even a cow. One could always cook in and eat out of a mess kit. No, you never wanted to lose your mess kit.

Shadowy figures from all directions flickered through the dark, dodging between barracks and leaping obstacles to converge on the mess hall, accompanied by the loud clattering of aluminum mess kits held by their extended handles during the rush.

In all of our previous camps, even stateside, we'd had company messes. These were smaller, more easily served, and the men had a more relaxed mealtime. At Mourmelon-le-Grand we had a divisional mess, with cooks and kitchen police (KPs) from all units working together as though in a large factory, feeding eleven thousand or more men at each meal. Our division usually numbered around fourteen thousand men, but since our ordeal in Holland we had not as yet built ourselves back up to full strength. We still needed replacements.

Our cooks felt the same impact we did. Although they did not accompany us into combat, they too were shorthanded and had to pick volunteers to split firewood, fire up the woodstoves, and help prepare and serve the food. Coffee alone—just one cup per trooper times eleven thousand men—had to be brewed by the hundreds of gallons in large galvanized garbage cans. Then there were the dehydrated eggs, bacon, and bread. The amount of food consumed each day was mind-boggling. When we finished eating, we cleaned our mess kits in large pots of hot, soapy water and then rinsed them in hot, clear water. As we finished cleaning up, the cooks began preparing lunch while the last troopers to pass through the chow line were still eating their breakfast.

After eating we returned to our barracks, completed making up our seaborne rolls, packed our musette bags, and helped the new replacements get ready. Then we fell out for weapons and clothing issue.

It was still dark when we began forming up and, with blackout regulations in effect, there was no light anywhere. Still, we somehow managed to line up in single file and, as we passed the supply room, the supply sergeant would ask a trooper what he had and what he needed. After the man's reply the sergeant's helper would see if they could fill his requirements from the sparse supplies they had in stock. The sergeant handed things out over the closed bottom half of a Dutch door: a rifle to one man, a helmet to the next, a trench knife to the next, and so on down the line.

Fortunately, most of the men in my platoon still had their personal weapons—rifles, carbines, pistols, trench knives, and bayonets—but there were a few who didn't. And no one had all of the essential items needed in combat. This operation would be a matter of make-do before we started. The division was also critically short of ammunition. There simply wasn't enough ammo to go around.

Many of the weapons in the division had been badly damaged or worn during our battles in Holland and had been sent to ordnance repair shops for work that could not be performed by unit armorers. We were especially hurting in the area of crew-served weapons— the machine guns, mortars, and bazookas that provide the heavy punch in a combat platoon. Many of those weapons had been shipped off for badly needed repairs, and now there was an acute shortage of them in the division.

My squad still had its .30-caliber machine gun. It had been with us since we'd begun training in England and had outlived several gunners. It still retained its original barrel and working parts and had developed a personality all its own. Despite two bullet holes in its barrel jacket and other combat scars, the men thought of it as almost a living member of the squad.

The platoon's mortar squad still had its 60mm mortar, and the men had their carbines. Charley Syer, our bazooka man, still carried an old, beat-up bazooka. So, all things considered, my platoon was probably better armed and equipped than many others in the division.

Outside the supply room, the line of troopers would shuffle forward, stop briefly while a man was waited on, and then move forward again. Finally it was my turn. I stood leaning on the bottom half of the Dutch door and asked for an entrenching tool, gloves, and a knit wool cap. The supply sergeant's helper said there were no entrenching tools left, but he handed a pair of gloves and a cap to the supply sergeant, who handed them over to me. I moved off into the

darkness and waited for Speer, then together we walked back toward the barracks. There was a hint of light in the eastern sky. It was not raining, but it was still damp and very cold.

In the barracks, men sat around cleaning their weapons, sharpening their trench knives, and making sure everything would function when needed. Some men took their weapons apart and cleaned them again. Some cleaned them three or four times. Our lives depended on our weapons functioning properly when needed—and on our ability and willingness to use them.

We put on our harnesses and packs, made last-minute adjustments to our webbing, strapped trench knives to our legs, fitted pistols, knives, brass knuckles, and other personal weapons wherever they would be handy, and hung our seaborne rolls over our shoulders. After a final inspection of our bunks and the rest of the barracks to make sure that nothing was left behind or overlooked, we picked up our rifles or carbines, bazookas, machine guns with tripods, and mortars with base plates, and began moving outside in a more or less casual manner.

No orders had been given and no noncoms were yelling, "Let's go, let's hit it, hubba-hubba one time." Someone, it may have been Ted Vetland, said we had to assemble in the regimental area alongside the road; so there we were, meandering along in small groups toward the assembly area.

We talked to each other as we casually strolled toward the gathering of Eagle men. We would stop from time to time to greet old friends from other companies and exchange news about others we had known—all the way from jump school days to the present. Who was still alive. Who was dead. Who had been wounded and who had been sent home. It was a joy to learn that this man or that was still alive, and sad or unbelievable to learn of others' deaths or maiming.

Abraham Axelrod, my first sergeant back at Fort Benning, Georgia, had been killed—cut almost in two by a mortar round. Clute was also dead. There were too many dead, too many seriously wounded.

We had received a number of replacements in the last few days. Why so many men now, within such a short time? Getting replacements had always been a problem in the paratroops. Very few wanted to join an outfit that saw so much heavy combat and suffered such a high casualty rate. Why were we getting so many replacements now? We questioned the new men, knowing that not everyone wanted to be a paratrooper. It took a lot of nerve to go through the tough training it took to become one, to leap from a plane in flight with nothing but combat gear, weapons, and a parachute. We found that recently—after we had been so badly decimated under Montgomery's command—a call had gone out from higher up that anyone wanting to transfer to the "'Troops" would be given priority over any other outfit. The only requirement was that the volunteers had to make three parachute jumps in one day—and their chutes would be packed for them. All they had to do was put on a chute and go up and jump, put on another chute and go up and jump, and do it again a third time. Then, voilà, they received their wings and jump boots and were officially made paratroopers.

This brought in a lot of young men—especially guys fresh from the States who had read of our exploits in Normandy and Holland. After all, the war was all but over, or so they reasoned, so why not? They would receive jump pay and go home with wings and boots as paratroopers. Most of our new replacements were these "one-day paratroopers."

We old men felt a lot of resentment toward these invaders of our select order. We had worked hard for the privilege of wearing our wings and boots. We had given birth to new traditions and set new standards for armies the world over to strive for. We had made a name for ourselves and we were one of a kind: a new type of soldier who truly stood alone. Now we were reduced to taking in one-day paratroopers to flesh out our depleted ranks.

This resentment stayed with us until—sometime during our long truck ride to the Ardennes—we began assuming a father-like role and started advising them how best to stay alive in combat. We spoke from experience, not textbooks, and we were sincere in our concern for our fledgling Eagles. Our new men felt this sincerity and responded in kind. Perhaps it was the pride they felt when they looked at the "Screaming Eagle" patch on their shoulder. Perhaps it was the knowledge that they were fighting alongside a "big brother" who made them feel like they were part of an elite team. Whatever it was, in the next few weeks those one-day paratroopers proved to be an asset to our outfit and we were proud to have them with us.

Large piles of K rations had been dumped on the ground alongside the road in the assembly area. Noncoms standing nearby told us to help ourselves; they said we could have all we wanted. We stuffed as many of the Cracker Jack–sized boxes as we could inside our overcoats and jump jackets. We didn't particularly like K rations, with their dehydrated foods and hardtack, but we had gone without eating before—and when you're hungry, even Ks taste good.

At least they were better than D bars, which were rectangular-shaped, hard, nonmelting, moldy-tasting chocolate bars that measured about an inch-and-a-quarter wide, one inch thick, and about four inches long. One bar would last a man all day—if he could stomach an entire bar in a single day. The damned thing was so hard a dog couldn't gnaw it. It could hardly be broken up, even with a rifle butt. It couldn't be shaved down with a trench knife, and it absolutely refused to melt—even in boiling water. What kept a man going all day was trying to figure out how to get the damned thing inside. Even if he did, I'm convinced it would have passed clear through his body without changing form or shape. But I'll never know for sure. I never was able to eat one.

Many trucks were parked bumper to bumper alongside the regimental street, while others came up the road in their follow-the-leader manner to find parking spaces in the ever-growing line of trucks, motioned along by arm-waving military policemen (MPs).

It was getting close to noon. It wasn't raining, but dark, scudding clouds passed quickly overhead, making it a damp, dreary day. It was close to noon. We waited. Then word spread down the line that it was chow time again. A hot meal! We shrugged out of our gear, pulled our mess kits from our musette bags, left everything in a heap, and ran hell bent for election toward the mess hall.

Troopers were hastened through the chow line, and we found places at the tables and ate in a hurry. Some troopers ate from their mess kits while going through the line so they could be ready in case there were seconds. We didn't know when we would be ordered to mount up and leave or when our next hot meal would be, and we sure didn't want to leave on a long trip with empty bellies and nothing to look forward to but K rations and D bars.

Again we made our way back to our gear and the trucks. And again, we waited. We waited until the talk died out. Men found places to sit or lie on the ground. Some slept. And still we waited. Time dragged as we milled about in an ever-growing mass, trying to keep in some semblance of company groups. No orders had been given or received as yet, so we continued to wait.

"Ain't this always the way?" somebody wondered aloud. "They lean on us, make us get out of the sack early and hurry like hell, then they say, 'That's T.S., you gotta wait.'"

So we waited.

We all knew our division commander, Maj. Gen. Maxwell D. Taylor, was back home in the States for the Christmas–New Year holiday. Latrine rumors had been heavy that he was back there trying to get more missions for the division before the war ended. Or at least get the division transferred to the Pacific, where bigger and better missions could be found for him to command. Perhaps maybe even volunteer us to spearhead the invasion of the Japanese homeland.

When General Taylor first came to the division, just before the Normandy invasion, he promised in a speech to us in a prejump marshaling area in England that he would get us bigger and better missions. All troopers believed the latrine rumors to be true. They were convinced he was back in the States trying to get us transferred to the Pacific. General Taylor was certain, I remember hearing him say, that the 101st had "a rendezvous with destiny. We will keep that rendezvous with destiny."

General Taylor echoed Maj. Gen. William C. "Bill" Lee's prophecy shortly after the division was activated. Lee's orders read in part: "The 101st Airborne Division, which was activated on August 16, 1942, at Camp Claiborne, Louisiana, has no history, but it has a rendezvous with destiny."*

Some of General Taylor's exploits against the Germans before coming to the 101st were related to us in a "get acquainted with your new

---

* General Orders no. 5, Headquarters, 101st Airborne Division, 19 August 1942, as quoted in Leonard Rapport and Arthur Norwood Jr., *Rendezvous with Destiny: A History of the 101st Airborne Division* (101st Airborne Division Association, 1948).

commander" introductory speech. General Taylor's introduction to the 101st was in the marshaling area in southern England, shortly before our Normandy jump. Several months before coming to us to replace General Lee, who had suffered a heart attack, General Taylor distinguished himself by infiltrating deep behind enemy lines in Italy disguised as a captured American pilot under guard. There he met secretly with Italy's Marshal Badoglio in a behind-the-scenes political negotiation, obtaining agreements favorable to the Allies that would take effect after Italy capitulated. General Taylor did prove to be a hell of a leader, well liked and respected by all of us in the 101st. A nonqualified jumper before D day (he made one practice jump at Fort Benning), he earned his wings by leaping from a C-47 over France, leading his division into combat. He was one of us.

But it was apparent to us there were others who felt it was important that we be given as many missions as possible before the war ended. It also seemed that they believed—perhaps even feared—the war in Europe would end before this could be effected. Even General Eisenhower had bet Prime Minister Winston Churchill five pounds that the war in Europe would be over by Christmas. Apparently nearly everyone in the high command was of the same mind. Germany was in its death throes and they were certain the war wouldn't last much longer. We hoped they were right. We hoped the end was near. No one in his right mind likes war.

However, when it came to combat, we were the best they had. We could fight whomever, whenever, wherever, and for however long it took to win. We were a proud group. Our officers were all leaders, not pushers. They not only ran with us, jumped with us, and fought alongside us, but whenever they ordered us to attack, they could be counted on to be among the first ones up and running toward the enemy, calling for their men to follow them.

Brigadier General Gerald J. Higgins, our assistant division commander, along with several senior and junior staff officers, was back in England at this time. The general was lecturing and critiquing our recent Holland operations for the brass there. With Generals Taylor and Higgins away, Brig. Gen. Anthony C. McAuliffe, the division artillery commander, was the highest-ranking officer present, so he took command of the entire 101st Airborne Division.

General McAuliffe, a well-qualified and able officer, wasted no time. After a short briefing and map study, he took his aide, Lieutenant Starrett, and Lt. Col. Harry W. O. Kinnard, the division G3 (operations officer), and headed for Werbomont, Belgium, in a command car. He left Col. Thomas L. Sherburne, the acting division artillery commander, in charge of the convoy with orders to lead the rest of us Screaming Eagles there.

Meanwhile, General Higgins had been notified of what was happening, and he and several other division officers raced back from England by plane, hoping to catch up with us before we went back into action.

Our immediate need was trucks, enough big trucks to move an entire division. Our command ordered the MPs and subordinate commanders to commandeer all trucks in the vicinity. Trucks were intercepted on the roads throughout the region—no matter who they belonged to or what their priority—unloaded on the spot, and directed to our camp, leaving their cargoes piled alongside the road. By 9 A.M. on 18 December, cattle trucks (semis with long, open trailers) began pulling into our regimental areas, where men were already milling about, waiting.

Dismounted drivers and assistant drivers stood near their parked tractors, eyeing us curiously. A few of them approached and asked what the hell was going on. We had no answers; we didn't know any more than they did.

The cattle truck trailers were about forty feet long, open topped, with wood-slatted sidewalls about four feet high. Loose straw covered the floors several inches deep, with a couple of unopened bales of straw lying near the front for future use. The slatted tailgate or a section of sidewall was removed and leaned against the back or side of the trailer for us to use to climb aboard—at least fifty men and their equipment to each trailer. Men carrying crew-served weapons passed their machine guns, mortars, and bazookas up to the men already aboard the trailers, then the gunners took them back when they were aboard. Because we weren't jumping, we carried our seaborne rolls with us instead of leaving them behind to be delivered to us at a later date.

After a trailer was loaded, the sidewall sections were replaced and the filled trucks moved forward at spaced intervals so empty trucks could take their places and continue the loading process. Under normal conditions it takes several days to prepare and move a full division, but we had accomplished the maneuver in just a matter of hours. The 101st was ready to roll. The Eagles were going back into combat. Looking around the trailers you could see the excitement in our eyes. We were goin' back amongst 'em. We were gonna stack bodies. Germans, give your souls to God, 'cause your asses are ours.

It was late afternoon when Colonel Sherburne issued the order to move out. Drivers climbed into the cabs of their semis and the sound of powerful motors grinding to life filled the air. All down the line, men leaned against side rails or stood in the open trailers and yelled and waved at the men being left behind to clean up the area. It was their job to get our barracks bags and personal items into storage, to remove all files and records, and to remove any evidence of our ever having been there.

The first truck moved out and the second waited until it was the proper distance ahead before following. This process was repeated 380 times until the entire convoy, looking like a gigantic snake, was moving over the French roads, passing through World War I battlefields at places like Verdun and Sedan on the way to Belgium. I leaned against the trailer's side and looked out over the darkening land; my mind's eye could see hordes of World War I troops rising from the trenches and charging in great masses through a lethal barrage of artillery and small-arms fire toward the enemy. Their ghosts were restless. Theirs had been the Great War, the war to end all wars. They had died in vain. We were still at war.

Men finally tired of joking with each other or watching the landscape and began to settle to the straw-covered trailer floor to rest. The trailers were so overcrowded that we had to stand and take turns lying down or sitting. We munched K rations when we became hungry and drank water from canteens. The convoy didn't stop, not even for us to relieve ourselves. The tailgate served as our latrine; the steel part of one's helmet served as a thunder mug. We rolled steadily on.

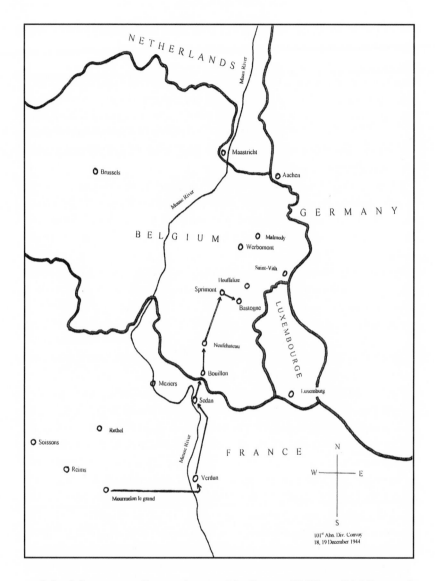

I had been standing—along with Speer, Phillips, Liddle, and
other old-timers—near the front of the trailer watching the passing
landscape. New replacements stood or lay scattered in among the
old men. Now I grew tired. The hustle and hurry had come to an
end. The adrenaline rush that came with Sergeant Vetland's an-

nouncement that we were going back into action had faded. Two-and-a-half months of hectic days and sleepless nights in Holland had taken a heavy toll. My body felt drained; my brain felt fuzzy. I inched my way to the floor, trying to shoehorn myself amongst the others who had already found their way to the floor and were vainly trying to sleep. The thick straw mat felt good, serving as an insulator between my body and the cold floor. The thought occurred to me as I lay there that this was the same way they shipped cattle and pigs to the slaughterhouse.

The cold wind whipping through the open trailer cut us to the bone and made us shiver uncontrollably. Most of us had overcoats, overshoes, and gloves on and had slipped our raincoats from the backs of our cartridge belts to lay over us in an effort to keep the wind from slicing through. But this, along with our being bunched together like so many seals gathered on a rock, was not enough. I shivered uncontrollably for so long that the muscles in the back of my neck pulled tight and gave me a bad headache.

Finally, with our legs over and under each other and men with coats sharing with those who didn't, we finally quieted down and began to rest somewhat. Occasionally a trooper would have to move, setting off loud grumbling when his movements disrupted the rest of us, allowing a surge of cold air to rush in between our bodies.

As I lay there, half asleep and half awake, my thoughts wandered back to Normandy and the sweet smell of apple blossoms mingled with the sickly scent of death. And to Holland, with its constant dampness and cold. I also pondered what lay ahead, wherever that might be. We still didn't know our ultimate destination. Perhaps Mourmelon-le-Grand wasn't so bad after all.

I thought of our new replacements. They had no idea what combat entailed. They would learn quickly or die. One such man was an American Indian from the Pacific Northwest. He was a stout, barrel-chested, friendly man who was visibly proud to be in our outfit. He was in the orderly room getting his paperwork straightened out when Speer and I walked into the barracks one day, wet and muddy from our daily drills and chores. We did not know that he had arrived, and as we began putting our gear away, I spotted a couple of tins of fish under an old closet that stood between our bunks, pushed against the outer wall.

"Hey, look!" I said. "There's some canned fish here on the floor. Some troops that were here before us must have left them behind. They can't be bad, they're still sealed."

Speer, always cautious and respectful of others said, "We better not touch them. They must belong to someone. Let's wait and see if somebody claims them."

"Aw bull," I replied. "We're the only ones here. These are our bunks and this is our area. There's no one else here. Somebody must have left these cans before we got here and we just didn't see 'em until now. Come on, let's have some."

We opened the tins with a trench knife and sat on the edge of our bunks eating them with some K-ration hardtack. While we were munching away, the Indian walked in and stood silently watching us. After a while he asked if he might sit and join us.

"Sure, sit down and have some fish," I said. "It's good. We found it under the cabinet there."

The Indian laughed. "I know; I put it there. My parents sent it to me from Washington State, and I was saving it for later."

Speer and I stopped in mid-bite and looked at each other, then at him. "Oh no, I'm sorry," I said. "We didn't know it was yours. We wouldn't have touched it if we'd known. We thought maybe some-body who was here before us left it behind. I'm sorry as hell. It's all my fault; I talked Speer into having some with me."

"That's okay," he said with a smile. "My parents will send more. Next time I'll have them send enough for the three of us."

We sat and talked for a couple of hours after that. He told us about his home on the reservation, his family, and what life was like back where he came from. He was glad to be bunking with two troopers who had been in combat and couldn't wait to join us on our next mission. He said he wanted to prove himself.

He was slightly shorter than I and stockier. As with most Indians, he had dark eyes and skin and straight, short-cropped, blue-black hair. We called him "Chief" (all the Indians I have ever known were called "Chief"), and he fit right in with us.

Not long after Chief joined us, an English lorry pulled into our company area. The driver checked in at company headquarters and then drove to our barracks, parked, and brought in several armloads of rum in gallon containers.

"Here's your back rum rations, mates," he said. "You blokes left Holland and didn't get all the rum that was due you, so they've sent it on."

Benson handed me a gallon jug and said, "Go ahead, take the devil off the top." His dark eyes flashed as he grinned.

I had heard this statement many times before from men from the South. Many of them were reluctant to take the first drink from a newly opened bottle. They claimed there was a devil in there and the one who took the first drink got the devil off the top. It never bothered me one way or the other. I figured I must have had a hell of a lot of devils inside me by then, so one more wouldn't hurt.

We all took a couple of swallows, but that rum was too potent to drink without something to cut it. Chief, on the other hand, accepted the proffered jug and drank more than three men's share.

"I ain't had nothing like that since I left the reservation," he said with a grin. We gave him all the rum, several gallons of it. I don't know what happened to the rest of that stuff, though. Nearly all of it was still lined up against the wall on the floor near the little stove when we pulled out.

Chief was one of the new men in our little group as we talked of our Paris experiences the night before we left Mourmelon. He seemed to get a big kick out of all the different stories we related. He was also huddled in our close-knit little group as we rolled over those French roads heading for Belgium.

The 82d Airborne Division, which had been resting and refitting at Suippes, also near Reims, preceded us down these very same roads. The 82d had been relieved from combat in Holland more than two weeks before us and therefore had more time back in the rest area to fit in replacements, repair weapons, and stock up on ammunition and other needed supplies. They were far more combat ready than we were.

It was only natural for the Allied high command to send out the better prepared and equipped of our two divisions first when news of the breakthrough came. The 82d was also headed for Werbomont, its long, strung-out convoy moving forward somewhere in the darkness ahead.

Blackout regulations were ignored and all of the vehicles had their headlights full on so we could make the best time possible. We were racing over the narrow, twisting blacktop roads in an almost reckless manner when our lead vehicles caught up to the tail end of the 82d Division convoy. As the two huge columns snaked along, it created a slow-down, speed-up situation as drivers tried to maintain the proper distance from the vehicle in front of them. At times it was even stop and go, but we moved steadily toward the enemy and the rapidly shifting front line somewhere in Belgium.

Soon we began seeing evidence of the magnitude of what we were heading into. Huge trees lining both sides of the road had been hewn into, leaving deep notches in their trunks facing the road. Engineers had done this so that the trees could be felled quickly, creating a crisscross roadblock called an abatis that would stretch for miles in case the Germans were to roll unchecked this far.

Some of the trees had TNT blocks and Primacord fastened to them so they could be toppled instantly. Most were cut deeply with axes and saws and braced with wood wedges to keep them standing. All the engineers had to do was detonate the explosives or knock out the wedges and they had an instant roadblock.

Where were we going? How bad and how big was this breakthrough? I tried to visualize masses of German troops and tanks, mentally comparing them with the crack SS panzer and SS panzer grenadiers that had come down on us in Opheusden, Holland. They had given us several fierce battles, and there had been a hell of a lot of them. We won all those battles, and we stacked one hell of a lot of German bodies doing it—but not without a terrible cost to us. I wondered if there were more German troops and tanks where we were going than there had been at Opheusden. There must be, I reasoned. After all, they were sending both the 101st and the 82d Airborne Divisions to the same place at the same time.

As we rolled along through the dark December night with every light in the convoy blazing, I imagined the 82d up ahead of us with just as many, if not more, trucks as we had. I realized that they had to be running with their lights on too for us to be going as fast as we were. We would make a beautiful target if the Luftwaffe (the German air force) should show up. It was a gamble, but we had to make time. We were in a race with the Germans for Werbomont, Belgium.

Our convoys were a fighter or bomber pilot's dream. Just imagine running into seven or eight hundred trucks filled with combat troops practically bumper to bumper on a single narrow roadway at night with all their lights blazing. The road was lined with hedgerows, fences, and ditches, so there was no escape. What a target! If the Luftwaffe had shown up, we wouldn't have had a chance. They would have raked us with machine-gun fire and bombs from one end of the convoy to the other. It would have been a massacre. We lucked out, though, because "Herman the German" didn't show.

Lying on my back and gazing at the stars (the overcast had cleared), I figured we were being thrown like sandbags into the breach in a broken dike. Our job was to stem the German flood until our armies could get back on their feet, reorganize, and return to the fight—regardless of the cost to us.

The green troops were excited. They acted like it was Christmas Eve already and that they'd soon be presented with all the war souvenirs they could carry.

"I want a Luger," I heard one guy say.

"Yeah, me too," said another.

"I'd settle for a P-38," another man put in. "It's a neat little pistol."

They all had something in mind they were going to look for when they got into combat. I guess Americans are about the greatest souvenir hunters in the world, even in battle. I didn't want to dim their spirits any but I did want them to realize this wasn't going to be a picnic. I wanted them to be on their guard so they'd stand a better chance of living.

"There's only one thing wrong with the whole setup," I said, interrupting them.

"What's that?" asked Gudbrandsen, one of the new men. He was young, lean, blond, and extremely proud of his Nordic heritage. But what the hell, we were all young and lean. The airborne was no place for the old, overweight, or timid.

"There's going to be one hell of a lot of us who won't be coming back," I answered.

The new men grew silent; some of them glanced at the other men around them as if to ask themselves, Who's it gonna be?

Speer, lying next to me, groaned audibly. "You shouldn't say things like that," he said.

"I know, but it's true, I'm speaking from experience—from Normandy and Holland." I glanced around at the other troopers in the trailer—Phillips, Benson, Don Brininstool, Liddle, Justo Correa, Chuck Gudbrandsen, Speer—old men and new. Fate was moving us all closer to our rendezvous with destiny.

We listened to the whine of engines as the trucks began going downhill, gathering speed as they went. Then there was the sound of grinding gears as nervous drivers double-clutched and shifted into lower gears as the trucks started up the next grade.

General McAuliffe's command car had passed over these very same roads earlier. Acting on a sudden impulse at the crossroads at Sprimont, he decided to turn there and head into Bastogne to see if he could find out what was happening from the staff at VIII Corps headquarters. Later, Colonel Sherburne, our convoy commander, stopped at the same intersection and asked the MP stationed there if anyone from the 101st had passed by there earlier. The MP told him about General McAuliffe going into Bastogne. Colonel Sherburne decided to follow him there—but not before ordering the MP to direct the rest of our column to Bastogne.

When the Germans first began breaking through, the 101st Airborne Division was ordered to Bastogne and the 82d to Werbomont. However, in the mass confusion that followed, the orders were garbled and we were mistakenly directed to move to Werbomont with the 82d. Now, through a quirk of fate and a snap decision by Colonel Sherburne, we were headed in the right direction.

We crossed from France into Belgium and at Bouillon the drivers were ordered to douse their headlights and taillights and switch on their narrow-slitted blackout lights. We slowed, but still the 380-truck column moved steadily onward. We couldn't see where we were going. Hell, we could barely see the trucks in front of and behind us. We were stuck there in the middle of the whole division—seemingly alone.

The column began lurching along in a stop-and-go fashion as we approached the crossroads at Sprimont. Standing in the trailer we could see the shadowy forms of the trucks ahead making the turn to the right and then moving out. Our truck slowed to a near stop at the corner. A small, glassed-in, one-room guardhouse with a single dim light inside stood on the northeast corner. Dim as the light was, it looked like a brilliant island in a blacked-out world. One MP sat inside, his feet propped on the desk. Another MP, a big man, stood outside and asked eaching passing driver, "You in the 101st?"

"Yeah," the driver would reply.

"Right. Follow the others then. Keep it moving."

Our truck completed the sharp right turn, jolted and moved into its proper place and interval with the others and began moving down a narrow, dark, macadam road. A little later we again came to a stop. Several dismounted officers appeared to be conferring at a T intersection up ahead. When they had finished talking and mounted back up, the convoy split. Some of the trucks ahead of us continued moving straight down the road into the darkness. Those containing the 506th PIR turned left at the road junction, traveled a short distance, and turned right again. We slowed to a near stop, swinging wide on the sharp narrow turns. We continued along at a very slow pace for I don't know how long. We were tired and spent our time sitting, standing, or lying there fitfully trying to doze. We lost all track of the time. Suddenly the convoy ground to a halt. It was still pitch dark and we didn't have a clue as to where we were. We didn't know if we had arrived at our destination or if the Germans were loose in the area and had forced us to stop. There were no sounds of fighting and nobody ordered us out of the trucks, so we just sat there and waited.

Finally some of the men got out of the trucks and began walking around, jumping up and down, swinging their arms, trying to loosen cramped muscles and restore circulation. Then, as always, men meandered forward to see what the holdup was. A short time later some of them returned mad as hell and wanting to kill somebody. Then we got the story.

Some dumb son-of-a-bitch captain commanding a heavy maintenance company that was retreating from the oncoming enemy had the road blocked with heavy equipment and refused to move it. He had bivouacked his unit overnight in an area west of Bastogne so it would be ready to move out before the Germans arrived.

In the meantime, after a hasty inspection of the Bastogne area, General McAuliffe decided to use that very same spot to encamp the

101st until he could assign the regiments to fighting positions around Bastogne. The captain objected, refusing to move without a personal order from Maj. Gen. Troy H. Middleton, the VIII Corps commander.

After that order was obtained and presented to the captain, he reluctantly moved his equipment out of the fields, then parked the vehicles across the road, blocking it completely and preventing the 101st from moving forward to meet the oncoming Germans. He claimed he was missing some men and thought the best way to intercept them would be to block the entire road and not allow anyone to pass in either direction until he had located them. Hell, even if he *was* missing some men, which we all doubted, they could have beaten him back to Paris and cozied up with some sweet mademoiselles while he was standing out there in the dark like the jerk he was, waiting for them.

Ol' Captain Son-of-a-bitch had parked his vehicles three abreast and seven rows deep across the narrow road and refused to move them into single file alongside the road so we could proceed into Bastogne and get ready to fight. It was another case of an over-inflated, self-appointed, egotistical nobody screwing things up. If he had died on the spot, no one would have missed him—although I'm sure the men in his command would have been greatly relieved.

General Higgins, our assistant division commander, had made it in from England and gone stalking through the dark looking for the captain. The general, a big, lean, muscular man, was formidable when angered. The captain, who must have suffered badly from mental poverty, continued to argue with the general, refusing to move his vehicles.

General Higgins angrily ordered the bullheaded captain to get out of his way, then the general personally ordered each and every driver blocking the road to move his vehicle to one side in single file. All the while, the captain, like a yapping mongrel dog, loudly protested the general's orders.

I had gotten out of the truck by this time and was standing there with a group of troopers, some of whom were so angry that they talked of making their way forward, waiting for the right moment, and then killing the captain in the dark with a trench knife. After that, they figured they'd commandeer his vehicles to take with us and set his retreating men afoot.

Four or five troopers slid their trench knives from their leg sheaths and started moving slowly forward in the dark. At that moment we got orders to mount up. General Higgins had finally gotten the road cleared. We climbed aboard our trucks and the convoy moved slowly on toward Bastogne. That self-centered, egotistical captain never knew just how close he came to meeting his maker that night.

Suddenly the trucks stopped again. We were in no mood to be hassled again. Then we saw them. Mobs of retreating Americans—walking, running, stumbling, and riding in all sorts of vehicles—clogged the road up ahead. They moved toward and then past us like a thick, wide river of lava coming up out of the dark and flowing back toward France. On and on they came in ever-increasing numbers, a wave of human lemmings pressing into the front of our trucks and around the sides, filling the road, the ditches on either side, and the fields all around us. They shambled along in shock and fear, blocking the road completely, eyes staring straight ahead, mumbling to themselves. This mass of fear-stricken humanity blocked the road ahead so completely that for long periods of time it was impossible to move the convoy forward a single foot. We were stalled there on the road. Had we been ordered to dismount, we might well have been swept back by the flood of humanity flowing around us.

I had never before—or since—seen such absolute terror in men. Their fear was so great, so consuming, that I'm convinced they would have walked right into our trucks had we been moving. They came up out of the dark and swept by on either side of us, then disappeared like shadowy ghosts into the dark to our rear.

We stood massed in the trailers and called to the men as they passed. "What's going on up there? How many Krauts are there? Which way are they coming from? How close are they? Do they have tanks?"

Most of the men did not bother acknowledging our questions; they just kept stumbling back in the direction from which we had come. The few who did respond nearly always had the same answer: "You're going up; we're going back. You'll all be killed! You'll all be killed!" Then, tired and disoriented as they appeared, they would take to running again. Many had weapons. We asked them to give us their weapons, or at least give us some of their ammunition. All of them refused.

We had passed the village of Givry and slowly began to move again. The flood of human flotsam seemed to have ebbed, for a while at least. Again our convoy slowed, then stopped. Following orders, we dismounted one company at a time to form up in loose company formations along the roadside. It was about 4 A.M. As each truck emptied, its driver would move a little farther down the road, make a U-turn, and then head back the way we had come.

Before our truck moved out I asked the driver where we were.

"This is Champs," he replied. "Bastogne is straight ahead about three miles."

So this is Champs, I thought. In the gloom we could see that we were in a small village. A few ancient, gray, fieldstone houses, some sort of leaning one against the other, were gathered together at a lonely spot on the road. It was no more than that.

"Why don't you give us a lift the rest of the way?" I asked.

"Not me," the driver said. "This is as far as we go. We shouldn't have come this far; we might've run into the Krauts."

He floored the accelerator and the engine roared. The truck began rolling, gathering speed, back the way we had come. Officers were calling out orders and the noncoms repeated them, bringing us into company formations. We began walking down the road in the dark of night. Stragglers continued passing us in ever-growing numbers, calling out to us as they passed, "You'll all be killed! You'll all be killed!"

We could no longer see the stars, and a heavy mist made the air damp and cold as we walked toward the enemy through the quiet, dark, cold night.

Word filtered down through our ranks that the whole division was to bivouac in a triangular area between Bastogne, Mande-Saint-Etienne, and Champs. The 501st PIR was to camp nearest Bastogne, the 506th PIR just to the west of the 501st, the 502d PIR just to the west of the 506th, and the 327th Glider Infantry Regiment was to set up farthest west of all.

We moved down the road in complete silence. The only sounds were those of our creaking harnesses; the light metallic clanking of machine guns, mortars, base plates, and bazookas being shifted on shoulders; and the soft shuffling of jump boots on the blacktop road, punctuated by the rattle of an occasional pebble being kicked over the hard surface.

We went up a side road to our right, then turned through a gate into fields on our left. Each company was assigned to a different field. We moved into ours, scattered out, and lay down in the wet grass to catch what sleep we could. This was the first time we had carried our seaborne rolls into combat with us but we couldn't unroll them and remove our blankets because we had to be ready to move out on a moment's notice. Instead, we used the rolls for pillows and curled up on the open ground like so many dogs.

We lay there shivering uncontrollably, not caring to move any more than we had to for fear of losing body heat from under our jackets and overcoats. We talked a little in low whispers, mostly about warm fireplaces, sizzling steaks, cold beer, warm beds, good booze, and women—all the good things that soldiers the world over have talked about for centuries.

Some men spoke of home, families, the end of the war, and what they were going to do when they got out of the army. One man said he was never going to work again as long as he lived. Then another man spoke out clearly enough for all to hear: When the war was over and *he* got out, he was going to get a big barrel of cold beer and an acre of bare titties. Titties of all sizes and shapes. Then he was going to pull off his shoes and socks and walk barefoot through those titties and squeegle his toes in them while he drank cold beer. I tried to picture an acre of bare titties in my mind. It sure would be a sight to behold.

At the first hint of dawn we were ordered back onto the road in company formations. Our clothes were soaked from lying on the wet ground, and movement brought new chills to our bodies. We marched back out to the blacktop road and turned in the direction of Bastogne. As we moved along the road we again began passing Americans headed the other way. Men had been passing by all night long, even while we were lying in the fields. They represented many different outfits: infantry, armored, maintenance units, office personnel, truck drivers, communications, Services of Supply (SOS) troops—every kind of unit from a number of different divisions.

They walked, ran, and stumbled past us singly, in twos and threes, and in large gangs of men—all of them in wide-eyed shock and terror. Most were silent, although some mumbled incoherently. The few who did speak clearly repeated the same thing we'd heard during the night: "We're goin' back; you're goin' up. You'll all be killed! You'll all be killed! The Germans are coming! The Germans are coming! You'll all be killed!"

Others could do nothing more than mumble over and over, "Tanks, tanks, tanks."

Tanks! That didn't sound good. We had gone up against German tanks in Holland—an entire division of enemy tanks and armored infantry—and it wasn't good at all. That explained the lemming-like hordes of Americans jamming the roads, heading back toward France. The Germans were coming at us with a mass of armor, and we were heading straight into them.

One grimy young man wearing an overcoat and hugging his rifle to his chest shuffled past looking dazed and tired. Luke Easly walked up and asked him, "What's going on up there?"

"I don't know," the man replied. "All I know is that you're goin' up and I'm goin' back. You'll all be killed."

"We could use another man," Luke said. "How about going back up with us?"

"Hell no!" the man answered, shaking his head. "Everyone's getting killed up there. The Krauts are coming. They're running all over everything. No one can stop them. I'm getting the hell out."

"Then at least give us your rifle," said Luke. "You don't need it and there are a lot of us who don't have weapons."

The young man clutched his M1 close to his body, his arms wrapped tightly around it as though he were cradling a baby, and started running down the road. He kept glancing back at us in wide-eyed terror, fearful that we might pursue him and take his rifle.

Thinking back on it, if I had been in the same situation, I wouldn't have given up my rifle either.

Who could blame those men for being scared? Many of them were fresh from the States, pumped up with the idea that the war would be over by Christmas. Then thirty-eight heavily armed and armored

German divisions had suddenly broken through their lines in a predawn surprise attack in a last fierce attempt to save their country from defeat. Many Americans and their units were obliterated before they even knew they were under attack. These men had found themselves in the valley of death, and their faces showed it.

Unprecedented heavy shelling had suddenly rained down on several divisions filled with green troops. One, the 106th Infantry Division, had landed in France just two weeks earlier. Another, the 99th Infantry Division, had been in Europe barely a month. Thirty-eight German divisions followed the artillery bombardment, driving over American positions, smashing all opposition, killing or capturing everyone who tried to stop them. There was total chaos. In some instances the Germans murdered American prisoners. Fear reigned. Once fear strikes, it spreads like an epidemic, faster than wildfire. Once the first man runs, others soon follow. Then it's all over; soon there are hordes of men running, all of them wild-eyed and driven by fear.

That was what we saw. Those men were not to blame. They had been through hell. They had seen the elephant. They needed time to reorganize, and it was up to us to give them that time. They would be back.

I doubt if all of this confusion and bloodshed could have been averted, but certainly we could and should have been better prepared. Our high command was informed. What were our leaders thinking of, putting inexperienced divisions alone in a vulnerable spot where the Germans had successfully begun two world wars, smashing through this very same terrain? Of course, there was the matter of that five-pound bet that the war would be over by Christmas.

The 28th and 4th Infantry Divisions, both combat-experienced divisions that had participated in the Normandy invasion, had repeatedly sent back reports of excessive vehicle, armor, and infantry movements on the enemy side. Even the 106th Division, which had been in the front lines only four days, sent back reports of enemy movements. All of these reports were written off by SHAEF as the exaggerations of green, inexperienced, and nervous troops. Those in command made no attempt to even investigate properly. Nothing was done at all except to become alarmed and make plans to move SHAEF farther to the rear, out of harm's way after the breakthrough occurred.

The 106th Infantry Division didn't stand a chance. It had never been in combat before, it had been at the front only four days, and it lacked proper support, proper ammunition, and was assigned a sector so wide and over such rugged terrain that it should have been covered by no less than three fully experienced combat divisions. To top it off, the area where the 106th Division was stretched so thinly was astride the same route on which the Germans had launched two previously successful invasions into Belgium and France.

Two of the 106th Division's regiments—the 422d and 423d—were almost immediately surrounded and pounded mercilessly by heavy and light artillery. Blasted at point-blank range by enemy tanks, and hammered by 81mm mortars and overpowering small-arms fire, the men of the 106th fought fiercely against overwhelming odds. Only when there clearly was no hope whatsoever did they surrender—and then only after they had destroyed their weapons so the enemy wouldn't get them. The men of these two regiments were ordered by their commanding general, in the name of humanity, to cease fighting, lay down their arms, and surrender.

Their surrender was the second largest capitulation in American history, second only to that of the surrender of Bataan. More than eight thousand men from the 106th Division's 422d and 423d Infantry Regiments were delivered into enemy hands on 18 December 1944. Every one of them was a hero.

The combat-experienced 4th Infantry Division stayed mostly intact in the face of that onslaught, absorbing much of the Germans' initial thrust and stalling them long enough for us to reach Bastogne. Now, here we were, battle weary and poorly armed, moving to meet the enemy again—this time in Belgium.

Some of our men were armed with nothing more than a trench knife. One trooper marching with us had only a stick—a tree limb he had picked up from the ground. He waved it menacingly and declared that he would replace it with a German weapon before nightfall. Time after time as we were marching along he would step to the center of the road, swing his heavy stick over his head and bring it down with a hard blow on the blacktop surface.

"You'll see, I'll have a rifle by tonight," he declared.

I couldn't help but admire him. But he wasn't the only man without a weapon; there were others. All of the men who weren't armed were confident they would pick up a rifle, pistol, or something to fight with from either a dead German or one of their comrades just as soon as we went into battle.

Most of us were armed but we had little or no ammunition. We had been promised ammunition ever since we'd left the trucks in Champs. We still hadn't seen a single round.

We passed through the tiny village of Hemroulle, a scattering of a few ancient houses that looked much like Champs. Most of these European villages looked the same. A little farther down the road somebody called another halt. It would be daylight soon. We were ordered to stack our seaborne rolls in platoon and company formations alongside the road. We would pick them up in a day or two, just as soon as we mopped up the Germans who were giving the rest of our army a hard time.

We felt a little reluctant about this. Many of the men had personal things such as pictures of their wives, families, and girlfriends in their rolls—not to mention valuable articles and souvenirs. I had no photographs, for I had no wife or girlfriend. But I did have a new, fairly expensive camera and several rolls of film I had purchased while on pass in Paris. I bought it with the idea of getting some combat pictures—on-the-job photos, so to speak. Of course I hadn't known at the time that we'd be going into combat again so soon.

But as the French say, *"C'est la guerre."* We stacked our seaborne rolls alongside the road as ordered. It was the last time we ever saw them.

Just before daylight on the morning of 19 December 1944 we started walking the last couple of miles to the city of Bastogne. In the first gray light of dawn my eyes searched ahead, our men looking like dark, bobbing shadows as they moved in long, scattered lines down either side of the road. No one talked, no commands were given, we just played follow the leader. We had a good bunch of re-

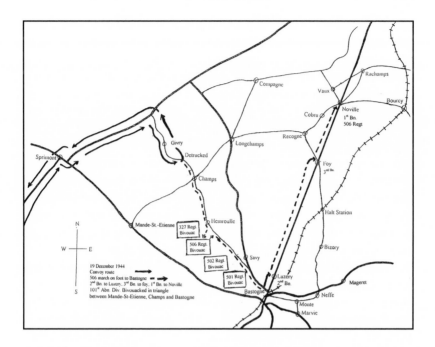

placements. They took their cues from us as we moved silently down the road; it was hard to tell the greenhorns from the veterans.

The 506th PIR entered Bastogne early that morning, right behind the 501st PIR, with our 1st Battalion in the lead, followed by the 3d Battalion, the regimental headquarters company, and the 2d Battalion bringing up the rear.

We took special precautions to keep our identity a secret, just as we had on our previous mission. We were ordered to remove or cover our shoulder patches with a scrap of cloth sewn over them. As we entered Bastogne itself, many of the civilians remaining in the city came into the streets saying, "Welcome 101st, we knew you were coming."

That was always the way it was, even in the States. If a GI wanted to know what was happening to his outfit, he could go to the nearest town and ask the first civilian or barmaid he saw. They always seemed to know.

Many of the people, men and women, went through our ranks with large and small pots of hot, black coffee, pouring it into troopers' outstretched canteen cups. Drinking hot, scalding coffee from aluminum canteen cups is not the easiest thing in the world. One sip brings instant pain, and as you jerk the cup away you invariably slosh hot coffee onto your hand, burning the skin. You eventually learned how to sort of inhale a sip of hot coffee without actually touching the metal with your lips.

Half an hour after our arrival on the western edge of Bastogne, General McAuliffe ordered our battalion to Noville, about five miles north of Bastogne. The full might of the German forces was thought to be coming out of the northeast like a storm. We were the ones anointed to meet the bastards head-on and hold them long enough for the rest of the division to dig in around Bastogne.

We moved out in company, platoon, and squad formations, followed by the 3d and 2d Battalions. We marched in long, strung-out, staggered single-file battle formations on either side of the road. We continued our march eastward into the north center of Bastogne, turned left on the Houffalize–Neufchâteau road, and headed north toward Noville.

Most of us wore heavy overcoats, overshoes, woolen scarves, and gloves in an effort to keep out the winter cold. We carried our rifles at sling arms. Gunners carried mortar tubes, bazookas, and machine guns on their shoulders, while assistant gunners packed the weapons' bipods, tripods, and base plates in a similar manner. A man cannot carry a mortar or machine gun for too many miles comfortably. A .30-caliber machine gun weighs forty-two pounds. That's a lot of weight for one man to carry, especially when you factor in a thirty-five-pound pack, ammunition, and other necessary gear. So we all took turns lugging those weapons. When a man became tired, another would spell him for a while. In addition, every man carried extra machine-gun ammo, mortar shells, bazooka rockets, TNT, and so on. Nobody complained about it, either. We all knew our lives depended on those heavy weapons.

I looked around at the other men as we headed north toward Noville. Phillips, who was trudging along in front of me, was a good man in combat. One could depend on him to cover his flank or back and to be with him in the attack. Benson, from Tennessee, was single, but I never heard him talk about a girl back home the way most of the others did. He carried our platoon's small walkie-talkie radio set, which never worked when we needed it. It seemed like he always had it torn apart in a bag so he could work on it.

Then there was Jack Bram. He had that unmistakable accent one associates with New Yorkers. He was a damned good man to have on your side in combat, something he had proved in our attack on Ravenoville in Normandy and many times since then. Bram had a ruddy complexion and a hooked nose. He was about five feet six or seven inches tall, stocky, and had a don't-give-a-damn attitude. He claimed to be a German Jew and that his main goal in life was to kill Germans.

Charles Horn, from Indiana, carried our platoon leader's large SC300 radio set. He was tall, slim, and very broad-shouldered. Horn often told me his shoulders got that way because he always slept on his back, never on his side. He had thick, black hair, light skin, and a face that seemed to sharpen down from a wide forehead to a narrow chin. He had also been with us since before Normandy.

Jerry Janes, striding along behind me, had a narrow waist, broad shoulders, dark hair that he combed straight back, and a wrinkled forehead, pug nose, and receding chin. A rugged man, Jerry was strong and tough as hell. He was from Wyandotte, Michigan, and he used to tell us of his rum-running days in the downriver communities during Prohibition. He had been with the 101st since the day it was activated at Camp Claiborne.

Ted Vetland, our platoon sergeant, was rugged and muscular. He had brown eyes, light-brown hair, and a jutting jaw. He hailed from Brooklyn, and it seemed like he was born for his job. He carried his .45-caliber tommy gun with ease and used it with expertise. As always, his hair hung over one eye and he kept brushing it back with one hand.

Our platoon mortar man, Jackson, was a huge Texan. He was strong as a bull, with hands as large as mallets and fingers that looked like a bunch of bananas. He had led a cowboy's life on a ranch back home and dearly loved a good fight. One night, after a drinking bout in Swindon, England, we got into a disagreement with some "legs" (paratrooper slang for regular infantrymen), and Jackson started swinging. Every time one of those huge fists would land, a man would crumple and go down. He kept us busy dragging unconscious men out of the street and stacking them on the sidewalk so they wouldn't get run over by a truck or a jeep in the blackout. His best buddy, "Whiskey" Wisniewski, was killed at Opheusden. Jackson became sort of a loner after that.

Charley Syer, our bazooka man, was tall, husky, and well built. He had a round face and wore those oddball-looking, GI-issue, stainless steel–rimmed glasses—only on him they didn't look bad. Syer was an expert with a bazooka. I never saw anyone who could out-do him with a bazooka—or who could match his coolness when killing a tank with one. It was like David and Goliath. He would stand his ground, fire a rocket, and carry on as though standing up to one of those metal monsters with nothing but a single-shot rocket launcher, as if it were the most natural thing in the world.

And of course there was Liddle, my Mormon friend from Utah. I never saw him take a drink of beer or alcohol. He was husky, curly-haired, cool, and quiet. Don had been severely wounded in Holland, nearly losing an arm to shell fragments in Zon. It must have taken an entire spool of catgut to sew up his wounds. He had healed quickly, though, and was now stalking into Noville and combat with us again.

Don Brininstool, a native of Jackson, Michigan, was a little shorter than I and about four years older. Like Liddle and Janes, Don was one of the men at Camp Claiborne when they formed the division. He fought well in Normandy and Holland, killing many Germans. I was glad he was still with us—guys who stuck their necks out usually got it sooner or later.

Then there was Sherwood Trotter. We all called him "John Scott" Trotter, after a well-known '40s musician. Trotter was one of the most fearless men I have ever known. In battle he would simply stand up, fully exposed, and head into the enemy, flinging grenades and firing his weapon at the same time. How the hell he missed getting killed, I'll never know.

I saw long-legged Walter Dobrich from Pennsylvania striding right along with Bill Rary of South Carolina, Frank Gaddy of New Mexico, and my buddy Siber Speer, another New Yorker. There were many others, too many to list them all here. They were all good men, all men you could trust your life to—which, in fact, we did.

Siber Speer was the one who more or less talked me into buying the camera and film I picked up while on pass in Paris. I would have spent the money on booze and women if it hadn't been for him. Speer bought a hand-carved tortoiseshell comb for his invalid mother back in New York.

At times I noticed he would flip open the top of a silver ring he wore and look at it. I never bothered to ask him what was in it. Then one day he showed me. It contained a small photo of his girlfriend. He told me they were going to be married when he got back home after the war was over.

Then there were the new men, most of whom I never got to know very well because most of them died or were wounded badly enough to be sent home during our first hours in combat. New men usually got hit first, in bunches. If they lived past three days, it seemed they stood a pretty good chance of lasting much longer—sometimes long enough to eventually become one of the old men.

Among our latest crop of replacements was Don Straith, another Michigan native. He was tall, slim, and had a sharp face with lean features. Gudbrandsen, whom I described earlier, was one of the few lucky enough to stay with us to the end of the war.

We all kept moving, walking forward to meet the enemy, to test them and see who would live and who would die. The trooper with the stick no longer stepped to the center of the road, but stayed close to his buddies who were better armed. If they killed a German at close range or one of them went down, he would at least have a chance to get a rifle. The stick wouldn't run out of ammunition, but a rifle is a lot more effective as long as it has rounds, then it can be used as a stick. But a stick is a stick is a stick.

As we passed Luzery on the northern outskirts of Bastogne, the 2d Battalion fell out to dig in there. They, along with several other battalions from other regiments, would form a defensive ring around the city of Bastogne.

The 1st and 3d Battalions of the 506th PIR marched on toward Foy and Noville. About halfway between Luzery and Foy we came upon a jeep parked in the middle of the road. A lieutenant wearing

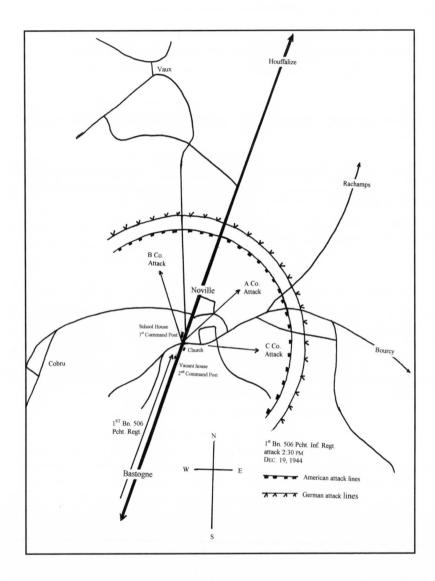

Vaux

Houffalize

Rachamps

B Co.
Attack

A Co.
Attack

Noville

School House
1st Command Post

Church

C Co.
Attack

Bourcy

Vacant house
2nd Command Post

Cobru

1st Bn. 506
Pcht. Regt.

N

1st Bn. 506 Pcht. Inf. Regt.
attack 2:30 PM
DEC. 19, 1944

Bastogne

W ——|—— E

American attack lines

German attack lines

S

a 10th Armored Division shoulder patch was standing in back of it talking to two of our officers. The jeep was piled high with ammo of all kinds. The 10th Armored officer, 2d Lt. George C. Rice, had heard and seen that we were virtually without ammunition, so he borrowed a jeep and drove all around the Bastogne area scrounging, begging, and borrowing various types of ammo from tankers, truckers, and anyone else he could find. Most of it came from the 10th Armored. Lieutenant Rice personally handed out bandoliers of .30-caliber M1 ammo, doling it out sparingly to riflemen. He also had .45-caliber ammo for those with tommy guns and .45-caliber pistols. There was a limited supply of bazooka rockets, mortar shells, and hand grenades in the jeep, too.

We slowed as we walked by. I reached out and accepted two bandoliers of M1 cartridges, which I slung around my neck over my right and left shoulders, as did the rest of our riflemen. I also got a handful of .45 ammo for the nickel-plated Colt .45 pistol my father had given me, and which I carried throughout the Normandy and Holland operations. We all thanked Lieutenant Rice for his efforts on our behalf. We never did receive the ammunition promised by the army command.

Some of the men began pulling off the condoms they'd placed over the muzzles of their rifles. There was always a plentiful supply of the contraceptives in company orderly rooms. We used them to tie around our boot tops to blouse our pants legs and also to pull over our weapons' muzzles to keep out rain, snow, and mud. I've often wondered how we looked to civilians as we marched through their villages with condoms hanging loosely over the muzzle ends of many of our rifles.

# 2 Attack

We moved forward again, more cautiously, more spread out. The sound of heavy and light artillery boomed in the distance; small-arms fire echoed and reechoed through the hills. We were moving toward a battle in the north. Who was it? Who was catching hell? Who was winning? Who was losing? With all the firing going on, we knew Americans were making a stand. We had to get there in time to help them.

We had moved forward another mile, maybe less, when the order to halt filtered down through the ranks. We fell out alongside the road and rested in the ditches. Some of the men dipped small handfuls of fresh snow, letting it melt in their mouths. On the other side of Bastogne, where we had spent the night in the field, there had been no snow on the ground. Here, it was at least two inches deep and covered everything as far as we could see to the north. It seemed quite fresh, and the men had no qualms about eating it to quench their nervous thirst. Going into battle, one's throat is nearly always dry.

John Bielski, our machine gunner, stood on the bank overlooking the road. Most of the rest of us sat on the road's edge with our feet in the ditch that ran beside it. The carbine Bielski was holding in his right hand suddenly went off, causing troopers to start and to finger their own weapons nervously. The carbine had been pointing down, and the bullet had cut a perfect half-moon in the edge of his boot sole. Bielski appeared far more surprised than the rest of us. He stood there wide-eyed, obviously wondering what the hell had happened. We knew what happened: a faint wisp of tell-tale smoke trailed from his carbine's muzzle.

"Too bad it didn't go through the middle of your foot," Benson drawled in his raspy voice. "You could've gone back to the hospital and had a good rest while we do the dirty work."

"The hell with you," Bielski snapped. "I'll take my chances. A bullet through the foot could cripple a man for life."

Heavy and light gunfire still sounded to the north of us. Someone was catching hell. Then came an order for us to re-form on the road and move out. We moved up the road a short way, then turned off to our right into a field on the east side of the road. Spruce trees grew tall and thick in cultivated woodlots on three sides of the field, which was covered knee to waist deep with a sort of heavy shrub. Snow lay fairly thick in the more open spots, mantling the shrubbery in white.

While we were there our new company commander ordered us to shed our overcoats, overshoes, and other heavy clothes. It was hard to keep track of the company commanders' names. We'd had several different ones since jumping into Holland. It seemed they either kept getting knocked off or new officers would come into the outfit and they'd shuffle them around. A couple of times we even got back a commander we'd had before.

We stacked our heavy winter clothing into piles in platoon and company formations. We stripped down to jumpsuits, jump boots, helmets, and gloves. This was getting to be a habit, stacking our personal stuff along some roadside or out in a strange empty field. The captain told us we were going into the attack and would have to be able to move fast. Besides, he told us, there wouldn't be time to get cold, and we could come back and pick up our heavy winter clothes the next day, after we'd whipped the Germans back to where they'd come from. Right then and there we began having some reservations about our new company commander.

While we were fighting we weren't supposed to get cold, but at that moment we were feeling pretty damned chilly. We knew from seeing news photos of the action on the eastern front that the Russians did quite well in winter wearing overcoats, but evidently someone up at headquarters didn't think we could handle it. We were stripped down to jump clothing that we normally wore in the summertime. The sky was overcast and a misty fog was settling in over the snow-covered fields. It was damp and it was cold.

Leaving the field, we formed up on the road in battle formation: 1st, 2d, and 3d Platoons in order, squads in order, men strung out on either side of the road no closer than twenty to thirty feet from one another but mostly farther apart than that. Continuing northward we entered and passed through the village of Foy, which was no more than a small jumble of houses at a crossroads. The 3d Battalion, which had been following along behind us, fell out there to take up defensive positions and form a secondary line of defense between the enemy and Bastogne. Our battalion continued to march northward toward Noville, expecting to engage the enemy there.

We marched the full five miles from Bastogne to Noville, not counting the three miles from Champs to Bastogne. The closer we got to Noville, the louder the din of battle became. First we heard the artillery and mortar shells crashing down ahead of us, then, as we drew closer still, we could hear the staccato rattle of machine-gun fire and the characteristic popping of rifle fire. Someone was *really* catching hell. On our previous missions we had come upon combat and death with the suddenness of jumping into a cold shower—a sudden shock and we were in the middle of it. First there was the plane ride, with antiaircraft shells bursting around us and strings of tracers rising up to meet us like writhing strings of fiery pearls. Then, after the short parachute drop, we were amongst them, fighting for our lives.

This was different, I thought, as we walked along. This is how the infantry gets into it. It was as though we were out for a Sunday stroll and walking into a thunderstorm up ahead.

We kept getting closer and closer, and the noise kept getting louder and louder. Men became silent, more intent, their eyes searching ahead, anxiously scanning the woods on either side for movement, for any visible sign of an enemy. We all listened intently, wary of the first change in sound that might indicate the Germans were drawing within range. We spread out even more so that a burst of machine-gun fire or a shell burst wouldn't get too many of us. We also moved closer to the ditches on either side of the road and assumed an instinctive crouch, the way a boxer does when he has to dodge, duck, or move fast.

I felt a slightly sick feeling in the pit of my stomach. I knew it was the same with the other men around me. We had talked about that and other intimate things that combat veterans experience and rarely confide to anyone but each other.

The road we were on ran very slightly east of north from Bastogne, through Noville, and on to Houffalize. Near the center of Noville, another road came in at an angle from the east, intersecting the Houffalize–Bastogne road, forming a Y. That road grew out of two other roads: one from Rachamps and the other from Bourcy. They joined together and became one before merging with the road entering Noville from the east.

Low, rolling hills surrounded Noville on the east, north, and west like a giant horseshoe. No farmhouses were visible in the countryside outside of town, just open fields, large and small, with patchworks of cultivated pine woodlots interspersed on the hills.

It was over those hills and down those roads that the enemy came. This was no probing action by the Germans; it was the main thrust of a full panzer battle group. The entire Fifth Panzer Army, with infantry, was coming out of the east toward Bastogne like a gigantic water head from a broken dam. The 2d Panzer Division was coming down on Noville itself. The German hordes were marching en masse with orders direct from Hitler to take Bastogne at all costs and without delay.

The Ardennes is made up of rugged terrain. Deeply carved valleys run between steep, heavily wooded, razor-backed ridges that dominate the country, leaving heavy, mechanized armies nowhere to maneuver but on the twisting roadways snaking along the centuries-old pathways in the deep gouges between those razor-backed ridges. Bastogne was the hub of that road net. The army that controlled Bastogne controlled those roads.

The fast-moving panzers heading westward were ordered to bypass strong islands of resistance and towns held by the Allies and mop up later. But Bastogne, with its seven roads projecting like the spokes of a wagon wheel to all points of the Ardennes, had to be taken. Those seven roads came together in one of three major communications hubs—if not *the* major hub—in the Ardennes, so Bastogne and its seven roads had to be taken or the entire German offensive would fail. They would not be able to move their mechanized armies or the supplies needed to maintain their momentum without it.

When General McAuliffe arrived at VIII Corps headquarters, he carefully studied the large maps of the area in the war room. The general quickly realized Bastogne's importance to the outcome of the oncoming battle. He decided then and there that this was where we would make our stand. We would hold Bastogne. We had to halt the German advance and hold Bastogne and its seven roads or die trying. For the Americans and the Germans alike, the seven roads to Bastogne became seven roads to hell!

Noville was a typical European town with an assortment of gray, fieldstone buildings—houses, shops, sheds, and other structures—built onto and squeezed between each other, all jumbled haphazardly together and interlaced with a web of narrow, winding streets and alleys. A church with a tall spire sat next to the main intersection near the center of town. A long, low two-story building that appeared to be a school stood on the west side of the main road across from the church, facing the Bourcy road coming in from the east. The many large windows in this building offered a commanding view in all directions, especially up and down the connecting roads.

Lieutenant Colonel James L. LaPrade, our battalion commander, immediately set up his command post (CP) in that building, along with Major Desobry, commander of a battalion-sized task force consisting of tanks and armored infantry from the 10th Armored Division, who was already installed there.

In Holland, Lieutenant Colonel LaPrade (then a major) had distinguished himself by swimming the Wilhelmina Canal in Zon with a lieutenant and a sergeant in the face of withering enemy fire to establish a foothold on the enemy-held side. Many times after that he proved himself to be a leader and not a pusher.

Colonel William Roberts, commander of the 10th Armored's Combat Command B, ordered Major Desobry to force march his task force, which consisted of a company each of tanks and armored infantry plus a collection of engineers, medics, and reconnaissance troops, to Bastogne all the way from Remeling, France, on 17 December. Desobry and his men arrived in Bastogne the next evening. He was then ordered to take his task force straight to Noville, set up roadblocks outside town, and hold it until ordered to withdraw. Major Desobry and his men arrived in Noville at 11 P.M. on 18 December, after fighting their way through swarms of demoralized stragglers fleeing from the pursuing Germans.

Major Desobry did all that was ordered of him. He set out roadblocks to the north and northeast, each a half mile out of town. He ordered his men to hold those positions until daylight, then withdraw into Noville to consolidate their lines and hold that town.

The Germans attacked out of a heavy fog before dawn on the nineteenth, hit the roadblocks, and were smashed to a standstill by the 10th Armored men. The Germans, unable to dislodge the Americans, finally withdrew back the way they had come. Then, at daybreak, just as they had been ordered, the armored men fell back into Noville, where they could make a better stand.

The Germans evidently didn't know what size element they had encountered. They had been feeling their way westward through the fog that had settled in and so far had overrun everything in their way without much trouble.

Now they withdrew, licked their wounds, counted their losses, and made plans to attack in force and obliterate these Americans who didn't know any better than to stand in the way of a rolling Nazi blitzkrieg.

Major Desobry waited anxiously for the Germans to strike again. From what direction would they come? he wondered. With what? Tanks? Infantry? Both? What was their strength? When would they strike? Would he and his men be able to hold? One thing for certain, he vowed to himself: he was sure as hell going to give it his best. If he went under, the surviving Germans would know they had been in one hell of a fight.

An hour or so after daylight, two Tiger tanks approached Noville from out of the fog in the north and were blasted into junk. Then, at 10:30 A.M., the fog lifted like a stage curtain, revealing that the whole countryside was covered with enemy armor—Panthers, Tigers, armored cars, half-tracks, everything. Desobry's men counted thirty-two German tanks in one field alone. It seemed the whole damned

German army was out there. This small battalion from the 10th Armored sure had its work cut out for it.

The fog shifted, lowering and rising to and from the ground, stretching and reaching out toward the defenders like long fingers from gigantic ghostlike hands. The enemy was hidden and then revealed again as the fog rolled and lifted. Tanks would appear at one spot, then the fog would lower, and when it rose again the tanks would be gone, only to reappear at another spot when the curtain lifted again.

Then, Dame Fortune entered the picture. Word of the breakthrough had reached many scattered armored units, and those that were able made their way from all compass points toward strategic Bastogne. Some of them fought their way through or skirted the vanguard of the Germans forces to get there.

So it was that one platoon of the 705th Tank Destroyer (TD) Battalion arrived at this moment in Noville. The TDs, with their hefty 90mm guns, joined with Major Desobry's little task force and for more than an hour the big guns roared. Muzzles flashed, sending shrieking, flat-trajectory shells from villages and fields toward targets both seen and unseen. Tanks wheeled, ploughed, and maneuvered, seeking cover and positions that would give them a firepower advantage. Exploding tanks filled the milky fog with their luminous glow, and their burning hulks spewed oily, black smoke, adding to the blanket that obscured the battlefield. Buildings caught fire and burned, adding still more heavy smoke to the confusion and inspiring fear and anger.

The heavy battle noises gradually faded. A few machine guns chattered here and there, joined by sporadic rifle fire and punctuated by the sounds of an occasional tank round being fired and slamming into a target. The small American armored force had succeeded in halting the Germans, who withdrew to the other side of the high ground to the east, from whence they had come. They had encountered their first major obstacle since jumping off on 16 December. An enemy willing and able to stand and slug it out toe-to-toe with them had just kicked their butts.

This battle was the thunderstorm we had heard up ahead as we made our way toward Noville. Now we were on the outskirts, lying in the road ditches, waiting for the command to attack. Lieutenant Colonel LaPrade had made his way into Noville and was conferring with Major Desobry. Until he gave the order, we had to lie where we were and wait.

The 10th Armored Division troopers consolidated their positions and dug in deeper. Major Desobry no longer had questions about the Germans. All had been answered. Now that we had arrived he no longer wanted to wait for the enemy's next move; he wanted to mount an attack. As soon as Lieutenant Colonel LaPrade and he got together in the schoolhouse CP they agreed that LaPrade, by virtue of his rank, should assume command. They also agreed we would jump off in a coordinated attack head-on into the German lines to gain possession of the high ground overlooking Noville. The armored vehicles and their ground troops would take the Vaux, Houffalize, and Bourcy roads. Our B Company would attack toward Vaux, C Company would attack toward Bourcy, and A Company would attack northeast between B and C Companies. Our attack was scheduled to begin at 2 P.M., but due to our receiving ammo on the way up and other delays, we didn't get into position in time and the attack thus began at 2:30 P.M.

Our pace was slower than it had been on the approach march because we were walking in the ditches on either side of the northbound main road. As our lead men entered Noville, those of us on the right (east) side crossed over to the western side. It had become extremely quiet; no one was shooting at anyone. We came to a halt and, as we did, the sound of artillery shells arcing toward the town and our lines reached our ears. The big shells moaned high overhead; we could almost count their rotations by the sound they made. They came screaming in, louder and louder, shriller and shriller, on their downward path, seeming to gain momentum the closer they came. The sounds of big guns booming in the distance reached us. We hit the bottom of the ditches as one just before the volley slammed into the town. The explosions sent up clouds of dust, and the smell of cordite filled the air. Orange flames and black smoke erupted at their impact.

New fires started as older ones burned. Calls for medics to move up front sounded above the din. Cries of pain and fear mingled with the crash of exploding artillery shells. Buildings collapsed into piles of rubble. Vehicles burst into flames. Pockets of fog lying here and there were interlaced with streamers of wispy fog. It moved as though alive, rising and falling like a suffocating, breathing thing. "Screaming meemies" (German multibarreled, electrically fired rocket launchers called Nebelwerfers) joined in, sounding like the savage shrieks of a thousand giant wildcats. The rockets screamed on their way over and down, exploding violently in and around our positions, shaking the ground and jolting us—even those who were in foxholes.

Flat-trajectory shells fired from German high-velocity, self-propelled guns and tanks added to the shock and confusion.

Word was passed down from man to man, "Attack! Let's go, let's go." None of us were briefed as to details; we were just told to attack. That was it. Up ahead, men rose up and ran forward in the crouched position of men under fire. They yelled back, "Let's go, let's go, come on, let's go." We rose up to join them, starting forward as one. Now that we were in it, the sick feeling left my stomach, as I had known it would. My body returned to normal, my senses sharp and active. Glancing back at those behind us, we too yelled, "Come on, let's go, let's go," and gestured for them to follow. We raced forward through exploding artillery and automatic weapons and rifle fire. Dust, smoke, and fog obscured our view of the ground ahead. We didn't know the details of our attack; all we knew was to go forward, follow our platoon and squad leaders into the German lines, and kill anybody who got in our way.

Brininstool, our present squad leader, was several men up ahead of me. He had been looking out over the road, evaluating what was going on. Then I saw Liddle, his big frame moving steadily forward. Nothing seemed to faze him. Well, almost nothing. On occasion I had seen him grin his white, toothy grin, especially when things got bad or dangerous. He was one hell of a man.

A couple of new men rushed forward behind Liddle. One of them was a husky, young blond who had boasted back in the barracks about wanting to get into combat and kill a German with his bare hands. He was joined by his constant companion, a small, thin, dark-complected trooper who looked up to the husky blond. I don't recall their names for they had just arrived in our outfit only a few days before. Both were one-day paratroopers.

I glanced back. About five men behind me I saw Royce Stringfellow kneeling on one knee, a tommy gun in his hands. He was tall—six feet or more—and slim. More shells screamed in, blasting the area with explosions, dust, and shell fragments. At this point the blond braggart turned and began running back the way we had come. He rushed past, almost running me over, screaming wildly in a pell-mell race toward the rear, away from the enemy.

Stringfellow leaned forward as though making a bayonet thrust with his tommy gun and caught the running blond in the stomach with the muzzle, knocking the wind out of him. Stringfellow glared and screamed at the blond kid to get back up in front or he'd blast him right then and there. The new replacement begged and pleaded to be let go. Stringfellow took deliberate aim at him and said, "Now!" The man crawled on hands and knees back to the front of our squad, crying all the way. It was the only time I ever saw a man in our outfit act that way. His actions were completely foreign to us. His was an isolated case; our other one-day paratroopers took their cue from the old men and advanced without hesitating. It was as though they too were veterans.

We were all moving forward now, dispersing, getting more distance between us. It is natural to want to be close to someone else when death reigns, but training and past experience dictated getting away from each other. Speer hung fairly close to my right rear, although at a respectful distance. I felt a comfort in his presence there and drew strength from him.

A 10th Armored Division GI's body hung out of a wrecked jeep where the first road from the east joined the road we were on. He was still seated behind the steering wheel but his body was bent far left over the side, head down, arms outstretched, his life's blood dripping into the water-filled ditch alongside the road. The water, which had turned red for a hundred feet back down the ditch, stood in stark contrast against the white, snow-covered banks.

The Bourcy road came in from the east alongside the church at the next intersection. We crossed the exposed main road a few at a time, running in a low crouch, and made it past the church, spreading out on either side of the Bourcy road.

"Burgett, Phillips! Scouts!" Brininstool yelled, motioning for Phillips and me to move out. He wanted us to scout ahead a good distance in front of the rest of the company. Making contact with the enemy with scouts out front prevented the main body from being trapped in an ambush. It's cheaper to lose one or two men than to lose half a company. We rotated this dangerous duty so that each man in the company had a turn at it at one time or another.

Phillips looked at me with a half smile on his lips and shrugged his shoulders; I involuntarily shrugged mine and grinned back. He gathered his legs under him and took off running toward the north side of the street. I let him get about a hundred feet ahead and then followed.

German artillery was smashing heavily into the streets and houses. Wrecked American vehicles were everywhere—some of them burning, sending heavy black smoke into the gray mist and overcast. American dead lay in and out of many of the wrecks. Even more were in and between the buildings. The stench of death, along with the acrid smell of burnt powder and the dust, made breathing difficult.

Major Desobry's task force had done well holding back the German tide until we arrived, but many of his men died in the process. The bodies strewn in and about the carnage and destruction attested to the ferocity of their stand. I could only shake my head as we ran past.

German artillery shells and rockets continued shrieking and screaming into the city, blanketing every square yard with heavy explosions. Rifle and machine-gun fire swept the ruins and surrounding area. My throat was dry and burning as we made our way from doorway to doorway, leapfrogging up the road. First I would run past Phillips to a doorway ahead, then he would make a dash to a protected spot past me. Other A Company men were charging up the road hard on our heels. Still others had spread out toward our left flank, moving beyond the houses and into the fields.

Next to the last house on the right edge of the village, we saw the backs of two tanks between the rear of the house and a scattering of trees to its right. They were American Shermans. Phillips and I ran crouched over to the left rear of the house and flopped on our bellies on the ground behind it. A red-faced captain wearing a 10th Armored shoulder patch and carrying a carbine came running around a corner of the house, climbed on the nearest Sherman, and yelled down through the open hatch to the crew inside. The tank backed up, spun left, then wheeled to the right and slowly approached the left front of the house, poking its bow carefully out to get a clear field of fire. The captain leaped off the back deck of the tank and ran to the cover of a doorway in the house across the narrow street to our left front.

Several German tanks were clanking down the road, and we could see several more starting down the hills to our left front. Still more appeared on the forward slope of the hills to our far left, and we could see and hear even more in the trees to our right front. I counted sixteen Panthers and huge Tigers rumbling toward us. The enemy artillery barrage stopped. They couldn't keep plastering us with high explosives with their tanks and infantry moving into our area or they would wind up killing their own men.

The Sherman in front of us fired, and the one on the right cut loose a split second later. We could see German infantry swarming over the hills in front of us, still out of rifle range. Several 75mm and 88mm shells struck the house and the trees beside it. Orange balls of fire exploded around us. Bricks, stones, dust, tree limbs, and shrapnel flew through the air. Phillips and I hugged the ground.

The Sherman in front of us fired again; the third German tank back exploded, sending black, oily smoke mushrooming skyward. A second later the tank just behind it also exploded—probably hit by a round fired by the American tank on the right side of the house. I didn't hear its 75mm gun go off, but with all the explosions it was impossible to make out who was firing. Other enemy tanks returned fire. High-velocity tank shells rifled point-blank in our direction. They were so close we could smell the burnt powder and feel the shock waves of air from their muzzle blasts slapping us. Still more enemy shells slammed into the house and trees to our right, exploding all around us.

The Sherman in front of us rocked violently and was momentarily obscured by a cloud of dust. Suddenly it churned in reverse, headed toward where Phillips and I lay watching the tank duel.

"Look out!" Phillips screamed. We rolled over and over to our left, then scrambled on hands and knees, and finally rose to our feet and leaped headlong out of the way. The Sherman ploughed right over the spot where we had been lying.

The tank on the right moved into the woods on that side of the house and the first tank, the one that almost ran us over, swiveled into the spot the second Sherman had vacated. It fired a couple of rounds and then raced back to its previous position and fired again. While making this second maneuver, the driver backed into the left-rear corner of the house and became wedged there with the weight of the tank's right rear against the stone building. The tracks spun forward and then reversed, kicking out dirt, dust, and rubble. Several times the driver slammed the gears forward and back. The tank rocked and the lower corner of the house crumbled and gave way, freeing the Sherman from its grip.

The Sherman that had entered the trees would move forward fifty yards or so, fire, then move back and fire again. Those 10th Armored tankers worked so fast that even we thought there must have been at least four tanks there at the entrance to town and in the tree line.

All this time their captain had been standing there in the open, directing fire. The surviving German tanks started backing up the hill, firing as they withdrew. The infantry that had been following them also retreated back over the hills and out of sight. The tank captain stood glaring at the crest of the hill, his face red and bathed in sweat despite the cold December air. I walked up and congratulated him on the nice job he and his tankers had done repulsing the German attack.

He stared blankly at me for a moment, then cocked his head a little as though favoring his right ear, and said, "Sorry, you know, with those big guns going off, I can't hear too well."

He was breathing heavily, as though he had just run a mile, and his head swiveled quickly to the right and left as we talked, his eyes focusing on and searching the surrounding hills. When he removed his helmet to wipe his face with a sleeve, he revealed a thick head of bright-red hair.

Phillips and I wished him luck and then started forward again. German artillery, as though on cue, began plastering the area just as we stepped out. We could hear the shells coming in, some whistling loudly as they arced high above before screaming downward, louder and louder on their way in, shredding human nerves as well as the air in front of them on their path to death and destruction. Other shells screamed on flat trajectories from muzzle to target, with loud explosions marking their violent impact.

Artillery is the most horrible, death-dealing, feared instrument of modern war. More men have been wounded, maimed, or killed by artillery than by any other means since the advent of gunpowder. When you are being pummeled by artillery there is nothing you can do to strike back. All you can do is lie there and listen to the shrieking, screaming shells coming in and the loud explosions they make when they hit. Your throat dries up and your lungs burn as you breathe in the burnt powder, dust, and acrid smoke caused by the blasts. You instinctively hug the ground as hot, ragged steel fragments and splinters of shrapnel tear into trees, stone walls, and human bodies. There is nothing you can do to fight back while all around you flesh is being torn to red, bloody scraps.

Some men pray, some yell at the enemy, and some just lie there quietly in their holes, being bounced and jarred around while they await their fate. At times under heavy, prolonged shelling I found myself yelling, screaming at the enemy to stop. I would scream for the shelling to stop, for the enemy to come out face-to-face with us and get it over with. On the other hand, when it was our shells rumbling overhead toward the enemy, I would yell, "Give it to them! Give it to them! Don't stop until you've killed every goddamned one of them."

The fog was still with us. At times it would rise up to hang in a low ceiling over the battleground, then drop suddenly to cover everything like a thick, white blanket. At other times it would ebb and flow in patches, filling the low spots. All of this added to the confusion and fear on both sides. Men and tanks moved about in this nightmarish mess, firing small arms and cannon at whomever they thought might be the enemy.

Phillips and I ran forward through the fields the German tanks had just abandoned, pushing toward the enemy-held hills through the mist, fog, and explosions to a small, low-roofed stone hut a little farther ahead. Phillips dove headfirst through the small doorway, with me right on his heels. The place turned out to be a chicken coop. Shells slammed into the ground just outside of it. We could hear the not-too-distant booming of the big guns, followed by the shriek of high-trajectory shells coming right at us. The floor was covered with chicken manure but we hugged it close as the explosions and hot steel fragments rained around us. We breathed burnt powder and the dust of dried chicken manure that hung thickly around us deep into our lungs. I looked at Phillips. He was wide-eyed, bewildered, and I knew I must have looked the same to him, for I too was suffering shock from the hammer blows of the artillery. The shelling finally stopped briefly, and we broke from the doorway and ran low to the ground to another place that looked almost like the one we had just left.

We figured we would wait there just long enough for the Germans to make adjustments to their big guns, then take off running as soon as we heard their distant booming and head for the next spot that afforded some measure of cover.

We had long since learned that it takes long-range artillery a good bit of time to reach the target. Sometimes you can hear the booming of the guns before you hear the sound of the incoming shells. Other times you don't hear anything until you pick up the sound of shells rotating and screaming just about at the top of their arc from cannon to target. If you live long enough, you can learn to almost pinpoint the spot of impact where high-trajectory shells will hit, just by the sounds they make.

On the other hand, a high-velocity, flat-trajectory round fired from a rifle or field piece reaches the target before the sound of its firing. If you hear the report of a rifle or 88mm gun, the bullet or shell it fired has long since passed. A man never hears the rifle that fires the bullet that kills him because the bullet travels much faster than the sound.

While we were racing toward the second chicken coop, the chicken coop we'd just left was obliterated. The second chicken coop suffered the same fate when we abandoned it, and our third haven, a pigsty, was smashed to rubble around us. The Germans were dogging our footsteps with heavy artillery, or so it seemed to us.

Finally, they either lost interest in us or lost us from view, for the fire directed at us let up somewhat when we raced forward again and flung ourselves into another dung-filled pigsty.

"Man, I'm hurtin' for a cigarette," I said, gasping for breath as I reached with fumbling fingers into a pocket of my jumpsuit for a pack.

"Me too," Phillips replied.

We leaned back against the filth-covered wall, lit up, inhaled, and relaxed while a heavy concentration of enemy artillery shells continued to rain down on Noville and the surrounding area without letup. We smoked about half a cigarette each, then peeked out of the low door of the stone pigsty, evaluated the strike of incoming shells, and made our break, running low and fast. We made it safely to one of several haystacks on the north side of the road, almost at the foot of the enemy-held hills. The haystacks looked like giant mushrooms. Cattle had eaten into the undersides all the way around, leaving rounded tops lapping protectively over. We were making our way as best we could toward the enemy. We had to make it to the hills, climb them, and then close in on the bastards who were killing us.

Others from our platoon caught up to us here. Brininstool and two other troopers, Speer and Liddle, hunkered down under a nearby haystack while others scattered around us, taking whatever cover they could find.

Snuggling in close to the base of the haystack, Phillips and I lay flat, surveying the crest of the hill in front of us. From here on the sloping ground was completely without cover or concealment. It had been grazed over by livestock and was now blanketed with a couple of inches of snow. Our dark jumpsuits stood out starkly against the snow, making us easy targets for the enemy.

The bows of several tanks appeared on the hillcrest facing us. A huge, lone Tiger rolled over the top and rumbled slowly down the slope toward us. The other tanks stayed where they were. It was too late to do anything but squeeze down as low as possible and hope for the best. There was too much open ground between the haystacks and the town or any other protection. We didn't have a snowball's chance in hell of making it across the fields to safety. It would have been certain death to try. My head spun; I felt like a trapped animal. We were all trapped animals.

"If we had a bazooka we might be able to knock it out—or at least go down trying," Phillips said.

"Yeah," I agreed. "Maybe we could hit it in the ribs a couple of times, at least let them know we were here. Look at the size of that son-of-a-bitch! It's as big as a house."

The Tiger was always something to behold. It was monstrous, dwarfing the Allied Shermans, Churchills, and Cromwells, and even its cousin, the Panther. Its 88mm gun looked like a telephone pole sticking out of a moving two-story house.

The Tiger stopped about a hundred yards from us, not doing anything, just sitting there with its engine idling, the bow and turret machine guns pointing right at us. Maybe it wasn't really after us. Maybe its crew didn't know we were there. Or perhaps they were trying to figure out if we had a bazooka with us or not. Why didn't they just open fire and be done with it?

Suddenly the fast, ripping burps of a machine gun split the air and a string of bullets stitched the haystack across the middle. The tracers started a fire that quickly spread to the mushroom-like upper part of the stack. Soon the heat was uncomfortable and getting hotter. We scooted backward on our bellies around the base of the stack to the rear part, away from the tank. But it would be just a matter of time and we would either be cooked alive or exposed to the direct fire of the tank's guns again.

Brininstool yelled at me to return the way we had come, find the company commander, and ask for permission to withdraw the squad from its exposed position. "Are you nuts?" I yelled. "If I try to cross that field they'll blow me to bits."

He just glared at me and again ordered me to move out.

I knew better than to argue, so I crouched like a runner ready for the starting gun, then took off on a dead run, keeping the haystack between me and the tank. Bullets and tracers whizzed around me, but I kept going. I found our company commander on the outskirts of town in one of the houses and relayed Brininstool's request.

"No, we've got to go forward, or at least hold where we are," the captain said.

Without waiting I spun around and went running back up the road toward the edge of town, passing the redheaded 10th Armored captain, who was standing in the same doorway where I had last seen him. Then I was racing back over the exposed, snow-covered ground through shellfire, exploding mortar rounds, and lancing bullets. The haystacks seemed so far away, but I kept zigzagging toward them. I finally reached the haystacks—still in one piece, much to my amazement. The haystacks were really burning as I slid in beside Phillips.

I yelled over to Brininstool, relaying the captain's order to continue the attack or hold where we were. Attacking was impossible. Staying there much longer seemed equally impossible. Our entire haystack was ablaze. Pieces of burning hay began falling on us. We had to leave.

"It's now or never," Phillips said. "I'm going."

He leaped to his feet and took off running toward the rear of the houses lining the road. The tank opened up on him with its machine guns, but he kept going. Suddenly the rest of the men lying around me exploded like a covey of quail flushed in a hunt. They ran fast and low, zigzagging toward town. The tank's machine guns hammered away at them. I could see bullets kicking up little geysers in the snow all around them but no one fell.

I guess this is it for me, too, I thought. Maybe I can get some distance between us before he sees me. With that I darted out, racing back toward Noville and the protection of the houses. In the back of my mind was the thought of the two Shermans we'd left behind at the entrance of town on the south side of the road.

*If this son-of-a-bitch decides to follow me he's going to be in for a surprise, I thought.*

Sprinting low to the ground and angling across the fields, I reached the road leading into the center of town. I don't recall seeing anyone else from my squad during this run. Machine-gun bullets crackled past my head. Then I heard the roar of a big engine. I glanced over my shoulder and caught a glimpse of the Tiger lurching forward like some prehistoric monster intent on catching me. I made it to the road and ran straight down its center with every ounce of strength and speed I could muster. The Tiger was only a couple of hundred yards or so behind and gaining. I didn't try to zigzag; I just wanted to put as much distance as I could between that metal monster and myself and make it to the safety of one of the houses in town.

Bursts of machine-gun bullets lanced past me, splattering the pavement around and ahead of me before whining off in different directions. I could see sparks fly where the bullets struck the pavement to my front. Glancing over my shoulder and seeing the muzzle of the big 88mm gun pointed straight at me sent a feeling churning through the pit of my stomach that is impossible to describe. Goose bumps rose on my arms, and I could feel the hair crawling on the nape of my neck.

I passed the first house on the left and saw that the Shermans were gone.

*Son-of-a-bitch, where in the hell did they go, and why now?* I wondered.

Enemy shells still rained on the city, exploding with deafening crashes. Smoke and dust filled the air among the buildings, and many raged with fire. Then, just as I approached the first house on the right, the 10th Armored captain I'd seen earlier stepped from his doorway with his carbine at port arms and shouted, "Halt!"

"Halt hell, get out of my way," I yelled as I sailed past him. He looked down the road, saw the tank coming, and dove backward into the doorway. I was going too fast to make the same door, but I was able to dive into the third or fourth one past him.

Phillips and Liddle were standing in the second room talking. I was glad to see they had made it and were still alive. The corpse of an old civilian lay on an ornate brass bed in the far-left corner of the room.

"Get out the back door fast!" I yelled.

Neither Liddle nor Phillips waited for an explanation. All three of us squirted through the entrance at the same time, diving right and left away from the door opening. The big tank pulled up broadside to the front of the house, rotated the turret until the cannon's muzzle protruded through the front door into the living room, and fired.

There was one hell of an explosion inside the house, nearly ruining it completely and blowing away most of the back wall. Then the driver reversed the gears and backed up, pivoted the chassis around while the turret remained pointed in our direction, and raced back up the hill and out of sight over the crest.

The three of us reentered the house. The old civilian's corpse had been splattered against what was left of the far back wall, and his bed was a twisted pile of scrap metal. Goose down from the bedclothes mixed with plaster dust and filled the rooms like a fine snow. We sat on the floor leaning against an outer wall, lit up cigarettes, and looked out a back window. We could see more German tanks burning in the B and C Company sectors, sending black columns of smoke billowing into the low-hanging overcast. We obviously weren't the only ones who had been busy.

The B and C Company attacks had carried them to the crest of the hills before they ran into enemy armor backed by infantry. The overwhelming firepower from the tanks and panzer grenadiers stopped their advance, killing many of the paratroopers as they pressed their attack. Their frozen bodies lay on the snow-covered crests for several weeks before they were finally recovered. The survivors of those two companies had to withdraw, just as we did, back into Noville.

Our company encountered German armor almost immediately, and we did not get to close in on the enemy one-on-one as we had hoped. The German infantry in our sector chose to stay behind the hillcrests, well behind their armor. However, the Germans remained patiently behind the hillcrests in B and C Companies' sectors, letting them advance until they were within point-blank range of their tanks' big guns and the infantry's small arms before they opened up. The effects were devastating, and many of our brother paratroopers were slaughtered on the spot.

When our attack stalled and we were caught well out forward under the haystacks, we had had little hope of making it back alive. Fate and the whim of that Tiger crew, whatever that may have been, spared us. There was no doubt in any of our minds that the men in that tank could have killed all of us right there if they had been intent on it.

Orders came down the line verbally. The 10th Armored men were to move back to the center of town and dig in for a last defensive stand. We paratroopers were ordered to dig in and form an outer perimeter around Noville as a first line of defense. Wrecked tanks and other vehicles were scattered around our perimeter, through-

out the open fields, and in the village itself. The bodies of tankers
and paratroopers lay everywhere. Fog continued to settle and rise,
and explosions and fires glowed through the mist. We dug in to await
the next German attack.

Smoke from the burning tanks and houses blended with the fog
and haze that was settling over the low ground between the houses
and the hills. The deep-throated thudding of American machine
guns answered the fast-ripping burps of German automatic weapons.
Mortar shells made their familiar *whoomp* sound as they hit and detonated. Artillery shells whistled overhead and slammed around us
in devastating volleys, while screaming meemies shrieked down, exploding in violent volleys that jarred the whole countryside. White
phosphorous shells landed in and around our positions, bursting in
fountains of white smoke that showered flesh-burning chemicals into
our foxholes.

"My God!" Liddle exclaimed. "They're using American artillery.
The Krauts don't have white phosphorous of their own. They're using our own ammunition against us."

Our area was being plundered of life and buildings by the heavy
shelling. The three of us talked a little while, wondering what was
happening. For once we were bewildered, and we were becoming
more bewildered by the minute. The words of the retreating Americans the day before came back to haunt us: "You'll all be killed!
You'll all be killed!"

I wondered why that enemy tank had chased me down the street
and then backed off. There was no doubt in my mind that the men
inside could have blown me away at any moment if they had *really*
wanted to. Maybe they were just toying with me. Maybe they thought
I would lead them to our CP—or at least to a larger group of men
so they could kill more of us.

The Tiger approached our haystacks, spraying them with machine-gun fire, setting them ablaze to flush out the men the crew
knew were in there, then they had picked one man to follow. They
didn't choose one of the men running through the open fields; they
chose me: the one man running down the main road into town.
There was a purpose in their method of selection, even in the way
they had fired machine-gun bursts around me as I ran, but I failed
to comprehend it.

Speer came up to the house we were in and looked through the gaping hole in the back wall. "What did that tank do?" he asked. "He made a mess out of that old civilian and his bed," Liddle answered, nodding his head sideways at the scrambled corpse smeared in the corner. "I hope his kinfolk won't think we done that to him when they come back to bury him."

We left the house to join the rest of the men in our company as they began occupying positions along a bank that ran more or less east and west in back of the houses and parallel with the road. Speer, Liddle, and I ran crouched over through exploding artillery and small-arms fire raking the area along the line back toward the still-burning haystacks. We were instructed to dig in at the farthest point to the northeast in A Company's part of the perimeter. We were given the positions closest to the enemy.

We were halfway to the haystacks when the Germans cut loose with everything they had this side of hell. We dove for cover in a ditch behind a stone building. Artillery shells were landing so thick and fast that one would have been hard pressed to throw a helmet into the air and have it hit the ground in one piece. We hugged the bottom of the ditch next to a cobblestone wall with several other troopers and waited for a letup. Men were being hit. Screams of pain and cries of "Medic!" could be heard above the deafening roar of exploding shells.

A new replacement, a young man of Italian descent who looked like an actor named Leo Corillo, ran around the corner of the building screaming, his guts trailing in the dirt behind him. He was holding most of them in his arms. Frank Gaddy leaped from the ditch, tackled him, and had to fight to keep him on the ground until we could reach him.

Shells still pounded the area and shrapnel still shredded the air all around, but three of us held the little guy down until he quit fighting. He lay there sobbing and whimpering, shaking his head from side to side, his eyes wide and glassy, staring at nothing.

I took the raincoat off my belt and laid it on the ground. Gaddy wet his hands with water from his canteen and then poured some of the water onto the coat and piled the man's guts on it. Together we washed his entrails, picking off the largest pieces of dirt and stone with our fingers before forcing his guts back into his belly. Then we bound him up tight around the midsection with strips cut from my raincoat, shot him with morphine, and dragged him into the ditch to wait for a medic.

The barrage let up a little and we made it to our positions beyond where the haystacks had been. We took possession of some nearby foxholes dug by men who had fought here before us. I found a slit trench and lay down in it. I didn't like slit trenches; I preferred foxholes. But I had no entrenching tool, so I had little choice.

Midafternoon came on and with it came another German attack. Seven tanks—a mix of Tigers and Panthers backed by infantry—approached our lines, belching fire from their 75s and 88s and raking everything in front of them with machine-gun fire. More tanks were moving in the B and C Company sectors, sixteen tanks in all, followed closely this time by their infantry.

They moved at a slow pace, the long barrels of their cannon looking like huge snouts as they swiveled around, seeming to sniff every shadow, every corner, and every ditch. They stopped often, sometimes turning a little to the right or left, then moved forward again. Slowly and relentlessly grinding toward us. We watched over the edges of our foxholes with bloodshot eyes glaring from beneath the steel rims of our helmets as they plodded inexorably onward, their firepower laying waste everything in front of them—everything they thought might harbor a bazooka man, antitank gun, or infantrymen. As I lay there at the bottom of my slit trench, I felt the heat of an engine as a tank passed close by, its tracks crumbling bits of earth from the edge of the hole down on top of me. We didn't have a bazooka—not even a rocket or a Gammon grenade. Even the large rocks were frozen to the ground, so we couldn't push them between the bogie wheels and maybe cause one of the metal behemoths to throw a track. Our rifles and carbines were about as effective against those steel monsters as a handful of sand thrown against the backside of an enraged bull elephant.

So we did the only intelligent thing left for us to do: We lay in the bottoms of our foxholes and let the enemy armor pass through our line, the German infantry following a safe distance behind—quietly and methodically firing at random, working their rifle bolts, and firing again.

Fires from burning vehicles and houses flickered and glowed, casting weird shadows in the gloom of smoke and fog that caused the advancing infantry to appear as though they were dancing and weaving. They seemed to grow in size, then blip into nothingness. They appeared from and disappeared into wisps of fog and smoke, ghostly forms moving toward us with fire flashing from the muzzles of their weapons.

The fog, haze, and smoke that shielded the enemy from us also hid us from them. Had it been clear, the enemy tanks would have seen our dark-suited bodies against the lighter snow and the tanks could have run their tracks over us, crushing out our lives. I have seen this done.

Still we waited. We waited for the tanks to pass us and for the oncoming infantry to get close enough so that every one of our shots would count. Every time we pulled the trigger, there would have to be meat on the table. We could not afford to waste a single round.

At last the panzer grenadiers were within effective range—so close that nervous sweat soaked my clothes, even in that cold, wintry air. We always yelled and screamed like Indians or animals whenever we attacked, but these Germans came on quietly, methodically, in a military fashion, doing a job they had been trained for since childhood.

We opened up instinctively, without command. Our small-arms fire lanced into their ranks, raking them with a deadly hail of hot steel (our combat rifle ammo consisted of copper-jacketed, armor-piercing rounds). I was firing at shadows, but the way they grew, shortened, and wavered in the light of the fires in the fog, it was hard to tell whether we were hitting accurately or not. I could see them in and out of the flickers and shadows and fired each shot deliberately at individual figures, rather than fire several snapshots at clusters of men who happened to bunch up.

After every eighth round fired the clip ejected and I would reload, aim, and fire again. My rifle bucked against my shoulder and a figure would spin away or drop. Then I would aim and fire again and again and again. I never noticed the recoil of my M1 as it bucked with each shot. The barrel grew hot and oil oozed from the wood stock. Still I fired. All up and down our line rifles and machine guns kept up a steady roar. We could hear some tank fire in town but that was not our concern. Bullets cut close, spattered the frozen ground around us, and cracked sharply as they passed close by our heads. We didn't duck or think about them; we just kept firing. We had to kill to live.

The enemy tanks, which had been moving so ponderously, suddenly sprang to life, pivoting around, churning the ground and snow as they spun back in our direction. Engines whined with the surge of power. The huge machines thundered, the ground shuddered under them, high-velocity shells screamed from gun muzzles, and shells exploded indiscriminately amongst us. Screams and shouts broke out and men could be seen running in all directions. Hundreds of fiery tracers laced the air. Confusion reigned.

Several shells skimmed above the top of my slit trench, exploding near the opposite edge of my hole from the direction in which they had come. I was thrown bodily out of the hole by the concussion, hit the ground hard, and rolled quickly back into it. The left sleeve of my jump jacket was torn from cuff to elbow. More shells screamed straight at me. It would be close. My God, it would be close!

Again and again big rounds landed close around my shallow trench, exploding violently. Several more times I was blasted from the hole, but each time I managed to roll back into it. The hair on my left arm and the left side of my face was singed. My skin was blackened by burnt powder. The enemy's big guns roared uninterrupted. Volleys of shells screamed toward us, rending the air with their sudden passage. Most of them, it seemed to me, were coming directly at me. Why me? Of course, that wasn't true at all, but when you're alone in a hole with very limited visibility and under extremely heavy shelling, it sure seems that way. All of Noville was getting its fair share of the pounding. The German infantry had pulled back to evade our accurate shooting. Their tanks had overrun us and reached the center of Noville but they could not remain there without a screen of their own infantry to guard them. The Germans lost several tanks to our Shermans and TDs hidden in town, and the rest pulled out, back over the crests of the hills from which they had come. Again the enemy artillery took over.

It had grown totally dark. Suddenly I felt alone. Where were my comrades? I felt helpless. I couldn't fight back. I was alone in a fiery maelstrom, choking on burnt powder, dust, and smoke. The German tanks were no longer in our midst but I knew they were still out there somewhere in the fog and dark, waiting. If it had only been men attacking us it wouldn't have been so bad. You can use rifles and knives to close in on and fight a man. Even tanks could be destroyed with the right weapons: bazookas and satchel charges or grenades. That was something we understood and did not really fear. But long-range artillery was something else. It was hidden safely on the other side of the hills where we couldn't see it. We couldn't strike back. All we could do was lie there and be pounded mercilessly into the ground. We truly were cannon fodder. Amidst all that had been the monstrous tanks running over us, crushing the life from men and firing large-caliber cannons at point-blank range.

I stared vacantly into the pitch-black darkness around me and shivered.

"Pull back! Pull back!"

The Germans had launched yet another attack, and the words came down the line, shouted from man to man in the inky darkness. I was confused; my head spun. We had closed with enemy tanks before but never against so many and with nothing at all to fight them.

I could vaguely make out shadowy forms rising out of the ground and heading back toward town. I couldn't tell who they were but I could see that they were bent over and moving in the direction of our CP in the schoolhouse. Never before had we fallen back in the face of the enemy. It wasn't right; we couldn't be defeated. It was impossible. This was a battlefield, a life-and-death struggle of individuals among thousands, with no one knowing who or what was where, how many there were, or why they were there.

Where were my buddies? Where was the rest of A Company? I called out amidst the crash of artillery fire. It was like yelling into the teeth of a hurricane—no one answered. Our lines were stretched so thinly over such a long span of front facing the enemy that we had lost contact with each other. We'd had to stretch out our line to make up for our losses. I called for Speer, who was always near me. No answer. I called for Phillips, Liddle, Brininstool, Bielski, Vetland—anybody. Still there was no answer.

The fog, laced with smoke from burning fires, hung thickly all around. I could hear the screams of wounded and dying men amid the shrieking of incoming artillery and the crash of tank guns. My mind was still addled from being blown out of the ground. I could smell my burnt hair. The clothes on my left side were torn and ragged from the close artillery blasts. I was cold and alone. Where in the hell *was* everybody?

I wasn't about to be left out there to die alone amid such confusion. I wanted to be with the others to make a last stand. From what I could make out in the darkness and fog, they were falling back to the center of town to regroup and make their stand there. I slipped out of my slit trench and ran after them in a low crouch, darting through the night, the dust, the heavy smoke, and the explosions. I could hear the angry snapping of small-arms fire and make out forms in the light of burning fires moving back toward the center of town.

When I arrived at the intersection near the schoolhouse, I could see the figures of men. Were they fellow troopers? 10th Armored men? I didn't know. The fog, dust, and smoke were so thick that the fires in burning buildings appeared as orange glows, with the shadowy forms of men moving about them. The moving shadows could have been friend or foe. It was impossible to tell until you were close enough to reach out and touch each other.

Some of the groups of men, I discovered, consisted of both troopers and armored infantrymen milling about and talking amongst themselves. A few, probably officers and noncoms, were yelling above the din of battle: "It's all a mistake! Go back to your original positions. Our orders are to hold this goddamned town, and by God, we're going to hold it."

I remember wishing they would make up their minds. I had heard the order to pull back into town and now I heard the order to return to the line. I had to hurry. I realized my buddies were still back there, and I felt the need to be with them. I wanted to get back before they missed me. I didn't want them to know I had left our lines. I didn't want them to think I had quit or let them down.

Once again I found myself running in a crouched position through burning Noville, my torn sleeve flapping behind me—running back toward the foxhole I had just left.

• • •

The second German advance had ground to a halt. The battle was still going on, but with both sides having to grope their way around it had quieted down some. The enemy tanks weren't moving now. They had withdrawn out of town and were sitting on the outskirts in the fields in front of our lines, their engines idling, waiting for a chance to use their big guns.

After the German armor overran our outer foxhole positions and entered the streets of Noville, Major Desobry's tanks and the 705th TDs that had previously pulled back and occupied strategic positions in town blasted a goodly number of them clear into Valhalla. Now the surviving Germans sat in the fields outside Noville waiting for the fog to lift before making their next move. It dawned on me that the two Shermans I had been counting on to save me earlier, when I was being chased down the road by the Tiger, had moved to positions where they could give a better account of themselves.

A barrage of small-arms fire from GIs and Germans blasting at each other from all directions scythed through the air as men from both sides cautiously felt their way about, looking for someone to kill. Men were relying heavily on grenades because they are more effective in a heavy fog than trying to fire accurately with a rifle, plus there was no tell-tale muzzle flash to give away one's position to the enemy. It was hard to believe that just three days before I had been living it up in Paris without a care in the world.

Moving back down the street I came to the very last house on the road. I hadn't run into or passed anyone on my way back. Then I saw them: the shadows of men gathered in the dark area close to the ruined house. Evidently they had already seen me. I approached warily, my rifle pointed in their direction, my finger on the trigger with the safety off. They turned out to be several troopers lurking in the deeper shadows. After I identified myself I asked if any of them knew the whereabouts of A Company's 2d Platoon. They told me my buddies were in a house on the south side of the road. I made my way to where it stood—dark and foreboding but untouched by fire. From the outside there didn't seem to be any sign of life. I entered quietly, my feet crunching on broken glass scattered on the floor, and made my way to the cellar. There I found most of the men from A

Company. They were being briefed on the situation and instructed where to dig in to form a new line connecting with B and C Companies.

Once again, A Company was stretched sparingly along the ridge running northeast from the houses and past the smoldering ruins of the haystacks. This ridge and our line ran about two hundred feet from and parallel with the road. The ground was level from the road to the edge of the ridge, then it dropped away, forming a bank about four feet or so high that ran down to a flat table of farmland stretching to the foot of the enemy-held hills. Foxholes dotted the edge of this bank, dug by infantry units that had been there before us. A Company reoccupied these holes, and this time Speer and I got the one on the company's far right flank, nearest the remains of the haystacks. Liddle was somewhere nearby. I didn't know quite where but I knew he was alone. I also knew he would be there when needed; we could count on him.

Artillery had been raining down steadily during our move back out to the ridge, exploding in and around Noville and in our sector on targets probably unseen by the enemy. They were blanketing the entire area, destroying and killing as much as possible in preparation for their next attack, whenever that might be. Suddenly the artillery fire intensified. The attack would probably be soon.

As the shells again poured down heavily around us, we hugged the bottom of our holes. The concussions from near misses bounced Speer and me around ours like the pea in a whistle. Orange balls of fire from exploding shells blossomed in the dark and fog, and the smell of cordite filled the air. The German tanks edged closer behind this protective curtain. Seemingly on cue, probably thanks to adjustments called in from the tanks, the artillery began to zero in on our positions.

We were again compelled to leave our holes and take cover in the basements of the houses. This time Speer and I moved back with the others in short, running spurts through the darkness, racing from cover to cover as explosions and shell fragments filled the air.

The house in which most of the men from 2d Platoon were taking cover had a basement that was in semidarkness, a lone candle flickering pitifully on a box or small table near a root cellar that was half filled with sugar beets. An old woman and three young children lay huddled together on the sugar beets. The old woman whimpered, sobbed, and cried constantly as explosions rocked the city and the house above us. When shells landed close to our house, shaking the walls and foundation around us, she would cringe and pull a short blanket up over her head while her body convulsed with wails and sobs. She certainly couldn't have been much comfort to the little ones gathered close to her.

A woman of about thirty wearing a black sweater stood stoically in the corner, her arms folded across her chest. A young man, perhaps fifteen years old, stood nervously next to her. He was a little shorter than she was and very thin. He wore no coat or jacket, and his white shirt stood out in sharp contrast to everything else around the cellar. He kept shuffling his feet nervously but he never left the woman's side.

They were the first live civilians we had seen since the ones who had given us coffee back in Bastogne.

Sergeant Vetland rested with one butt cheek atop a barrel at the foot of the stairs leading into the basement. I guess he wanted to be the first to see anyone entering our newfound bunker. He held his tommy gun at the ready, with the muzzle pointing toward the opening at the head of the stairs. He constantly checked his watch to note the time, all the while listening intently to the artillery coming in around us. If the artillery let up, we knew the enemy would begin moving on Noville and that we would have to rush back out to our positions to meet them. Most of the rest of the men were here, too. Bielski sat on the floor with the squad's .30-caliber machine gun leaning against his husky body. He was a good machine gunner. Although I hadn't been in a position to witness his actions during our last few firefights, I knew he must have wreaked havoc on the enemy.

Benson, Phillips, Luke Easly, and Hassle Wright were there, too. Luke was from Peoria, Illinois; Hassle Wright was from Kentucky, and a crack shot. I don't recall seeing Liddle. I remember hoping he wasn't still out there on the line alone. But, knowing Liddle, that wouldn't have mattered to him.

There were others there, scattered about in different spots and positions in the cellar. Speer and I made our way through the sprawled troopers, stepping over arms and legs to flop in the first clear space we came to. We did not move around to see if there might be a spot where we might make ourselves more comfortable. I noticed that our new replacement, the Indian who had shared his fish with us was not there. I asked if anyone had seen him. He was dead, killed in the first five minutes of our attack by shrapnel. So were the husky, blond braggart and his small sidekick. Many of the old men had also been hit—most wounded, some killed. Since I had been one of the scouts out in front of A Company's main body, I did not see who got it in our first attack.

Watching Vetland's face in the flickering glow of the candle and seeing his eyes look more frequently from his watch to the door, I knew that it must be close to dawn. We would have to return to our foxholes before it was light. I watched his expressionless face in the light of the candle.

A few minutes later he stood up and said, "Let's go." Without looking back to see if we were following, he led the way up the stairs. As I passed the root cellar, I noticed the young woman staring woodenly at us. There didn't seem to be any feeling one way or the other in her eyes, just a dull, vacant, far-off stare.

Outside, the artillery was still coming in at a steady pace, but not as heavy as it had been during the night. The early morning air was heavy with fog. The damp, windless air caused the dust and smoke to hug the ground. The whole city of Noville was in flames; the buildings were in ruins. Great holes gaped in the walls of the houses we had taken refuge in, and the floors were scattered with broken glass and debris. Piles of bricks, stone, and rubble amidst the burning shells of buildings were all that was left of the town. The burning hulks of tanks, half-tracks, jeeps, and trucks were scattered throughout the ruined city. Some of them were funeral pyres for the cremated crews trapped inside.

The broken and torn bodies of GIs lay haphazardly throughout the village. Others were huddled in foxholes and in the corners of buildings, where they had died seeking refuge from the holocaust around them. Countless German corpses formed a ghostly perimeter around Noville, scattered in uncomfortable, grotesque heaps or cremated in burned-out tanks and other vehicles of war.

It was still dark and foggy as we made our way in a long, scattered single file back across the north side of the road to our original positions along the ridge running from the houses to the haystacks. Again Speer and I took our place in the foxhole at the extreme right flank of the company line. Phillips found and teamed up with Liddle. Others were in holes by themselves in order to cover a wider area. Speer and I chose to buddy together because, being closest to the enemy, we would be the first ones to get hit when the attack came. We needed to be able to cover each other.

There was very little small-arms firing and even the big guns had slowed their booming. An explosion close to our left, toward town, shattered the air and a dull orange glow of fire appeared, barely visible in the fog. Everyone was at the edge of their foxholes, their eyes straining. Minutes later there was another explosion, followed by another dimly visible burst of flame in the fog. Again the minutes dragged by, then a third explosion rent the air. Then there was nothing more than occasional bursts of small-arms fire and the sound of heavy artillery rounds rumbling overhead toward targets in our rear.

Word came down from foxhole to foxhole to watch out for Sergeant Vetland. German tanks had halted just in front of our positions before we pulled back during the night, and he sensed they were still there, although it was impossible to see more than a couple of feet in the dense fog. He borrowed Charley Syer's bazooka and three rockets and went hunting out front in no-man's-land. He was amongst them.

Groping his way quietly through the fog, he listened for the sound of enemy tank engines idling. Locating the first tank, Vetland crept forward until he was right next to it, laid his hand against the armor, then felt back and forth along the full length of the tank until he found its midsection. Keeping the bazooka pointed at the spot, he backed slowly away. When he figured he was at a safe distance, he knelt, took careful aim at the spot that he couldn't see but knew was right in front of him, and fired a rocket. The tank exploded violently, erupting in flame and incinerating the crew.

That wasn't enough for Sergeant Vetland, though. He still had two rockets left. Again he went quietly among the enemy until he located another tank in the same manner. Following the same procedure he let fly another rocket and another German tank went up in flames. His third try was less successful, and the crippled tank limped away through the fog, back toward its own lines.

Ted Vetland returned to our lines and crawled back in his foxhole after returning the bazooka to Charley Syer. The burning tanks glowed dully through the heavy fog. When daylight finally filtered down to us, it was still so foggy that I felt like I was trying to look through a glass of milk. Thus began our second day in Noville, 20 December 1944.

It was still early when we heard the sound of high-velocity tank guns firing away back in the center of Noville. A couple of German tanks had made it into town and, after an exchange of shots, were knocked out by our armor. The morning wore on with little happening. Very little small-arms or artillery fire was going out or coming in. Then, just before the fog lifted, a Tiger tank ran all the way into the center of town and ground to a stop right in front of a damaged Sherman. The Sherman's turret had been hit and could traverse only a few degrees to the right or left. The tank commander had backed his tank just off the main Houffalize road into a narrow street that intersected the main road coming in from the east. He parked it between two ruined buildings right at the intersection and waited.

The Tiger had stopped about thirty-five to forty feet in front of the Sherman's 75mm gun. The Sherman fired. The shell hit the Tiger right in the ribs and ricocheted off. The Sherman pumped out two more armor-piercing shells in rapid succession. Despite the close range, both shells careened off, whining end over end into the distance. The Tiger took the hits without apparent damage. But, when it tried to back out the same way it had come in, it ran into a parked jeep and a wrecked half-track. The driver rolled up on them, smashing them flatter than cow pies, and got stuck on top of them. The crew abandoned the Tiger, running like hell through the fog and out of town. Our tankers destroyed the Tiger with a thermite grenade. Later they caught hell from General McAuliffe. That captured Tiger and its fearsome 88mm gun had been in perfect condition. It would have been a hell of a boon to our defense of Noville.

Not long after that incident, about midmorning, the fog lifted like a stage curtain. It didn't blow away with a breeze or dissolve, it rose straight up in a matter of seconds and hung there, about forty feet in the air. In front of us, scattered throughout the snow-covered fields, was a swarm of enemy tanks. I counted twelve just to our immediate front. Still more were visible in front of the company sectors to our right and left. I counted up to thirty-two and then quit. They were just sitting there, their engines idling, vapor clouds drifting up from their exhausts.

One of the tanks, a Panther, wasn't more than ten feet in front of the foxhole Speer and I shared. The tank commander's head was sticking out of the turret, and I could see him talking on his radio, holding the mike in his hand. His eyes turned in our direction and in that very brief instant he ducked inside his tank before either of us could get off a shot at him. Damn! I would have liked to put a bullet through his head and see his body fall onto his crew inside.

Another tank was just to our left, nearer the houses. All of them began backing toward the hills across the field. None of them turned around; they kept their bows toward us, backing slowly all the way to their own lines on the other side of the hills.

When they started backing away, the tank to our left nearest the houses must have spotted our foxholes dotting the edge of the bank. Stopping his vehicle's rearward flight, the Panther's commander traversed his turret and fired 75mm shells into the bank about two feet below the edges of several holes. Shell after shell was slammed into hole after hole. They tore through the thin bank and exploded violently inside. The men of A Company were being butchered right down the line without a shred of defense.

Zygmunt Chmiliewski leaped from his hole, went over the bank, and started firing his carbine directly at the front of the tank. The big 75mm gun fired point-blank at him, the huge shell narrowly missing him. It exploded in the rubble of houses behind us. Chmiliewski rushed forward, closing on the tank, firing his carbine all the while. The tank churned in reverse, its treads plowing snow as it ran at full speed backward toward its own lines.

"Stop that tank! Stop that tank!" Chmiliewski roared. He was so frustrated with rage that he ran after the tank, firing his carbine at the heavy armor. He stopped only when the tank had outdistanced him and he realized the futility of his attempt to catch and destroy it. When he returned to us we could see tears streaming down his face.

"Why didn't someone stop that tank?" he asked, knowing full well that none of us could have done a thing about it at the time. With the tanks gone and the artillery strangely silent, Chmiliewski continued to stand there facing us, his arms outstretched as though pleading. "Why didn't someone stop that tank?" he asked again. Tears of frustration continued to flow freely down his cheeks. For the first time in years, I felt tears well up in my own eyes.

Several of our men had been killed outright. The tank's heavy gun blasting away at point-blank range was the last thing they saw.

The fog remained suspended high enough that a short time later we could see the enemy massing on the crests of the hills. Enemy tanks spread out and then slowly started down toward us, their infantry following close behind. Another battle would soon be joined. We crouched low, glaring at the enemy over the edges of our foxholes from under the steel rims of our helmets. We knew our .30-caliber armor-piercing ammo would be useless against the tanks, so we would concentrate on their infantry and try to kill as many as we could before going under.

Seldom did we ever have tank support. When we were fortunate enough to have tanks fighting with us, we would precede them on foot, acting as a screen to protect them from mines, *Panzerfausts* (disposable German antitank rocket launchers), antitank guns, or enemy tanks lying in wait around a corner. We used our tanks as fast, mobile artillery that would follow us closely and give us heavy firepower when we needed it. Here, the German infantry was following their armor, using the tanks as mobile shields.

The enemy bore down steadily across the open ground on three sides of Noville. Word passed down the line to again let the German armor penetrate our lines without firing on them. Once they were past us, it would be up to the Shermans and TDs tucked away in strategic locations in town to take care of them. Our job was to take care of their infantry.

At least twenty tanks moved into our positions. One of them, a Panther, headed straight for our foxhole. Its left track crunched over our hole, crumbling dirt down on us. Speer and I crouched low in the bottom of our hole, tucking our heads close to our chests, making ourselves as small as possible. We didn't dare look up. We could only clutch our rifles and wait for it to pass. It stopped. We were trapped in a hole in frozen ground, and the only way out was covered by the steel track of an enemy tank.

"If he gets hit and burns, we'll be roasted alive," I told Speer.

He already knew that and said he didn't want to hear it. "Just pray," he mumbled.

Speer was a devout Catholic and he shared his beliefs and convictions with me. Although I could understand his feelings, I did not accept them. I have always been an agnostic—at least ever since I was old enough to reason and think for myself. I don't know if there is a god or there isn't a god. I really don't care. If there *is* a god and he is as good and as forgiving as people say he is, then I shouldn't have a problem. If there isn't a god, then it doesn't matter.

The tank's engine revved slightly, and then it began to move slowly toward town. Our hole was open again. We poked our heads cautiously up and saw the German Panther moving toward the center of Noville. It felt like we'd spent an eternity trapped in our foxhole, although it was probably not more than a few seconds. But the tank went on without noticing us. If its crew had suspected we were in the hole the driver would have locked the track over us and churned around and around, grinding our foxhole and us into a mixture of dirt and human flesh. The day before a German tank had ground a paratrooper into the dirt, and there wasn't enough left of the poor man to leave for the graves registration team. Later, when the ground was frozen too hard to grind a man up in his foxhole, tank commanders would maneuver their vehicles into a straddle position over the hole, have the driver gun the engine, and gas the trooper with carbon monoxide from the exhaust. If the trooper tried to escape by crawling out from under the tank, he would be shot to pieces by the German infantry following behind. No quarter was given.

When the Panthers and Tigers again reached town, the hidden Shermans and TDs opened up and enemy tanks erupted in flames.

It was our turn again. We rose up and tore ragged holes in the enemy's lines with rifle and machine-gun fire. All up and down the line I could hear small arms popping. Speer was to my left, and we were both firing as fast as we could. We could see the Germans fire their weapons, work their bolts, and fire again. We could see them fall as our withering barrage tore through their ranks. Some kicked and thrashed, others screamed, and some just went down hard and lay still.

Then we could hear our own artillery roaring overhead. The shells bridged us, coming in from somewhere back near Bastogne, arcing high, then screaming down to crash into the enemy to our front. Their lines were decimated.

Although our airborne artillery had arrived in Bastogne with our convoy and set up there, they were so short of ammunition that they were only allowed to fire a limited ration of shells at a time—and then only at a heavy concentration of enemy and under dire conditions. Our situation had to be critical and in doubt before headquarters would allow a few shells to be fired on our behalf. This was the first artillery fire support we had received since arriving in Noville the previous morning. With the German tanks and infantry coming down on us en masse, it did look pretty bad for us. But it must have been even worse than we thought for our command to allow our artillery to fire scarce shells at our attackers.

The German infantry could not get past us to their tanks, which—feeling naked without their infantry to protect them—began to withdraw. They lost several more vehicles to cannon fire from the Shermans and TDs, but not without exacting a toll. Several of our troopers were killed or wounded, as were a number of the armored infantrymen. We also lost a couple of Shermans and their crews.

Again the German tanks backed away toward the hills over which they had come. The surviving infantry slowly preceded them back up the slope, keeping the tanks between them and us.

We had managed to hold our ground in the face of yet another determined attack. The enemy's artillery, seemingly chagrined by the setback, began a more or less token shelling of our positions. New fires started as old ones smoldered. Noville was little more than a smoking ruin, but it was still our town.

The morning wore on. We hadn't eaten since we'd left the trucks early the day before. We'd left our K rations with our overcoats and overshoes in the field on our way up here, so we had no food, and only a little water remained in our canteens.

Our regimental commander, Col. Robert F. Sink, realized from the beginning that the 506th PIR was overextended and that we were in a bad position to make a stand. He knew that in time we would be overrun and lost to the enemy. After visiting our lines the day before, he had returned to General McAuliffe's headquarters and asked that we be withdrawn to where the rest of the division was digging in around Bastogne.

Brigadier General McAuliffe agreed fully with Colonel Sink and relayed the request to Major General Middleton, who was in overall command of the units in the Bastogne area. General Middleton denied the request, saying, "If we are to hold, we cannot keep falling back."

We were ordered to remain in place and hold to the last man.

However, after this last attack, it must have become evident to General Middleton, who had moved with his staff and set up a new CP several miles to the rear in Neufchâteau, that we would be far more effective as live soldiers than dead heroes. At noon on 20 December he finally issued orders for the 506th to withdraw from Noville and rejoin the rest of the 101st at Bastogne.

# 3 Withdrawal

The Germans had been driving in a wide pincers movement around Noville. This was their normal mode of operation. The main task force in one of their blitzkrieg operations would flow around strong pockets of resistance and keep attacking forward. Follow-up units would then do the mopping up by laying siege to the enemy forces in a pocket until it collapsed, then moving forward to the next, and so on.

Bastogne, along with its smaller satellite towns and villages, was the exception to this rule. Bastogne, with its seven-road hub, was a priority target. The Germans needed this network of roads to achieve success in this battle of battles. Nine armored and mechanized infantry divisions were given the sole mission of taking Bastogne as quickly as possible while the rest of the huge force pouring into the expanding bulge in the American line raced toward the Meuse River.

We knew Bastogne was being surrounded. We had expected it on our way up to the front. It was nothing new to us because paratroopers routinely are surrounded as soon as they hit the ground behind enemy lines. It's the nature of the business. What we didn't know was whether or not Bastogne's encirclement was complete at this time. We were also unaware that the enemy had already surrounded us at Noville. We'd been given orders to hold Noville at all costs, and that was exactly what we were doing. It was up to the generals to worry about us being cut off from the rest of our division. The 3d Battalion was holding Foy, so we at least knew we had an avenue of withdrawal if or when the time came.

We could see the Germans moving through the woods and hills surrounding us. But we weren't going to move out until we were ready—not until we were sure there wouldn't be anything of value left behind for the enemy, and not until we had all of our wounded ready to move. There was nothing we could do for our dead but leave them where they fell.

B and C Companies pulled out of the perimeter line and fell back into the rubbled center of burning Noville, where they joined the battered remnants of Major Desobry's gallant task force. That left A Company stretched out to cover what had been the entire 1st Battalion sector.

We were Noville's first line of defense. The 10th Armored task force's infantry and tanks would hold the center of town in case the Germans broke through our line. B and C Companies worked to get the wounded ready to transport and to make serviceable whatever vehicles could be salvaged for the convoy. Any vehicle unable to move under its own power was destroyed in place. The B and C Company troopers also gathered up all the ammunition we could not use or carry and piled it around and over TNT charges and other explosives stored in the base of the church tower. The church was the only building left standing that could be considered nearly intact. The Germans had purposely avoided hitting it during their artillery barrages so they could use its steeple for artillery observation when they took over the town. The rest of the town was in ruins.

Paratroopers worked at a fever pitch to get vehicles ready to move, our wounded stabilized and loaded into vehicles, and everything being left behind prepared for destruction. Two Shermans were in good condition with partial crews, but there were no drivers to operate them; they had been killed during the shelling. Tank officers moved among their infantry asking for volunteers to operate the tanks but could not turn up a single man with the slightest idea of how to operate a tank. Two paratroopers finally stepped forward out of our 1st Battalion and volunteered to drive the tanks and lead the convoy back to Bastogne.

At last the defenders of Noville were ready to move out. We were called in from the outer perimeter to the center of town, where the rest of the troops had already gathered. The torrent of shells had slowed to a trickle, with only occasional artillery, tank, or mortar rounds falling in the vicinity. The thick fog had obscured our movements from the enemy holding the high ground surrounding Noville—a blessing that probably averted our slaughter by artillery.

The Germans had changed their tactics. They were pushing around Noville in a wide arc running to the west, south, and back to the east on one side, and in an arc that ran south to west on the other side. This time they stayed close to the high ridges on either side of town before launching their main effort with troops, tanks, and a violent artillery barrage against our 3d Battalion in Foy, just to the south of us.

Using the same blanket of fog that concealed us from them in Noville, the Germans moved troops and armor around the town to both sides of Foy, slamming into our 3d Battalion's positions with all the force they could muster. The onslaught of tank and artillery fire, coupled with a strong infantry assault, drove the battered remnants of our 3d Battalion out of Foy to a line just south of that town. The Germans had been pressing their attack since 8 A.M., and by noon were entrenched in Foy.

Back in Noville we were completely surrounded, cut off altogether from the rest of the 101st Airborne Division and the other defenders in and around Bastogne to our south. We no longer had radio contact. We were on our own.

That was the situation when we, the men of A Company, straggled in from the perimeter around Noville, gaunt, ragged, dirty, cordite-splotched, and hungry. Most of us old men had been virtually without sleep since our trip to Paris on 14 December. It was now the twentieth. We came in small groups, wary, watching, and listening for "incoming mail," ready to hit the ground at the first hint of another barrage.

As we made our way past the foxholes along the bank for the last time I looked into them to catch a last glimpse of my buddies who had died there. Ollie Barrington was one of them. A tiny piece of shrapnel had smashed into the right side of his head at the temple, just under the rim of his helmet. He died instantly.

As I stared down at his body, memories of the day Trotter, Barrington, Hundley (who was killed in Holland), and I were ambushed in Normandy filled my mind. Barrington had been shot through the right forearm by a 9mm Schmeisser bullet but he healed up fast and managed to survive seventy-two days of hard combat in Holland. Now he lay dead, a tiny shrapnel hole, no larger than a BB, in the right side of his head.

Many of our 1st Battalion comrades were left behind in Noville. A large percentage of our new replacements were dead. The numbers of older men continued to shrink. This was the third mission for a lot of us. Our luck couldn't hold forever; sooner or later we were bound to get it, too.

Lieutenant Colonel LaPrade's body was loaded into one of the vehicles for burial back in Bastogne. During a heavy barrage on 19 December, an 88mm shell exploded in the street just outside of his CP, which had been moved to a house several doors south of the school building on the west side of the road. Shrapnel tore through the barricaded windows, killing him and seriously wounding Major Desobry.

We left the rest of our dead where they fell—in foxholes, fields, houses, and alongside the roads in ditches. We always left our dead where they fell. It was the job of men from the graves registration team to take care of our dead whenever they could get to them. It wasn't that we were heartless. Many of these men were like our own brothers, but we had a war to fight and win. We could not do it and take care of the bodies of fallen comrades at the same time. It was hard enough simply to care for our wounded—even our walking wounded. If a trooper stopped for a dead comrade, it would give an enemy soldier enough time to aim and fire. Then there would be two dead Americans.

The wounded and unconscious Major Desobry was evacuated from Noville to the field hospital near Sprimont during the afternoon of the nineteenth. That field hospital—with all its doctors, technicians, and patients—fell into German hands that same night when the Germans, encircling Noville to the west, overran it. Major Desobry, along with many others, became a prisoner of war.

We found out about it from three survivors—two dental officers, Captains Jacob Pearl and John Breiner, and a medical officer, Capt. Roy H. Moore—who hid in the woods when the Germans made their attack on the hospital at 11:30 that night. These officers later made their way back into Bastogne, where they related the story to our division intelligence staff.

More than a hundred German shock troops running well ahead of their main force and supported by six armored vehicles, including tanks, half-tracks, and an American tank destroyer, were skirting Noville to the west that night. The Germans came down the Houffalize road, attacking without warning. Minutes earlier, a convoy of American trucks had pulled into the area. They didn't stand a chance. The German infantry opened up with rifles and machine guns, backed by machine-gun fire from the tank destroyer, half-tracks, and tanks. The Germans deliberately machine-gunned medical tents marked with large red crosses, as well as ambulances and other vehicles in the area that were loaded with wounded GIs. They kept up the barrage for more than fifteen minutes, killing as many of the wounded as they could.

Every truck in the convoy was set ablaze. One Negro truck driver climbed up behind the big .50-caliber machine gun set in a ring mount over the passenger's side of the cab and opened fire at the Germans, killing and wounding some of them. The Germans turned their machine guns and rifles on him, riddling his body until he was all but cut in half, and nearly tearing the cab away from the rest of the truck.

Later, many of the attacking Germans who had been killed were found to be dressed as civilians, only they were wearing German dog tags and carrying German military identification.

Several other Americans managed to escape into the night with the three medical officers when the shooting started. Some of them were wounded. These men later ran into a patrol from B Company, 327th Glider Infantry Regiment, which had been sent to destroy a German roadblock near Sprimont. The survivors told the 327th GIs about the massacre, then proceeded on into Bastogne.

The Germans took the survivors prisoner, but not before entering several of the tents and cutting the throats of many of the wounded paratroopers clear to the bone as they lay there helpless on cots. They took only a few paratroopers prisoner, along with all of the surviving tankers and armored infantrymen, doctors, and other medical personnel.

After destroying the roadblock and killing all the Germans there, the 327th Glider Infantry patrol made a sweep toward the hospital area on their way back to Bastogne. They were guided to the area by the loud, continuous blowing of stuck horns on the still-burning trucks.

As they approached the site the patrol spotted nearly a hundred of the Germans who had butchered the wounded in the hospital. The Germans, confident no Americans were in the area, stood around some of the burning vehicles talking loudly and laughing.

The company commander quickly plotted an ambush. He ordered the bulk of the company to move quietly by a roundabout way, and set up in front of the Germans. At a prearranged signal from the troopers who had gone ahead, the platoon that waited in place raced noisily forward, yelling and shooting at the surprised, panic-stricken Germans, who immediately took off running toward a nearby woods on the far side of a clearing. When they reached the center of the clearing, they were in the killing zone. Caught in a deadly crossfire, they didn't have a chance. The glidermen took no prisoners.

It was getting late in the afternoon where we waited in Noville. The fog had lifted somewhat, but the sky and sun were shielded by thick, low-hanging clouds. It was cold. The temperature had plummeted sharply throughout the day. Smoke rose up from the burning town and spread into and thickened the gray overcast. We stood in the center of a dreary, bleak battlefield surrounded by destroyed and burning houses, shattered war machines, and the dead.

Torn and broken bodies were scattered around in grotesque, uncomfortable positions. It looked as though a child throwing a temper tantrum had mutilated her dolls and had thrown them down in a fit of rage.

A Company was gathered near the schoolhouse and the church. We mostly just milled around awaiting orders. The work of getting the wounded ready for transport and the convoy ready to roll had already been accomplished by the troopers and armored men who had stayed in town. They had hidden the operational vehicles behind and in between the ruined buildings in such a manner that when the convoy started, they would move out in the proper order onto the main road. We didn't want to line all of the vehicles up in the open before we were ready to move because they would have made an inviting target for artillery spotters on the hilltops around town. The bulk of the armored infantrymen also stayed scattered amongst the ruins in case of another heavy shelling or an enemy attack.

Suddenly, Jerry Janes leaped aboard a burning half-track and struggled to take the .50-caliber machine gun off its bent and twisted pedestal mount. Several of us yelled for him to get off and leave the gun there because the half-track might explode at any moment. Besides, a fifty was too damned heavy to haul around on our shoulders.

"Nobody asked you guys to carry it," Jerry shouted. "I'll take care of it myself. Just get the ammo for me."

Three men jumped up with him. One of them, Trotter, began helping Janes with the heavy machine gun. The others began throwing boxes of ammo off to other troopers who had gathered nearby to watch. Flames licked all around Janes and Trotter, but Janes was determined to get that fifty. Finally it came free of the twisted mount, and he cradled it in his arms as he leaped to the ground. He swung the big gun up, balanced it on his shoulder, and fell in with us, his ammo bearers trailing along behind him.

"Now," he muttered, "just wait till those Krauts come again."

Jerry Janes—tall, narrow-waisted, and broad shouldered—balanced the gun on his shoulder and seemed to carry it with ease as he strode with us through the rubble. It would be a comfort to have a big gun like a fifty with us, if only we could hang onto it.

C Company, which had dug in on the southern edge of town, was the natural choice to lead the advance of our southbound convoy on foot as we withdrew from Noville. This was not a rout or retreat; it was an ordered and orderly withdrawal to strategically better positions, with full control and deliberate execution. Officers and noncoms were in complete command at all times, and the men, paratroopers and armored crewmen and infantry alike, acted as though they were on routine maneuvers.

The order of march called for C Company to lead the convoy on foot, followed by an M8 armored car, four half-tracks, and five Sherman tanks. The vehicles loaded with the wounded were next, followed by the main body, which was made up of all types of vehicles, and had B Company troopers and 10th Armored infantrymen riding or walking beside them. The rear guard consisted of four tank destroyers from the 705th TD Battalion carrying A Company troopers on their decks.

Fog had settled in again. This was a blessing, for it would keep us from being observed by the Germans on the high ridges and hills surrounding us. C Company marched out first, followed by the assigned vehicles in the proper order and interval as each pulled out of its hiding place into the growing, slow-moving convoy on the main Houffalize–Bastogne road. Like a gigantic snake slithering from its shattered nest, the convoy grew longer and longer as it headed south down the road toward Bastogne.

When the column had advanced far enough and was evidently well underway, A Company's paratroopers clambered onto the decks of the TDs, the last to leave the small, ruined, and burning bastion we had fought so hard to hold. We had been the first airborne troops to enter Noville; now we were the last to leave.

"Last man out, don't forget to close the door," someone shouted.

"And don't forget to turn off the light," called another voice.

All this clock-like work reflected the abilities of Maj. Robert F. Harwick, who succeeded Lieutenant Colonel LaPrade as our battalion commander, and who had taken charge of the 10th Armored men too after Major Desobry was evacuated.

I was sitting on the starboard deck of the lead tank destroyer with several other troopers, some of whom I did not know. The TD commander slipped down inside, the big machine lurched into gear, and with the other three TDs following in single file with the rest of A Company's men aboard, we clanked down the macadam road toward the rear of the southbound convoy.

Just barely after clearing the town we again came to a stop. The turrets and big guns of the TDs we were riding on pointed to the rear, to the north and northeast. The explosives covered with abandoned ammo stored in the church were set to go off now. The 101st had been critically short of ammo on the way into Bastogne, while the armored units carried an abundance of the stuff. The ammo we

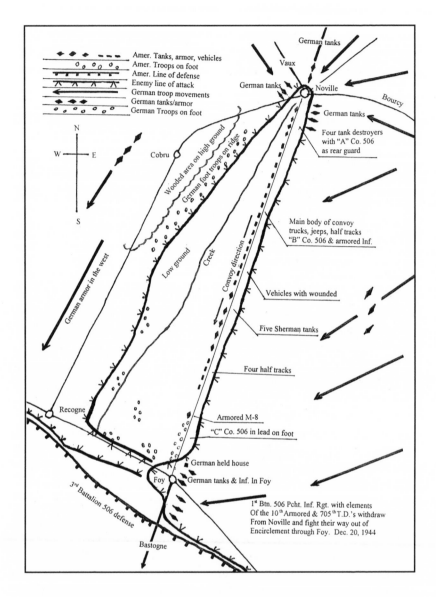

Amer. Tanks, armor, vehicles
Amer. Troops on foot
Amer. Line of defense
Enemy line of attack
German troop movements
German tanks/armor
German Troops on foot

German tanks

Vaux

German tanks

Noville

Bourcy

German tanks

Four tank destroyers
with "A" Co. 506
as rear guard

N

W — E

S

Cobru

Wooded area on high ground

German foot troops on ridge

Main body of convoy
trucks, jeeps, half tracks
"B" Co. 506 & armored Inf.

Low ground

Creek

Convoy direction

German armor in the west

Vehicles with wounded

Five Sherman tanks

Four half tracks

Recogne

Armored M-8

"C" Co. 506 in lead on foot

German held house

Foy

German tanks & Inf. In Foy

3rd Battalion 506 defense

1st Btn. 506 Pcht. Inf. Rgt. with elements
Of the 10th Armored & 705th T.D.'s withdraw
From Noville and fight their way out of
Encirclement through Foy. Dec. 20, 1944

Bastogne

couldn't take with us had to be destroyed. We couldn't afford to let
any usable ammo, vehicles, or weapons fall into German hands or
to leave the church steeple standing. Now the two needs worked to
our advantage.

We waited, and the minutes dragged by. The low layer of fog and haze blended with black smoke to blanket the sky just above the hilltops. Small and large patches of fog drifted slowly over the area, at times obscuring the high ground, the lower road, and the column ahead from view. As rear guard it was one of our assigned duties to see that the explosives in the church detonated on schedule. If they didn't, some of us would have to return and set them off using whatever means necessary. We couldn't use an electrical wire hooked to a battery to trigger the detonation because the shelling had been so heavy that the wire would almost certainly have been severed by a shell burst or fragment. We had to use a slow-burning fuse set safely inside the building, protected there by the thick stone walls.

As we sat there waiting we laughed and kidded each other about who would have to go back and detonate the explosives if they failed to blow on time. Together, on a whim, we decided to let the TD commander choose which of us would have the dubious honor.

"How would you like to be just ready to pull the igniter and have the whole thing go up in your face?" someone asked.

"You'd never know it," somebody replied. "You'd never even hear it."

A couple of minutes after the deadline, while we were waiting for the TD commander to designate a detail to go back and set off the charges, one hell of an explosion tore the front of the church off, toppling the tower onto the road and forming a roadblock. Three purposes were accomplished in that one blast: The ammo we couldn't use was destroyed so the enemy wouldn't get it, the Germans were denied the use of the church steeple as an artillery observation post, and the road had been neatly blocked by the debris.

Major Charles L. Hustead and his 10th Armored Division engineers had done their work well.

"Let's go!" the TD commander shouted. Our four vehicles ground forward and we went racing for the tail end of the column farther down the road. We closed on the convoy, reduced our speed to theirs, and joined the procession.

Just as the first vehicles in our long, strung-out group started to enter Foy, all hell broke loose. Enemy troops hidden in the road ditches and in the fields to our left flank opened up with rifles and machine guns and let fly a hail of hand grenades. Bullets lanced through our ranks from the houses up ahead in Foy, and German 81mm mortars joined in. We had enemy to the front, rear, and east of us, with more closing in from the west.

It was now around 2 P.M. The day had started out badly, and it didn't seem to be getting any better, with unfriendly people on all sides giving us a hard time. Suddenly the convoy ground to a complete stop.

We weren't receiving too much fire in the rear of the convoy, but up front we could hear all kinds of combat noise filtering back through the wisps of fog. We stood alert, watching for an enemy that could come rushing down on us from the rear or on either flank at any time. We couldn't go running forward to give aid to those up front and leave our rear exposed and unguarded. All we could do was stay in place and wonder what in the hell was going on up there.

As it happened, when our lead vehicles reached the northern edge of Foy, the armored shutter designed to cover the driver's vision slit in the first half-track dropped down and the driver, unable to see, rose up to adjust it. Major James B. Duncan of the 10th Armored, who was riding in that vehicle, mistakenly thought the driver was wounded and yanked the hand brake, stopping the half-track on the spot. The second half-track, having lost its brakes sometime back, rammed into the rear of Duncan's vehicle. Germans hidden in the ditches and in the fields to the east then opened fire and began flinging grenades at the stalled column.

Major Duncan quickly dismounted from his lead vehicle and hustled toward the rear of the convoy. Half-track number four backed up a short way and stopped, leaving room to maneuver. Then the first three half-tracks, almost as one, made a break for it in single file, racing through the firing, through Foy, and all the way back to Bastogne without stopping.

Major Hustead, who had succeeded Major Desobry as commander of the 10th Armored task force in Noville, walked forward to see why the convoy had stopped and what all the shooting was about On the way he met Major Duncan, who was heading toward the rear. Taking Major Duncan in tow, Hustead led him back to the front of the convoy. Major Hustead then ordered the first two Sherman tanks to move forward and shell suspected enemy positions in Foy. The two Shermans moved forward and plastered the town, setting several houses on fire, then moved back to observe the results of their handiwork.

Again they moved forward. This time, however, they were hit by cannon fire from German tanks that had slipped in close to the road from the east through the fog. Sherman number one caught fire, and the driver of number two was wounded so badly he could no longer control the vehicle. Again the convoy was stalled. Captain William G. Schultz, the tank company commander, had been riding in Sherman number five, the last tank in line. He dismounted, moved quickly forward, took over tank number three, and drove it forward through Foy, hoping the rest of the convoy would follow him. It didn't. Just south of town, Captain Schultz's tank was hit by German tank fire and destroyed. The captain and his crew managed to escape and headed south toward Bastogne on foot.

After Schultz had gone on through Foy, the driver of tank number five, hoping to get things rolling, dismounted, ran forward, and took over tank number two. He drove forward toward Foy, was hit by German tank fire, and was destroyed on the spot. All this was happening while C Company paratroopers and armored infantrymen who had been riding in the forward part of the convoy engaged in a shootout and grenade-throwing contest with the Germans in the ditches. They drove the enemy infantry away from the road and back into the fields and fog to the east.

Up and down the stalled column paratroopers and armored infantrymen left their vehicles to take cover alongside the road, while drivers stayed in their vehicles, keeping them ready to roll.

A Company also left its vehicles for the safety of the ground. I recall leaping from the deck of the first TD and hugging the ground on the west side of the road as bullets and mortar shells began striking our ranks. I still couldn't see anyone to shoot at, so I held my fire, not wanting to waste precious ammo unless I was sure I could put meat on the table. However, the armored infantrymen up ahead poured out a withering barrage of small-arms fire through the fog. I don't believe the Germans on the east side of the road could see us very well either, or the death toll would have been heavier. I think most of them were firing through the fog in the direction of the sound of our vehicles' engines.

The fog cleared enough up ahead so that I was able to see Schultz's driver as he took the second tank with its wounded paratrooper driver and steer it around the first burning tank. While I was watching, the tank took a direct hit and the explosion and black mushroom cloud boiling up from it made it plainly evident we were in serious trouble.

Suddenly a young paratrooper near me yelled, "There's Krauts on that hill! There's Krauts over there!" He was pointing to the west, toward our rearward flank.

I looked and saw a lot of Germans dressed in gray-green uniforms moving from north to south in long, strung-out lines along the face of an exposed ridge that ran nearly parallel to our road. They were moving on the sloping ridge just below a wood line overlooking the low ground that separated us from them.

Watching our tanks being destroyed up front had diverted our attention just long enough for the enemy to emerge unseen from the north and walk along the ridge, until our young trooper happened to look that way and see them. Just why they did not open fire on us, I do not know. We were fully exposed out there on the open road. Maybe the drifting fog had obscured us from their view for a while. Or, more logically, they may have thought we were one of their own armored units traveling south on the road along with them. I just don't know.

"Let's get the goddamned Krauts off the hills!" the same young trooper yelled.

Several A Company troopers charged out into the open field, racing toward the Germans. I was among this group. We crossed the snow-covered field, jumped a small creek, and went charging after the enemy while the burning Shermans and other wrecked vehicles blocked the convoy from moving any farther.

There were no German tanks in view on the hills to the west, just infantry. If there was any doubt in the Germans' minds about who we were or what our intentions were, they were fully aware now. They didn't seem at all anxious to close in on us. Instead they scattered into the woods to the west. We settled in the snow along the crest of

the ridge and formed a defensive line parallel to the road to hold
them off in case they returned before the convoy was ready to move
again. We could see the tracks the Germans had made in the snow
as they moved along the ridge, as well as the tracks they'd made when
they scattered and fled into the woods.

However, the enemy on the left side of the road, coming in from
the east, was supported by tanks, and advanced slowly and steadily
toward the road into a hail of small arms from the troopers and armored infantrymen in the convoy. Meanwhile, German small arms,
88s, and mortars poured fire down on the convoy from the village
of Foy and the high ground to the east.

I heard an engine roar and turned to see the tank destroyer on
which I had been riding move forward on the right side of the road
past the vehicles to its front. As the TD approached the fourth Sherman in the column, which was manned by paratroopers, the tank
began backing up. The TD quickly reversed its forward motion to
avoid a collision and backed over a jeep, smashing it flat.

The Sherman stopped and then moved forward toward Foy. Moments later it was hit by German tank fire and exploded. The turret
blew off, went about forty feet up, did a flip in the air, and landed
upside down in the middle of the road, its cannon still in place,
blocking the road completely. I have seen tanks destroyed many
times but never anything like that. Of all the places for that turret
to land, why did it have to be in the middle of the road, blocking
our only route back to Bastogne?

The number five Sherman now sat driverless. Paratroopers stalked
through the heavy enemy fire, moving among the 10th Armored GIs,
asking each one in turn if he could operate a tank. All replied that
they'd had no training for the job. That was true, for most of them
were armored infantrymen.

"We'll learn to run the son-of-a-bitch," several paratroopers said,
and climbed aboard. After fumbling around inside for a while they
were able to figure out the controls well enough to permit them
to later drive it all the way back to Bastogne near the head of the
convoy.

The initial shock and surprise caused by the ambush of our convoy didn't last long. We had been hit so hard and so often in the last

twenty-four hours that we were pretty numb. The 3d Battalion was supposed to hold Foy until after we passed through their lines, but it was plain they had failed. It was equally plain that if we were going to get back to Bastogne, we would have to fight our way through.

Those of us who had attacked the German infantry moving along the west ridge were crouched in the snow in a defensive line. A clearing in the fog allowed us to see into the fields on the road's east side from our vantage point on the slope above the fields over which we had attacked. Just to the east of the three remaining rear-guard TDs, four German Panther tanks were nosing cautiously toward the road. The TD commanders had also been watching. They too had seen the approaching Panthers and were ready. When the Panthers hit a slight rise in the ground near the road their bows lifted slightly and the three TDs fired almost as one. Three of the Panthers exploded and the lone survivor backed quickly away, disappearing into the fog.

The enemy was closing in on our rear; the convoy had to get moving if we were going to break out of this trap. The three remaining TDs at the rear of the convoy then moved forward through the fields on our side of the road to engage the enemy up front. The fourth TD, which had moved forward earlier and had its advance stopped when the fifth tank's turret was blown off, peeled off and joined them. Together the four TDs circled around the west side of Foy and headed toward the southern edge of the village, where they met some of our 3d Battalion troopers who were mounting an attack to relieve the pressure on us.

A couple of 3d Battalion troopers stopped a tank destroyer and asked the driver to go after the German tanks that had been doing all the shooting from the northern edge of town. The troopers said they knew where the tanks were hiding. The driver told them he had no crew, so the troopers climbed aboard to man the gun. The TD crept forward to within two hundred yards of the enemy tanks. The big 90mm gun roared and knocked out the nearest tank with a single shot. The rest of the German tanks fled east into the fog.

Small-arms, mortar, and artillery fire continued to rake the convoy trapped on the road, increasing in intensity. Dark splotches of burnt powder left fan-shaped marks on the white snow where flat-trajectory artillery shells struck at sharp angles and exploded. Mortar shells left ragged, circular black powder marks on the snow after exploding. The low ground between Noville and Foy was fast becoming covered with these black splotches as shells of all sizes continued to pour in.

Four men in a jeep spun out from the right side of the trapped column, heading southwest on an angle toward the Recogne–Foy road. Their jeep bounced, slid, and skidded across the bumpy, snow-covered field. One man lay across the hood firing a pistol while another drove. They made their way alongside the stream amid flying bullets and exploding mortar shells, crossed over the high-banked, blacktop east-west road running through the center of Foy from Recogne, then raced south until they were past the village before cutting east, back to the main road to Bastogne. One man in the jeep was killed by machine-gun fire.

More men began moving out from the convoy. Some, bent on killing, headed in large groups toward the enemy on the east side of the road. Others were walking out across the fields to the west, following the jeep's tire marks in the snow. Trucks, jeeps, and half-tracks began leaving the road, trailing the men walking through the western fields.

Up till that moment, drivers had been reluctant to venture out onto the flat, low ground with a stream running through it for fear of getting bogged down and becoming stationary targets, to be picked off at will by the enemy. The jeep started the mass exodus. As drivers saw heavier and heavier vehicles leaving the convoy and striking out across the field without getting stuck, they too headed that way. The fog began shifting, moving close to the ground in large and small patches that looked like a large, slow ice flow on the move. Some paratroopers walking in groups through these fog patches ran into large and small gangs of German infantry working their way toward our right flank. Firefights broke out as men from both sides felt their way in and out of the heavy rifts of fog, meeting others who were out to kill them in sudden face-to-face encounters. The decision to shoot was instantaneous. During these hide-and-seek skirmishes our paratroopers captured two large groups of Germans who surrendered, but only after being outgunned by the troopers.

I sat watching in sort of a trance as trucks, jeeps, and half-tracks began peeling randomly away from the convoy to make their way individually across the fields to safety. It just didn't dawn on me that they were all leaving. We had been there so long it was starting to get dark. The handful of us who had mounted the attack to protect the convoy's rear flank still sat on the hillside guarding against surprise attack, watching from ringside seats as the drama below unfolded.

"Come on," the man next to me yelled. "The convoy's moving out; we've got to catch up or we'll be left here."

For several moments I had my doubts. They wouldn't just leave us here. But then it dawned at me that the men in the convoy really didn't even know we were back here protecting their butts. Who was going to protect the rear? I wondered briefly. Then the thought occurred to me that there was no rear left to protect. The TDs were gone and now the rest of the vehicles in the convoy were plowing across the snow-covered fields below as though it was every man for himself.

The trooper who had called for us to leave was running toward the road. Soon all of us were running back down the hill after him, jumping the stream and racing toward the trucks still on the road. I climbed aboard a six-by-six that was empty except for the driver. He asked me if I knew how to operate the .50-caliber machine gun in the ring mount over the passenger's side of the cab.

"Hell yes," I replied. "I can operate any weapon made."

I climbed up inside the ring mount behind the big fifty, jerked the bolt to the rear, fed a belt of ammunition into the gun, and slammed the charging handle forward so the gun was ready to fire. While I was doing this, the driver told me how his assistant driver had been killed back in Noville, leaving him with no one to operate the machine gun.

German infantry moved steadily out of the fog from the east headed directly toward us, some of them running, trying to get closer so they could get better shots at our retiring convoy. Most of them were wearing white camouflage jackets or coats, helping them to blend with the snow and fog. We had no camouflage, so our dark jumpsuits stood out like sore thumbs.

"Shoot, shoot!" the driver yelled at me.

Using nothing but lighter .30-caliber rifles and machine guns in combat caused me to develop the habit of waiting for the enemy to get real close before opening up. The driver must have thought I had frozen up on the gun. I thumbed the butterfly trigger and the big fifty hammered rounds toward the enemy. I blazed away at anything and everything moving in the open fields to the east of us—the fog, white-suited Germans, muzzle flashes, anything that caught my eye.

We were still on the road, waiting for the vehicles ahead to move out. My driver wanted to follow in someone else's tire tracks; he didn't want to blaze his own trail. He was worried about hitting a mine or an unseen hole. He was nervous, very nervous, but he was the driver, and his idea made sense to me. We began moving slowly forward, using as much of the macadam road as possible before taking to the snow-covered fields. A 10th Armored lieutenant grasped the truck's tailgate, hanging on and running erratically behind our slow-moving truck. He hollered at me to help him aboard.

He threw his carbine through the slats onto the bed of the truck and shouted, "Help me up; the Krauts just put a bullet through my ass and I can't raise my legs enough to climb up."

I slid down from behind the gun, jumped over the seat into the bed of the truck, grabbed the lieutenant by the collar, and yanked him bodily over the tailgate. The seat and legs of his trousers were soaked with blood.

"Thanks," he said as he collapsed to the floor and rolled to the side to brace himself. He grabbed his carbine, stuck the barrel through the wooden slats on the side of the truck, and began firing. German bullets were striking our vehicle and snapping through the air around us. Men were being wounded and killed up and down the column.

I made my way back to the cab, slipped inside the ring mount, and thumbed the butterfly trigger. The big gun hammered to life, again sending tracers and armor-piercing bullets toward the enemy. The heavy cordite smoke burned through my nostrils and deep into my lungs. I could hear other fifties booming amidst the lighter machine-gun and rifle fire. I just knew Jerry Janes was out there somewhere, even though I couldn't see him. I didn't know where he might be in that god-awful mess, but I was sure he was out there, hammering away with the fifty he'd ripped off the burning half-track.

I didn't know where *any* of my comrades were. I could only hope they were making their way the same way I was trying to do. We were heading back to Bastogne one way or another. Somehow we'd find a way out and the survivors would gather there.

Our truck was almost to where the wrecked vehicles that had been in the lead were still burning on the road. The tank that had its turret blown off sat square in the center of the road; its turret lay upside down at an angle across the road in front of it. Good men, paratroopers, were killed in that blast. Their flaming coffin, together with the other wrecked tanks and vehicles, blocked the road completely.

The men in the vehicles still on the road laid down a barrage of small-arms fire so intense it sounded like a steady roar. Tracers lanced toward the enemy, slicing through their ranks. Some Germans left the safety of the cover they had found and advanced toward us. They were driven by blood lust; they wanted to destroy what was left of the convoy before it had a chance to escape their trap. I was still firing, as were the rest of the men of the convoy. Some of the Germans fell kicking, trying to crawl or roll back into the ditch beside the road. Still others went down and lay still, not moving at all. Yet others dove or ran to the right or left, evidently trying to find a place of refuge or from which they might gain an advantage. The bodies of friend and foe alike lay scattered about. It was getting dark fast. It was still light enough to see, but it wouldn't be for long.

Suddenly the truck I was in lurched forward, swung to the right off the main road, and headed across the snow-covered field past the burning Shermans and other wrecked vehicles. The truck bounced so much that it was impossible to operate the fifty without endangering other GIs scattered throughout the fields and in other vehicles around us. I quit firing. Still, I stayed there in the ring mount, hanging on to the gun and bracing myself against the rough ride, just in case the gun was needed on a moment's notice.

The Germans continued to fire at us with small arms as the intensity of the shelling increased. Mortar shells arced high overhead, then came straight down, exploding all around and on us. Flat-trajectory, high-velocity shells slammed into our midst, joined by long-range artillery that screamed in from beyond the surrounding hills. There were explosions everywhere; shell fragments sliced through flesh and metal alike. I looked around and saw vehicles of all description spread out over the entire field from the road to the stream. Despite our driver's misgivings, none dared to follow in another's tracks for fear of getting stuck in the ruts they left in the soft pasture. Our truck had started out following a set of tracks, then, after we skidded a little, the driver steered clear of the tracks and began making his own way over unmarked snow. He talked aloud, explaining to himself and to me what he was doing and why.

All of the vehicles were spread as far apart as the field would allow. It would have been suicide to bunch up or travel nose to tail in single file. German gunners would have zeroed in on such a prize target, raking it with small-arms fire and everything else they could bring to bear. It was every vehicle for itself. At the last possible moment, men who had been engaging the enemy at arm's length from the ditch alongside the west side of the road left the safety of their covered positions and climbed aboard the last of the passing trucks. No one I know of was left behind alive.

What remained of the convoy made its way south through a barrage of exploding shells and streams of tracers and other bullets. The trucks and half-tracks bounced and rocked as they made their way slowly over the rough ground. Engines whined and wheels spun, but we ground on toward the narrow blacktop road running into the center of Foy from Recogne.

As we approached the road, the driver, who was hunched over the steering wheel so low that he was looking through it, said, "This is it; we either make it or we get stuck right here."

There were ditches running along both sides of the road. We would have to plow across the ditch nearest us at an angle, cross up and over the road, which was built up above the level of the surrounding fields, and then plow across the ditch on the other side at an angle. The driver tramped the accelerator pedal to the floor and the wheels spun on the snow-covered grass before biting into the soil underneath. Then we were charging toward the ditch-lined road. We hit pretty hard, fishtailed a little on the way over the top of the road, slammed down on the other side, swung forty-five degrees to the left, and went racing at an angle across the next field. From there we followed the vehicles ahead of us back onto the main road and headed south toward Luzery and Bastogne.

The jeep that had broken through first had alerted the 3d Battalion that we were coming through. The 3d Battalion in turn counterattacked north into Foy, forcing the Germans to split their forces. That relieved the pressure on us. In their attack, the men of the 3d Battalion took more than eighty prisoners and destroyed three tanks and self-propelled guns.

It was dark when we finally fought our way out of the German trap and passed through the 3d Battalion's lines. The vehicles slowed, then stopped and waited on the blacktop road until we were sure that every last man was clear of the trap. Once our leaders were certain that all who were able had made it safely south of Foy, we re-formed into a convoy and moved out toward Bastogne. Our officers were still in command. We were still an organized unit. The four 705th TD Battalion tank destroyers that had preceded us south of Foy stayed behind to help our 3d Battalion in their fight against the Germans there.

The convoy moved slowly at first, slightly faster than the pace of a marching man. The glow from Noville, burning like a gigantic sunset, lit up the night sky behind us. The trucks picked up men who had preceded us on foot. Then, like a huge, lumbering, wounded beast, the assortment of raggedy-assed, bullet-scarred vehicles began to speed up.

As we approached Luzery—located on the northern outskirts of Bastogne—men who had arrived in the vehicles ahead of us sat or stood beside the road, calling out their outfit's identification so the GIs in the convoy would know where to get off.

I heard Sergeant Vetland's distinct voice in the darkness calling for men of A Company of the 506th PIR. Looking in the direction of the voice, I vaguely saw him standing there with a small group of troopers next to the ditch running alongside the road. Some men were sitting on the edge of the ditch facing the road. Others leaned against pine trees that grew dark and thick nearby. Sergeant Vetland held his tommy gun in one hand and his helmet in the other. His eyes were searching through the darkness, anxiously seeking his own men among the faces in the trucks and half-tracks rolling by.

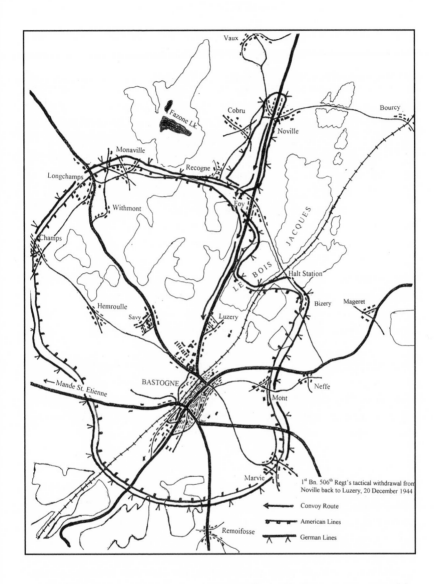

1st Bn. 506th Regt's tactical withdrawal from
Noville back to Luzery, 20 December 1944

← Convoy Route

American Lines

German Lines

"A Company, assemble here," he called. "A Company, assemble here."

I told the driver I would have to leave him here, and he thanked me for manning the machine gun on his truck.

I slid down from behind the machine gun in the ring mount, grabbed my rifle from the floor of the cab, and jumped from the truck to the road. In our scramble over the roads and fields I had completely forgotten about the lieutenant in the back of the truck. He hadn't made a sound in all that time. Even though the jouncing he took must have caused him considerable pain, he was lying there on his back in the bed of the truck, smoking a cigarette, holding his carbine across his chest. Blood caked his uniform but the bleeding seemed to have stopped. He was resting easy.

I moved down the side of the slow-moving truck to its rear, crossed the road behind it, and approached Sergeant Vetland.

"Hey Vetland, Burgett here," I announced.

Even in the darkness I could see the grin on his face. Other troopers warmly greeted me. It was like a homecoming.

I stood on the edge of the ditch with the other men and we took turns calling, "A Company 506th assemble here, A Company 506th assemble here," to the shadowy figures of men walking or riding in the passing convoy as the night grew darker.

Slowly our numbers grew. Each time a close friend or friends would show up there would be jubilation, backslapping, and handshaking. Speer, Phillips, Liddle, Benson, and others showed up in turn. Damn, that was good. In our counterattacks against the Germans on either side of the ambush, and during the rush of vehicles through the fields as we skirted west of Foy, squads and platoons had become fragmented. Men lost contact with each other as they made their way back the best way they could, just as I had.

Major Desobry had gone into Noville with fifteen tanks plus half-tracks and other vehicles carrying armored infantrymen, engineers, and other troops. That armored task force returned to Bastogne with only four tanks left, and one of those was manned by paratroopers. I don't know what their total losses were but they were heavy. Major Desobry's men had proven their bravery.

My unit, the 1st Battalion, 506th PIR, lost thirteen officers and 199 men killed. That figure does *not* include our wounded. It has been established that in our twenty-four-hour fight for Noville the paratroopers and 10th Armored men together destroyed well over thirty German tanks and other vehicles, and killed well over half a regiment of enemy troops in that battle. Up to three times that number of Germans probably were wounded. On top of those losses were the prisoners we took.

The battle for Noville proved to be one of the most crucial battles during the fight for Bastogne. One battalion of 101st Division paratroopers and the equivalent of nearly a battalion from the 10th Armored Division's Combat Command B met the entire German 2d Panzer Division head-on and fought it to a standstill. Their hopes of blitzing through us were shattered on the Houffalize–Bastogne road. We had bought the rest of the 101st and its handful of supporting units twenty-four vital hours in which to dig in and get ready for the coming siege.

The last of the convoy rolled past us heading toward Bastogne, and the road was suddenly empty, dark, and quiet. It seemed that everyone except us had gone on to Bastogne to seek refuge there, and then closed the door behind them. We were alone again, out in the dark, open countryside where it was getting increasingly colder. We were tired, dirty, hungry, and without food, winter clothes, or blankets.

Again we formed up into squads, platoons, and companies, shouldered our weapons, and moved out in the night toward some farm buildings on the eastern outskirts of Luzery. Their outlines could be seen vaguely against the slightly lighter sky. The glow of burning Noville was still visible in the northern sky.

Our platoon and squad leaders had been hastily briefed and led the way. I was tired and hungry and glad that someone else had the responsibility to lead us to our assigned positions. All I had to do was follow along with the others.

Soon we came upon a farmyard with its house, barn, and several outbuildings located just east of Luzery. Second Platoon entered the barn and, as we cleared the doors, three men from our regiment's 2d Battalion who were standing beside large boxes set on the ground handed each of us a box of K rations.

Men began pulling hay down from the loft and piling it deep along the outer walls, leaving a clear spot in the center of the dirt floor for a warming fire to be built. Most of us in the 2d Squad picked the north end of the barn as ours and piled hay at the base of the wall to sleep on. Then we joined the others around a small, smoke-less fire someone had started in the center of the bare spot near the barn's large double doors.

We used our trench knives to open the small tins of food we took from the K rations. The menus included breakfast, lunch, and dinner meals. I had drawn a "lunch," which meant cheese. I put the piece of cheese on the point of my knife and held it close to the fire to soften and warm it. Although I'd had nothing to eat since downing a box of K rations in the trailer on our way to the front on the eighteenth, I really didn't feel that hungry just then. Still, I did manage to eat.

Speer sat to my right, and Gudbrandsen was almost straight across from me. Gudbrandsen had handled himself well in combat for a replacement, fitting right in with the older men. Others were sitting—some on their helmets, some cross-legged—on the dirt floor, forming a tight circle around the small fire. We relaxed a little while we talked and ate, knowing that, for the moment at least, there were good troops between us and the enemy. Because of our shot-up condition, we were in regimental reserve and figured on being able to get some rest.

While we were sitting there, I pulled out my small sewing kit—the kind most GIs carried in their musette bags—and mended my torn sleeve.

Some other men from our 2d Battalion were in the barn with us. They had been there since our arrival in the vicinity on the nineteenth, when we in the 1st Battalion had marched north to Noville and they had dropped off here to help set up the main line of defense around Bastogne. They had not yet been anointed in this battle. We learned from them while we were eating that the 501st PIR had also been engaged on the first day.

The 501st had marched east through Bastogne ahead of us with orders to "develop the situation." That's army talk for heading toward the enemy until you run into them, then testing them in battle to see just how tough they are. The 501st ran into German armor just past Bastogne and fought in and around Bizory, Neffe, and Marvie. They didn't encounter as many German tanks as we ran into at Noville, but theirs was another decisive battle in which paratroopers again proved themselves as they held the German forces in that sector in check.

The men of the 501st had marched out at 6 A.M. led by their commander, Col. Julian J. Ewell. Their 1st Battalion led the way on the road toward Longvilly. Just west of Neffe the Germans opened up on them with machine guns and tanks. Some of our airborne artillery quickly set up close behind the 501st's 1st Battalion and began pounding the enemy tanks and surrounding German positions. The troopers also poured mortar and small-arms fire into the German positions. But the enemy was well established in Neffe and to the north of Bizory. The 1st Battalion could go no farther.

Colonel Ewell then ordered his 2d Battalion to take Bizory. In doing so he caused the westbound Germans to meet Americans attacking eastward into them across a wide front. The Germans to that point had run into only small, disorganized groups of Americans and quickly overran them. This action by Colonel Ewell and his 501st PIR caused the Germans heading toward Bastogne from Longvilly to halt, consolidate, and become cautious. That cost them precious time that they never recovered.

Finally, Colonel Ewell ordered his 3d Battalion to Mont while diverting one company to the village of Wardin to cover the regiment's right flank. He also ordered the 2d Battalion to take Mageret, northeast of Bizory, where a large German force was dug in on a ridge overlooking the area.

The 3d Battalion encountered heavy tank fire from Neffe and had to stop and dig in. It too could go no farther. By then the 501st was strung out on a front that ran in a rough line from north to south just east of Bastogne. The 3d Battalion's I Company was the outfit the battalion commander, Lt. Col. George M. Griswold, had sent on to Wardin, where Colonel Ewell had told him they would find a task force from the 10th Armored Division called Team O'Hara. Unbeknownst to the 501st officers, the tanks and armored infantry were about a thousand yards on the other side of Wardin, dug in astride the Bastogne–Ettelbruck road, where they hoped to intercept the Germans they thought would take that route from Longvilly. Unfortunately, most of the Germans had turned directly toward Wardin.

I Company's 130 troopers continued to plod along, blissfully unaware that they were about to run smack dab into the second prong of Lt. Gen. Fritz Bayerlein's Panzer Lehr Division's attack on Bastogne: a battalion of panzer grenadiers backed by seven tanks. The paratroopers reached the village at the same time as the Germans.

No attempt had as yet been made to fuse the airborne infantry and artillery into a single fighting unit with the armored forces, as should have been done immediately. This was only the first day of confused fighting in the battle for Bastogne. We needed each other very much as a working team. But at the start the paratroopers and men of the 10th Armored Division task forces in the area worked independently of each other. That was a mistake that was corrected by our battalion in Noville.

At the same time as I Company ran into the Germans in Wardin, Team O'Hara came under attack and had all it could do to take care of itself. The tankers and armored infantrymen could hear the fighting in Wardin but they were unable to disengage to help out.

I Company was wiped out except for a few men who managed to get back to friendly lines the best way they could. There weren't enough of them left to make up a platoon.

Early in the morning on 20 December, long before daylight, several tanks from the 9th Armored Division and four TDs from the 705th TD Battalion joined the 2d Battalion of the 501st in its defensive positions. Around 5:30 A.M., the Germans moved against the regiment's lines with seven assault guns and a battalion of infantry. Two hours later the battle was joined. Two of the 705th's TDs were disabled, as were two of the 9th Armored's Shermans. The Germans lost all but one of their self-propelled guns.

Artillery fire from Bastogne came in hot and heavy, blasting the German infantry to shreds as they advanced. Only a few escaped northward from the killing zone.

That night, while we were resting in the barn in Luzery, the Germans attacked in force out of Neffe, moving westward through the fields between Neffe and Mont toward the 501st's lines. Artillery from Bastogne again slammed in so heavy forward of the 1st Battalion's positions that the advancing German armor was smashed and their infantry were slaughtered. For weeks afterward, German bodies showed as mounds in the snow.

The crews of the 705th's TDs dismounted with machine guns and small arms and joined the paratroopers in raking the ground in front of their positions. All the attacks against the 501st that night came to a stumbling stop about three and a half hours after they began. Everyone wondered how the fire could have been so effective in the dark. Dawn the next morning provided them with the answer.

The Belgians had erected row after row of high barbed-wire fences running parallel throughout the area about thirty to forty feet apart to serve as holding pens for cattle waiting to be shipped out by rail. As the defenders looked out over the fields in front of their positions they saw the frozen bodies of hundreds of Germans draped over the fences or hanging in the wire, where they had gotten hung up while trying to climb over and through them with their heavy field gear. The bodies stayed upright there for weeks, hung on the fences in orderly rows, a grim reminder of the slaughter that occurred that night. It was an eerie sight to behold: those sentinels of death standing side by side in ghostly ranks, snow piled high atop their heads and shoulders.

I have since been asked, "How can you remember such details?" "How can one forget?" I invariably reply.

We of the 1st Battalion, 506th PIR, had fought our battles around Noville without sleep, food, and very little water. Many of our comrades were dead, and many more had been wounded. We were exhausted, and the deep hay piled along the wall looked inviting. But there was to be no rest for us just yet. The enemy was still attacking the outer perimeter in force at different spots. Luzery might well be their next target. A strong defense had to be established here immediately, and we had to man it.

Leaders called out names as men were picked to pull the first watch outside in the defensive positions. Half of us would be allowed to rest in the hay, then take a turn in the line in relief of the first shift. Duty would come around often and long. We were down to a total of fifty-eight men in A Company, out of the more than two hundred who had attacked into Noville with us on the nineteenth.

Three machine guns were to be emplaced on a railroad bank that ran north and south just east of Luzery, with three men each assigned to man them. Phillips, Speer, and I were detailed to set up a posi-

tion due east of the barn. We picked up our weapons, the squad's
.30-caliber machine gun, two boxes of machine-gun ammo per man,
and an armful of hay each, then started out the doors without looking back. Speer carried the machine gun and its tripod, while
Phillips and I hauled the ammo.

Outside, I noticed for the first time that there was more snow on
the ground than when we first came to Bastogne. It was over our boot
tops. Evidently it had snowed while we were fighting in Noville, but
try as I may, I cannot recall seeing it snow. I can only recall the tanks,
the enemy, the fog, the bodies, and the constant shelling.

It had turned colder than a well digger's ass. Being from Michigan, I knew the temperature had dropped well below zero. The snow
crunched and squeaked under our feet. Actually, it was ten degrees
below zero Fahrenheit. We plodded along toward the railroad tracks,
bearing due east. I thought of my warm overshoes and warm overcoat with its pockets stuffed with K rations that I had been ordered
to leave in a field outside Noville before our attack. It would have been
a lot easier to stand guard duty with a warm coat, overshoes, and something to eat. Then I thought of my seaborne roll with my blanket and
other goodies tucked away inside my shelter half. In my mind's eye I
could see a German soldier kicking through my looted things, picking out what he wanted—including my new camera and film. I hoped
the bastard would get shot through both kneecaps and live.

At last we came to the railroad tracks, made the machine gun
ready, and rechecked our weapons. We crept slowly up to the
bank—watching and listening, easing each foot carefully forward,
toe first, into the snow to soften the squeaking sounds. Then we
dropped to our hands and knees and eased our way to the top of
the bank, looking behind us to make sure that, when we looked over
it, our heads would not be outlined against a lighter skyline behind
us. That was a good way to catch a bullet through your helmet. We
were okay; trees and other objects blended darkly behind us, pro-
viding a safe backdrop.

Gradually we eased our heads up to peer from under the rims of
our steel helmets, out over the black steel ribbons of tracks into unfriendly land for long minutes. Our eyes searched every field, wood
line, and shadow. We could not make out much in the darkness. We

moved only our eyes as we swept our gaze back and forth over the enemy land, not daring to move our heads until we had to, and then very slowly. One learns and practices survival tactics or dies. Gazing at the steel tracks, I wondered if my flesh would stick to it if I touched one of them with my bare hand. I had heard of cases, true or not, of people sticking their tongues to cold steel only to have them freeze to it. It was just a thought.

We looked for anything unusual: a large, dark shadow that might possibly be a tank, a movement against the slightly lighter sky, a spark of light from a carelessly lit cigarette. Any kind of a light would shine like the beacon on a lighthouse out there in the open. It was a good way to bring an artillery barrage down on yourself.

We were quiet. We didn't dare to speak, not even in whispers. I learned that in Normandy when Hundley and I whispered to each other on D day in a hedgerow-wrapped field. Red Knight and Slick Hoenscheidt later told us they could hear us whispering from clear across the field. Here in the subzero cold the sound would travel even farther and clearer. Hundley was killed on 17 September at Zon in Holland.

So we didn't talk or whisper. We just listened. We listened for the squeak of someone else walking in the frozen snow. We listened for the sound of a tank engine idling. We listened for the accidental clink of a canteen cap tapping against the side of a canteen as a man stole a drink. We watched and we listened for long minutes, then we eased back down into the foxhole we'd found dug in atop the railroad bank, leaving one man to watch over the tracks while the other two curled up and rested inside, trying to get warm. We took turns watching in this manner. On arriving there we had quietly swept surplus snow away from the edges of the hole so we could get out and move around a little without making all the snow squeaking noises.

We had chanced on this abandoned foxhole dug into the railroad bank on our arrival. We set about digging as quietly as possible so as to enlarge it for the three of us, using Speer's and Phillips's entrenching tools. I still didn't have an entrenching tool of my own. I should have taken one from a fallen comrade back in Noville, but I didn't think about it at the time. We covered the dirt we dug and piled outside the front of the hole with snow; otherwise, when daylight came, the fresh dirt would stick out like a sore thumb, inviting anyone looking in our direction to take a shot at it.

It was getting colder by the minute. As we sat behind the gun we had to stay alert, watching and listening. The Germans were somewhere on the other side of the tracks. But where? We weren't sure. They could have been dug in on the other side of that same railroad bank just a few feet or yards away for all we knew. Probably daylight would tell.

We did not want to risk getting out of our hole to move around a little to get our circulation going again for fear any sound of ours, however slight, might bring instant death. We had to crouch there with our feet tucked up under us in our cramped burrow and wait.

I began to shiver. Just a little at first, then nearly uncontrollably as time dragged by. I shivered and kept on shivering. I shivered so badly that the muscles in the back of my neck drew tight, pulling down on the base of my skull. This continued until the back of my head was drawn back down toward my shoulders. The muscle tension became so great that I developed a splitting headache. Phillips and Speer fared no better, lying close to the sides of our hole shivering uncontrollably also. We cursed and swore under our breaths, shaking and shivering as time slowly dragged on.

Four hours later we heard the crunch and squeak of footfalls approaching from behind us. Sinking lower in the hole we brought our rifles to bear on three figures against the snow. We waited until they were within four or five feet of the railroad, keeping a bead on them with our rifles, then whispered the challenge word. They answered with the right password. They were our relief. We could return to the barn, with its warm fire and heaps of dry hay.

Climbing out of the hole I found my legs to be numb, stiff, and unresponsive. There was no feeling in my feet. My legs were frozen, my body and arms chilled to the bone. My fingers ached and my head hurt. We did high knee steps and shook our arms and legs to get our circulation going again. Then we headed back toward the barn. Each step felt like I was floating on air. I couldn't feel my feet or my legs to my thighs. It was as though I were riding atop someone else's legs. I had to watch my feet carefully so I knew when they were forward and solid on the ground.

Arriving at the barn we discovered most of the other men from A Company were gone. They had been ordered out into the line around Luzery after we'd left. A few men, I don't know who they were, moved around in the hay along the back wall of the barn. A sergeant I didn't recognize told us to return to the gun and send the other three troopers back. He said we were to tell the men who had just relieved us to join up with their own squad here at the barn and move to another place to stand watch.

I started to bitch. Spending eight, ten, or twelve hours' watch on a machine gun out in the open in subzero weather, wearing only light jumpsuits was quite a stretch. I didn't know it then, but there would be many more nights just like that one.

"Why bitch about it?" Speer asked. "If we gotta do it, we gotta do it. Bitching and complaining isn't going to change anything; let's go."

Phillips didn't say a word; he just looked first at Speer, then me as I complained and Speer talked. Speer stepped out toward the railroad bank and we followed. I still bitched, only a little more quietly. I felt it was my duty.

We headed back toward the gun, the snow squeaking under our boots. Our legs and feet had thawed and feeling had returned. With feeling came pain, intense pain in our toes and feet. Again we each carried an armful of hay from the barn with which to line the hole. We relieved the men there after exchanging the proper challenge and passwords and told them to report back to the barn for further instructions. At least they'd had some sleep in the warm barn. We eased our way down into the hole to await the coming of dawn.

Even with the hay it was damned cold. The three troopers we had just relieved hadn't brought any hay with them when they relieved us, so we didn't have as much of it as we would have liked there in the hole. I think each of us secretly wished an enemy patrol would come along, for in the heat of battle one does not feel the cold as much. Anything would have been better than that chilling, numbing torture. We were freezing to death. We knew it, and there was nothing we could do about it.

The sky gradually began to lighten on the morning of 21 December but the skies were still heavy with overcast. I looked at Phillips and Speer and they stared back at me. We could read it in each other's eyes: there would be no air support again today. As long as it remained overcast we knew our Air Corps would not show up.

Our eyes searched across the flat, snow-covered field to the woods on the other side. What appeared to us to be a huge Tiger tank moved a little way out of the distant tree line and stopped with its bow pointed north toward Foy. Its port side was toward us. It didn't do anything; it just sat there idling. We could make out a few men moving around the tank on foot, as though they were escorting the steel monster. Two other tanks—they looked like Panthers—moved about in the trees. It was hard to tell what type they were for sure with them inside the tree line, but none of them made an attempt to cross the open field toward us.

The "Tiger" could just as easily have been an American self-propelled gun accompanied by two Shermans. I can't be sure, but they sure looked German to the three of us there on the railroad bank. After a time the tank withdrew back into the woods. Then, with hardly a notice, they all just sort of faded away. We could no longer see any sign of the tanks or infantry.

We heard the snow behind us crunch again. We turned and saw three men making their way through the snow, coming in our direction. Even though it was daylight and they looked to be fellow troopers, we still challenged them. If they didn't know the password, we would have to kill them.

Our relief came and settled into the hole. This time they brought their own machine gun and each of them carried an armload of hay. Hay has a way of breaking down when you tromp on it, so it must be replenished—just like the straw in my mattress back in Mourmelon-le-Grand.

We shouldered our machine gun, picked up our ammo, and walked woodenly back toward the barn. We tried to walk in the footsteps made by the men who had relieved us in order to cut down on the amount of sound our feet made in the snow.

We watched our frozen feet carefully as we walked, for they were again so cold we could not tell by feel when they were solid on the ground. We watched each step to keep from stumbling and falling. It was as though I were floating. I could see my legs stride forward and hear the sound of my footfalls, but there was no feeling of contact with the ground. I had experienced the same feeling more than once when I was a kid in Michigan, wearing corduroy knickers and high-topped leather boots in the winter snows. The feeling had come back then, and I knew it would come back now. At least I hoped it would.

We were each handed a box of K rations as we entered the barn. Speer, Phillips, and I joined Benson, Gudbrandsen, Chmiliewski, Floyd O'Neal, and others from 2d Platoon around the small fire. We made coffee in our canteen cups and started heating the cheese, eggs, or chopped pork from whichever ration we happened to draw on the end of our trench knives. Once in a while a man would drop his meat, egg, or cheese dinner in the dirt from his knife end. He would scoop it up in his still-frozen fingers, laugh, and say, "Oops, fell right on a napkin," or some such thing, and then proceed to eat it. The men were in good spirits, all things considered, and we joked about our frozen toes, fingers, and ears as we sat there eating.

The pain would come later, when our frozen parts began to thaw. There's not a damned thing you can do about it but grin and bear it. Grin hell, it hurts.

We caught up on the latest news as we ate and warmed ourselves by the fire. Some of it was just plain latrine rumors—most of it, in fact.

One thing that wasn't a rumor was the fact that, during the night, the Germans had cut the Neufchâteau road running south out of Bastogne. We were now completely cut off, completely surrounded. Lieutenant Colonel Kinnard, the division G3, reported our situation to VIII Corps by radio this way: "You know what a doughnut looks like? Well, we're the hole in the doughnut."

A young hillbilly, one of our new replacements, was sitting close to the fire with us calmly eating.

"Did you know the Krauts have us completely surrounded?" I asked.

"Yeah," the southerner drawled, taking another bite of food. "Them poor bastards."

"What do you mean *them* poor bastards? We're the one's that are surrounded," I replied.

"Yeah, but we can shoot in any direction and hit them. They can shoot in only one direction and hit us."

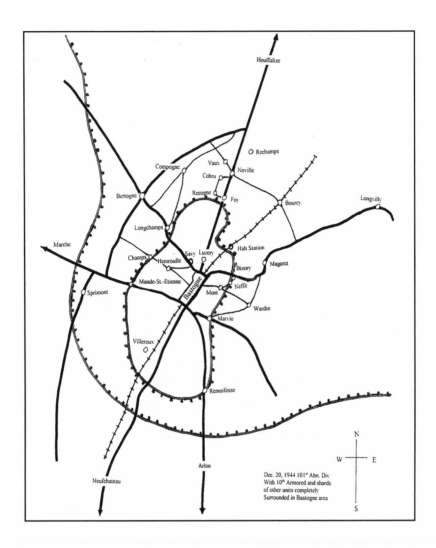

Dec. 20, 1944 101ˢᵗ Abn. Div
With 10ᵗʰ Armored and shards
of other units completely
Surrounded in Bastogne area

We all laughed until we had tears in our eyes.

Latrine rumor had it that some of the enemy had slipped through the 501st PIR's lines and were entrenched in a woods to our rear. Having Germans behind our lines presented a serious threat. Since A and C Companies of the 506th PIR were the only units in reserve, it would be our job to go and dig them out.

Actually, the German troops dug in behind our lines did not slip through the 501st's lines as we had been told. It all started when we marched into Noville on the nineteenth. Our 3d Battalion had remained behind us in Foy, and our 2d Battalion had dug in here at Luzery as part of the perimeter line the division was establishing to protect Bastogne. The 3d Battalion was supposed to extend its line to the south, then east through the woods to the Halt railroad station, where they would tie in with the 3d Battalion, 501st PIR's line, forming a solid defensive line around this side of Bastogne.* But the two battalions failed to link up, leaving a wide north-south gap in our lines along the railroad. This left a wide-open corridor straight down the railroad into the center of Bastogne through which the enemy could have slipped an entire panzer division unopposed. Fortunately they failed to do it. Only about a regiment of them got through in the fog on the nineteenth. We had passed them during our march to Noville like two ships in the night, with only the narrow strips of pines and brush of the Bois Jacques separating us. Platoons and companies of the 506th and 501st PIRs engaged in running battles in the fog with these enemies, who had managed, more by accident than design, to split their forces.

Colonel Sink, our regimental commander, grew increasingly worried about the lack of contact between our two regiments in this area. At his insistence, General McAuliffe ordered both regiments to make contact at all costs and close the gap. They did this by dispatching a number of patrols probing into the woods near the Halt railroad station.

In the end, contact was established and the line was closed, creating a solid defensive perimeter around Bastogne. However, more than a battalion's worth of Germans were cut off behind our lines, dug in somewhere in the Bois Jacques (Jack's Woods). It was now up to us, the reserve force, to dig them out.

---

*We thought the sign that read "Halt" outside the station was its name, so that was what we called it. We later learned that "Halt" meant stop. There were hundreds of "Halts" along the railroads in Belgium.

# 4 The Woods Fight

Sergeant Vetland was at a meeting in the company CP with the other platoon sergeants and platoon leaders when Speer, Phillips, and I returned to the barn from our all-night vigil. Now they returned.

"Okay, men," he said, "let's hubba-hubba, one time. Just leave your chow where it's at. We gotta go. We've got a little job to do. You can finish your breakfast as soon as we get back."

"Here we go again," somebody groaned. "We'll pick up our meals in a day or two, just like we did our seaborne rolls and our overcoats and overshoes."

We left our half-finished rations next to the fire and fell out in company formation outside the barn. It was about midmorning. We didn't bother to put the fire out. If the job was small enough the fire might still be burning when we got back.

Horn—the tall, thin, dark-haired kid from Indiana with the exceptionally broad shoulders—joined my squad as a rifleman. Normally he was armed with a carbine and carried the large radio on his back for the platoon leader. But we no longer had a radio and we needed every rifle we could get. When the time came for serious shooting, the carbine just didn't have the poop. I saw too many Germans get hit with the damned little things and keep on going. The carbine was a light, close-in defense weapon carried by machine gunners, bazooka men, mortar men, and officers who didn't want to carry a heavy rifle. They just weren't meant for heavy-duty combat.

We left the farmyard in our customary strung-out battle formation without being ordered. We carried our rifles at sling arms while machine gunners, mortar crews, and bazooka men balanced their weapons on their shoulders. Although we normally swapped the heavy crew-served weapons around during long marches, the gunners preferred to carry their own weapons when combat was expected.

We left the barn, trudging west through snow-covered fields toward the Noville–Bastogne road. We came out on that road and followed the leader northward toward Foy in long, single-file columns on either side of the road. We still didn't know exactly where we were going. Nobody took the time to brief us. All we were told was that we were going someplace to kill Germans. C Company led the way. They would take the left flank when we made the attack. We stopped about halfway to Foy and formed a line of skirmishers running north and south, facing east along the edge of the road. Then, with C Company on our left and scouts out front, we started moving slowly into the Bois Jacques. I glanced at my watch and noted that it was just before noon.

Siber Speer and Salome Alvarado moved out ahead of the rest of A Company. It was their turn to serve as scouts, just as it had been Phillips and my turn going into Noville. The woods was one of those cultivated plantations so common throughout Europe. Nearly all the lower branches had been trimmed, so there was nothing to conceal us as we moved amongst the trees. The Germans had been in the woods almost two days—long enough for them to dig foxholes and bunkers and camouflage them so that they were almost invisible.

As we moved into the wood line, Jack Bram and Bielski lowered their machine guns to their sides, carrying them at the ready. They had a box of ammo strapped to each hip, and another half a belt of ammo draped around their necks, over their shoulders, and fed into the guns. This allowed them freedom of movement while firing their weapons in the attack. Jerry Janes carried his big .50-caliber machine gun in the same manner, but with his long woolen muffler—which he'd kept with him when we dropped our overcoats and overshoes in the field outside Noville—wrapped around the barrel.

We had advanced into the woods only about a hundred yards, maybe a little more, with Speer and Alvarado fairly close together a couple of hundred feet up ahead, when Speer yelled, "There they are," pointing with his finger to where the Germans were dug in several yards to his front. Speer had very sharp eyes but was slow with his trigger finger. He had done the same thing before and we all had warned him to shoot as he hit the ground and then yell out a warning. We would know the enemy was there if he just fired his rifle as he hit the ground. It was a lot safer that way.

An enemy soldier who was so well camouflaged that no one saw him, not even Speer, fired his rifle from where he lay just a few feet in front of Speer. The bullet struck Speer in the mouth and plowed out the back of his neck. He was dead before he hit the ground.

Alvarado fired a round from his carbine into the German as the enemy soldier worked his bolt for another shot. The German grunted, slammed the bolt home, and fired blindly, hitting Alvarado in the body. Alvarado pitched forward, pulling his trench knife out as he fell atop the German. He plunged the blade into the man right to the hilt, killing him. Alvarado died a few seconds later. Just why he pulled and used his knife I do not know, for he still had his carbine in his left hand. It must have been an instinctive reflex after the shock of the bullet that slammed into his body.

All this took place in less time than it takes to read it. With Speer and Alvarado between us and the enemy, nobody had been able to fire in support of them during those first few seconds. If they had hit the ground first, we could have helped. Now, as the rest of the enemy opened fire, we began spreading out from where we'd flung ourselves down and returned fire.

Again all hell broke loose. Small-arms firing erupted so intensely from both sides that it became a deafening roar. Armor-piercing and tracer bullets lanced through the trees and ricochets whined all around, spinning off in erratic directions.

Jack Bram and Bielski ran forward, spraying bursts from the machine guns slung at their hips as they ran. Janes lumbered along behind them as best he could with his fifty, hammering out short bursts, the big gun jerking wildly around. But he kept at it, watching for the strikes of his tracers as he fought to keep the muzzle down. We laid down a barrage of covering fire with our rifles while they were on the move. Suddenly they hit the ground almost as one and switched to long, steady bursts as we rushed forward three and four at a time between and around them in quick, short spurts to positions well beyond them.

As soon as we were down and firing, Bram, Bielski, and Janes sprang up and leapfrogged forward, firing all the while.

We continued working our way forward in this manner, forcing the Germans to keep their heads down with our steady fire, until we reached their holes and began engaging them in hand-to-hand combat. Once again we were amongst them. Many of the enemy were shot as they cowered in their holes by troopers firing down on them as they ran past.

We gained overwhelming fire superiority early on, and the enemy's fire slowed to a trickle. Our machine guns and semiautomatic M1 rifles gave us a decided advantage over the Germans and their bolt-action Mausers.

Jack wasn't hitting the ground anymore. He remained standing even when the rest of us stopped and fired from the prone or on one knee. He fired his machine gun from the hip, governing the strike of his bullets by watching the tracers, like a man squirting a garden hose. All this while he was screaming at the top of his lungs. I was only a few feet from him but for the life of me I couldn't make out what he was yelling. Later someone told me that he was yelling, "I'm a Jew! I'm a Jew! You goddamned Krauts, I'm a Jew!" And he was killing them.

One German rose up from the ground in front of Dobrich and started to run toward our left flank. Dobrich fired once and the German went down hard, bursting into flames from head to foot. He was probably carrying a Molotov cocktail on him and the bullet must have exploded it, spraying him with flaming gasoline. The snow was melting around the German's body and I heard Dobrich yell, "Do you see that? Do you see that?"

I hit the ground hard after a short run and was searching for a target when another German, not more than three feet in front of me, raised his head up and looked me straight in the eyes. He had been lying face down on top of the snow, and I had thought he was dead. I jammed the muzzle of my rifle against his forehead and pulled the trigger. He was dead for sure now.

Bielski was lying to my left, just a few feet forward. He fired the last round from the box of ammo on his left hip and rose to his knees to reload. Taking the box of ammo from the sling on his right hip he slammed it down next to the gun, lifted the cover of the receiver, and laid the belt in place. Just as he started to close the cover, a single bullet smashed squarely into his forehead, ripped through his brain, and tore away the back of his skull. I saw steam issue from the back of his head and then he jerked back, staying upright on his knees with a shocked, wide-eyed expression on his face for a few moments, and then he fell forward over the gun. I rolled over to the gun and pulled Bielski's body off of it just as another trooper dove headfirst and slid in behind it. Bielski's body lay between me and the gun. The new trooper slammed the cover down and said he would take it from there. I felt rage boiling up within me. I shouted that it was my gun, that I would take it.

"Never mind," he yelled back. "I've already got it. I'll take it." He jerked the bolt to the rear, slammed it forward, and then did it again before firing a long, sweeping burst to the left and right.

This was no time to argue. I looked to the front, scanning the forest floor. There, just a little to the right and about two hundred feet out, I spotted two German-helmeted heads, one moving slowly to the right and the other moving to the left. Somehow I knew that one of those men had fired the shot that killed Bielski.

Taking careful aim at the helmet on the right I took the slack out of the trigger and squeezed slowly, deliberately, carefully. My rifle bucked; the head snapped back and disappeared.

"That's one," I muttered aloud.

Carefully aligning my sights on the other helmet, which was still moving toward the left, I fired another well-placed shot. He too went down hard.

"That's two," I said.

Second Lt. Anthony "Tony" Borrelli's 3d Platoon, our 2d Platoon, and men from 1st Platoon were all converging toward the ground where the main force of the enemy had dug in. The men from C Company were swinging forward on our left flank. We were amongst them. Fighting swirled around in a mad staccato of small-arms fire and paratroopers' yells. German bodies lay everywhere. We didn't look back to see who of our own we might be leaving dead in our wake. I saw an enemy head poke up out of the ground not more than fifteen feet away. I couldn't miss. I pointed my rifle like a shotgun, fired, and the head dropped straight down out of sight. Then I flopped on my belly next to a small tree, looked to see if I could spot any more Germans, and at the same time wondered if I had hit the German I'd just shot at. It dawned on me that he hadn't fallen right when I fired at him.

While I was lying there thinking about it, he suddenly popped up and, with one fluid movement, fired point-blank at me. The bullet passed between my head and the tree I was peeking around, cutting off a small, pencil-sized branch and my helmet's chinstrap. The chinstrap flipped up, striking me just under my left eye. The impact was such that I thought the bullet had passed through the left side of my head. I was stunned, more by the thought than the hit, and dropped my face into the snow, playing 'possum, pretending I was dead.

The German had slapped his bolt home and stood up in his foxhole, exposed from the chest up. I peeked at him through slitted eyes from under the rim of my helmet as he looked me over for a very brief moment and then took careful aim at the top of my head. My rifle was still in my right hand but lying out in front of me. I knew I could never get it up in time to shoot him. It was too late to do anything. Damn, I thought. Why did I have to go and miss? My body tensed in anticipation of the bullet strike.

At that moment something must have caught his eye, for he turned quickly to his right and fired at one of the troopers coming in from our left, one of Lieutenant Borrelli's men. Snatching my rifle up, and this time taking quick aim, I pulled the trigger as he worked his bolt. His helmet went spinning through the air and he jerked hard to one side and crumpled to the bottom of his hole. I ran over to where I could see him awkwardly folded over. I reached down and yanked him out of the hole with one hand. My bullet had entered his left cheek and taken his right ear off on its way out. I remember being amazed at my own strength. I could never have lifted a grown man out of a hole with one hand under normal conditions.

I let his body drop to the ground next to the foxhole and jumped in. I laid my rifle across his belly and used him like a sandbag while I fired. It was then that I noticed his belt buckle. It was not the square eagle stamped with the Wehrmacht's *"Gott Mit Uns"* motto, but the flying eagle of the Fallschirmjäger (paratroops). Was he a German paratrooper attached to the infantry? Or was he just an infantryman wearing a piecemeal uniform? I pulled his belt from him and fastened it around my own waist to save as a souvenir of our encounter. I still have that buckle to this day.

"Come on, we can't stay in one spot all day!" someone shouted. It was a squad leader, Sgt. Royce Stringfellow, lying behind and to the right of me. "Let's go, hubba-hubba, one time, get your asses going!" he hollered.

We didn't need him yelling at us right now. We had been forcing this attack but I guess he felt he had to say something. I could hear Sergeant Vetland also yelling for us to move forward, but he, Brininstool, and the other noncoms were up forward.

We were up and running, a little more to our left now, toward the sound and sight of continued firing. I dropped to the ground and rolled into a shallow depression. Liddle rolled into it at the same time, and we lay there side by side, firing at the enemy. Liddle was always calm and cool. Maybe being a Mormon made him that way, or perhaps it was his being raised on a Utah ranch. I don't know what it was but he looked at me, flashed about a yard of strong, white teeth in a wide grin that accented his sledgehammer jaw, and asked, "How you doin', Donny boy?"

"Okay I guess, but I sure wish I had a shovel to dig in with," I replied.

"Me too," he said. "It's too bad there weren't enough to go around when we came up here."

A machine gun blasted at us, then two of them, the strings of tracers crossing just inches over our heads. Bullets ripped and tore at the trees, limbs, and dirt around us. Bark flew from the tree trunks. I tried to crawl under my helmet. A tracer coming in from another direction, almost spent, stuck in a tree right in front of us, several inches above our heads. About half of the bullet was sticking out of the tree while sparks spewed from the back of it, like a miniature roman candle. We both stared at it, watching it burn. Again Liddle grinned at me. I rolled onto my back and took a deep breath.

Liddle rose to his knees, then jumped to his feet and cut out in a burst of speed for about fifty feet before hitting the ground. When he took off, something hit me in the right hip. I figured it was him kicking me as he left the slight hollow we were in, and I let it go at that. Later that night I found a bullet stuck in the flesh of my right hip. Evidently it had been spent, just like the tracer that had gotten stuck above our heads in the tree. I was able to remove it myself, so I didn't bother mentioning it to anyone else.

Troopers were all over the German-held area. A German and a trooper were locked arm-in-arm in a life-and-death struggle. They tumbled to the ground and, thrashing wildly in the snow, rolled into a large hole. The trooper was on top, gouging at the German's eyes. The enemy soldier was trying to choke the American. I ran toward them, crouched by the edge of the hole, and tried to get a clear shot at the German. The trooper gouged his left thumb deep into the German's right eye. The man screamed and convulsed backward, away from the trooper. I squeezed my trigger and the fight was over.

The trooper crawled out of the hole on his hands and knees, gagging and spitting blood into the white snow. "Thanks," he said.

I nodded silently and looked past him to where the German lay dead in the bottom of the hole. His one good eye was wide and staring, and his mouth hung open, twisted in a final scream of agony.

Troopers were swirling around the area as the battle entered its last stages. Turning to my left I saw that another of our men had a German facedown in the snow. He planted one knee firmly between the German's shoulders, grabbed the enemy soldier by his hair, pulled his head back, and slashed his throat from ear to ear with his trench knife. Warm blood spurted out, steaming into the snow.

*"Kamerad!"* a voice called out on my left. I looked and saw an older German sitting in the snow with a torn pants leg and a blood-soaked bandage tied to his left thigh. He caught my eye and waved weakly. I motioned for him to come forward, and he struggled to his feet and limped painfully over to me.

Of all the enemy soldiers I met face-to-face, only a few remain as individuals in my mind, as does this one. He appeared to be a mature, distinguished man. He had graying hair at the temples, giving him the appearance of a businessman, a father, or a grandfather, rather than that of a soldier.

I asked if he had a weapon.

Although he apparently didn't speak English, he must have understood me because he patted his body and then raised his arms to show that he was unarmed.

"Has he got a Luger?" someone asked from behind me.

"No, he hasn't," I replied, not taking my eyes off the German. There was a loud report. The trooper standing just behind and to the left of me had shot the German prisoner in the belly. The old man went down clutching his stomach and started cursing, glaring at me as though he thought *I* was the one who had shot him. He was in terrible pain.

The other trooper stepped up beside me and said, "We've got no choice. Actually, I've done him a favor. At least he won't freeze to death."

"He was my prisoner," I snarled, turning to face the other man. I stared directly into his eyes, pressed a finger into his chest, and said, "If you ever shoot another one of *my* prisoners, I'll blow *your* fucking head off."

The other trooper stepped back, shrugged nonchalantly, and swaggered off to join the rest of the men from our 3d Platoon. He must have been one of their replacements, because I didn't recognize him as being one of their old men.

The German was in terrible pain and dying. I knew he wouldn't recover. I knew he would die a horrible death, lying gut shot and exposed in the woods at ten below zero. Another shot rang out and a bullet tore through his head. Bits of his brains spattered the snow in a wide arc behind his body. Tiny puffs of steam drifted up from every spot where they landed. The German was dead. It had been quick and merciful.

Lieutenant Borrelli had led the 3d Platoon through heavy fighting on our left flank, then into the thick of it where we were. A rifle bullet struck him in the throat and he thought he was dying for sure. He called one of his men over to see how bad his wound was. The man looked but could find no wound. Borrelli put a hand up to his neck beneath his chin, then looked down. He spotted his second lieutenant's bar in the trampled snow and picked it up. The bullet had passed between the back of the bar and the clutch pin, shearing it from his collar and cutting a groove in the back of the gold bar. Borrelli put it in his pocket to save as a reminder of his close brush with death.

Although the battle was clearly in its last stages, a few diehards were still holding out. I pulled out my .45 pistol to conserve ammo for my M1 rifle. One does not have to be real good with a pistol in close combat, although there were times I remember wishing I'd had a twelve-gauge shotgun with double-ought buck.

We had finally reached the railroad tracks. A country lane ran just west of and parallel to the tracks. A German burst from a hole like a quail flushed out of hiding and ran northward on a gravel lane. His action took all of us by surprise and we watched, impressed by his speed. Then Charley Syer threw up his bazooka and let fly a rocket with a loud *whoosh*. The rocket hit the ground behind the running German and exploded. Snow, dirt, and debris flew up in a cloud, obscuring the fleeing enemy soldier for a moment. When it cleared, the German was nowhere in sight. He had evidently vanished over the tracks into the 3d Battalion, 501st PIR's sector. Some of us walked over and examined the spot where we had last seen the German. We found no chunks of flesh, scraps of uniform, or shards of bone. The man had gotten clean away.

Everyone began laughing.

"Did you see that son-of-a-bitch run? He was really hauling ass," someone said.

"I'll bet that Kraut will be picking gravel and pine needles out of his ass for the rest of his life," another trooper mused.

Then a few of the men began picking on Syer.

"Hey Charley," a voice called out, "what the hell were you trying to do to that poor son-of-a-bitch? Blast him clear back to Noville?"

And so it went. Charley just grinned. He knew that the less he said about it, the better off he would be.

The fighting seemed to be all but over. I stood there dazed, looking around at the carnage. How could this be? I was still alive. After all the battles I had taken part in, after seeing the deaths of so many comrades, I was still alive. Standing there amidst the carnage, the smells, the bodies, and the death, I was still alive. We always had men missing, killed, or wounded. Why was I always one of the few who survived?

I moved slowly to join a group of troopers from my platoon on the north side of the killing zone. I saw a young, wounded German in the bottom of a slit trench. He was unarmed. He'd probably thrown his rifle out of his hole. He was lying on his back, looking up at me. I reloaded my forty-five, jacked the slide back, and aimed carefully down the barrel at his forehead. Tears streamed down his cheeks.

*"Nicht schiessen,"* he babbled. *"Bitte, bitte! Nicht schiessen!"* (Don't shoot. Please, please! Don't shoot!) Phillips stepped up beside me. I lowered my pistol slightly and we stared at one another blankly.

"Are you still alive?" I asked, finally breaking the silence.

"I was just going to ask you the same thing," he replied.

It just didn't seem possible for both of us to still be alive after all we had been through together—Normandy, the seventy-two-day debacle in Holland, and now this. We'd both had the feeling that one of us would die in this attack.

For the most part, a soldier's premonition of death in battle is usually pretty accurate. I am not generally superstitious, but time after time I have seen men suddenly become quiet and withdrawn. Then they would announce they'd just had a feeling that they were going to get it. Some of them even forecast accurately the time, place, and manner in which they would die. It was eerie. All too often such premonitions proved to be only too true.

Whenever a man would declare his fate, others close to him would tell him, "Don't say that. You know what happens whenever someone says something like that. They always get killed."

Of course, there were also those who didn't expect it, and zap, they were gone to Asgard anyway. At least that was the way it seemed to us. But combat veterans are superstitious. If they aren't superstitious when they first go into combat, they get that way after they've been in battle awhile.

"What are you doing?" Phillips asked.

It was like I was coming out of a dream. My mind swirled. I was still pointing my pistol at the German in the hole, who by now was drooling and rocking his head from side to side, babbling incoherently.

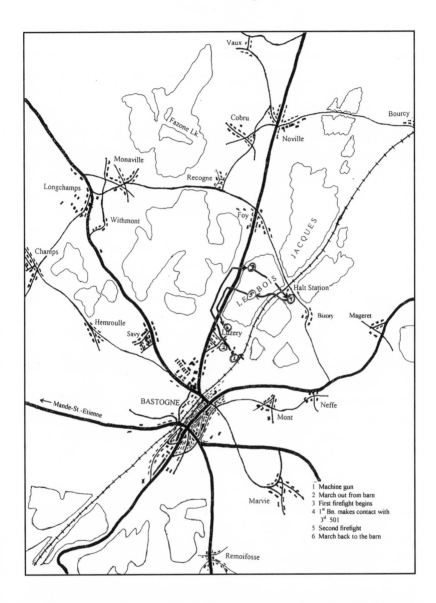

"I don't know," I mumbled. "Just getting ready to kill this Kraut I guess."

Phillips put his hand out and forced my arm down. "Leave him here. What's left are prisoners."

"But we can't take them with us," I argued. "We have no guards for them; we can't feed them. Hell, we don't have enough food for ourselves. We don't have medics—they've all been killed or captured. We can't even take care of our own wounded properly. We just can't take prisoners right now."

"I know," he replied, "but the only Krauts left alive here are the badly wounded, and they'll die tonight."

It was cruel. We had no choice; we had to leave them there. The temperature was well below zero. There would be no survivors. I holstered my forty-five, turned, and walked away from the man in the hole.

We wandered around the German battle position and began unloading and destroying enemy weapons by smashing them against trees. When the job was complete, we formed up in our platoons and moved out. Nothing but carnage lay about us. German bodies were everywhere, both in and out of the holes, sprawled in awkward, grotesque positions. Why did men have to fall crumpled up all the time? At times I had the feeling that someone should at least straighten out their arms and legs and place them in more comfortable positions.

The snow was blanketed with spruce boughs, twigs, and pine needles that had been shot from trees. Weapons, parts of uniforms, communication wire, German gas masks, helmets, canteens, and other equipment also littered the area.

Then there was the smell. It was an acrid mixture of burnt powder, fresh blood, and raw iron in human flesh. The powder smell was so strong it burned the lungs.

We were the victors. We were still alive, standing there alone among the death, the carnage, and the stench. After a while it began to grow quiet. The silence grew until it became a ringing in the ears. I looked around at the torn and broken bodies scattered all over the place in such a way as to make their presence known to the living. I hated the dead, but there was no escaping them. They were there wherever we went. Once again we had stacked bodies. There was meat on the table.

• • •

Leaving the scene of our victory, we followed a circuitous route to the south, gradually swinging west, back in the direction of the road. The woods here were thicker and heavier. They hadn't been manicured like the northern end of the Bois Jacques. Everything was covered with a thick blanket of snow. This area in particular reminded me of northern Michigan, where I had hunted white-tailed deer as a boy.

Ever since we had first gotten off the trucks in Belgium I had noticed a great similarity between this part of the country and my home state of Michigan. There were woodlots everywhere: large and small, hardwoods and pines—but mostly pines, and the majority of those were spruce. The countryside was gentle and rolling, except to the east, laced with creeks and streams, and with an occasional lake here and there.

But it wasn't Michigan. And I wasn't a boy hunting white-tailed deer. We were men in dark combat clothes, stark against the snow, spread out, making our way through thick growths of trees and brush. The slightest touch of the surrounding trees and foliage brought snow cascading over our heads and down the back of our necks. We had to constantly check the sights of our weapons to make sure they were free of obstructing snow.

Suddenly several machine guns opened up on us as one. Their familiar ripping burps tore through the crisp air. Thoughts of the German wounded begging us to take them with us a few minutes before were torn from our minds by the shattering machine-gun fire. Brininstool was walking up a little ways in front and to my left. Horn was also on my left, although not as far left as Brininstool, and a little behind me. We had just stepped into a small clearing when the firing began. Several machine guns fired from our right. At the same instant, a lone machine gun straight in front of Brininstool, Horn, and me cut loose with a long burst. The bullets cracked among the three of us. We instinctively hit the ground while at the same time trying to spot the gun. The second burst kicked up snow almost directly in front of the gun, then stitched its way rapidly toward us.

Brininstool, lying off to my left, looked at me and yelled, "Roll, Burgett, roll!" Then he glanced back to the front as he rolled away to his left.

"Look out Horn, roll to your left," I yelled as I rolled over and over to my right, just in time to avoid being hit by bullets kicking up little geysers of snow as they stitched the ground between me and Brininstool.

Horn seemed paralyzed and just lay there staring. I watched numbly as bullets again stitched a snow-geysered path between Brininstool and me right up to Horn, striking him full in the face. Horn rose to his elbows and buried his face in his hands, blood spurting from between his fingers, then eased facedown in the snow. He sobbed a little and then died.

Every rifle in the company opened up on the Germans on our right flank. Brininstool and I, who had been covering the left flank, spotted at least four men behind the machine gun in front of us. We fired deliberately at them, carefully aiming each shot. Brininstool took the two on the left and I took the two on our right. The Germans disappeared from sight and the gun fell silent. The firing continued for about two or three minutes on our right. Finally the enemy fire ceased, and gradually ours slowed, too. All became quiet. Everyone waited; no one moved. It was eerie lying there in the deathly quiet after the noise and din of our life-and-death struggle.

Far away, from along the outer perimeter surrounding Bastogne, we could hear the sounds of battle. The 3d Battalions of the 506th and 501st Regiments were intercepting the Germans who had quit the fight here and had slipped away through the woods to the east in an attempt to get back to their parent unit outside our perimeter. The Germans had stumbled right into the killing zone between those two battalions, and there they died.

The 3d Battalions of the 506th and the 501st had, in establishing a solid connecting line through the Halt railroad station, engaged in some bitter firefights. Now they faced a two-front battle. They had to face inward to meet the oncoming Germans who were fleeing our attack and trying to break out of our lines. At the same time they had to face outward to meet Germans attacking from the outside in an attempt to break through and get to Bastogne. Those troopers had quite a job on their hands for a while.

We could hear the firing in their sector gradually die down. They had pushed the enemy back from the railroad to the east and held their ground while at the same time slaughtering the Germans trying to get away from us. Some of our A and C Company men had made contact with the defenders in the outer perimeter just before we turned back toward the road and ran into this last fight.

Now all was quiet, deathly quiet. A voice from behind the stumps to our right called out *"Kamerad,"* breaking the spell. Jack Bram hollered out in German for them to come forward. The voice begged for us to come to them. Whoever it was said they were all wounded so severely that none of them could move.

"To hell with you," Jack shouted in German. "If you want to surrender, at least one of you will have to come out, even if you have to crawl. We're not sticking our necks out."

There was the sound of movement from behind the stumps. We saw a lone German pushing himself out backward in a sitting position, using his hands to move through the snow. His legs were twisted and limp and soaked with blood. They looked as if there were no bone in them. They trailed behind him—or rather in front of him, considering his backward position. He halted in the clearing, looked over his shoulder at us, and begged, *"Nicht schiessen, bitte, nicht schiessen."*

Jack Bram, with his .30-caliber light machine gun, and Jerry Janes, carrying his big .50-caliber weapon, were the first to step forward. Jerry still had his long scarf tied around the barrel to hold onto when the gun became hot from firing. He had been carrying and firing that monster all through the battle. It was a hell of a feat. Most men struggle trying to carry a fifty.

Then we all moved forward. The scene behind the stumps was almost like the one we had just left. The Germans were all in critical condition, begging us to take them with us. Bram told them we had no way to care for them and that we didn't have enough men to guard them, so we would just have to leave them there.

The man who had crawled out was talking again, with Bram interpreting. He said they had no bandages, no medicine, no food, no blankets, and that they would all die if we left them alone.

"We can't help that," Bram told him in German. "If you can crawl through our lines to the east and back to your own men, you may have a chance; but there's nothing we can do to help you."

The German doing the talking suddenly leaned forward, grabbed a burp gun lying near him in the snow, put the muzzle to his head, and fired. Several bullets ripped into his skull and with them went the top of his head. I saw gore, brain, and vapor steam out in the cold air and spatter red in the snow as he crumpled over. His troubles were over.

We policed up the rest of their weapons and smashed them against the trees. One of our troopers, a lanky hillbilly, took a loaded burp gun, test fired it to see that it worked, reloaded it, and leaned it against a tree about fifty feet away.

"This is for you," he drawled, nodding to the wounded Germans. "It's far enough away that we'll be gone by the time you reach it."

At first I didn't grasp his meaning, but then it dawned on me. The Germans seemed to understand at once, even though they couldn't understand a word he'd said. They accepted the offer in stony silence.

We walked away from the place and headed back toward the road. Our route back took us through the heavy pines. Spruce boughs laden with snow drooped as if in mourning, blotting out the daylight. It was ghostly quiet. There was no hint of wind or breeze. It had started to snow again. Large, silver dollar–sized snowflakes drifted quietly down and began piling up fast.

Stepping into small clearings on our way, where it was lighter, it began to look like the scenes pictured on Christmas cards: pine trees heavy with snow, snow covering the ground, nature in its quiet holiday grandeur. It was the evening of 21 December. Soon it would be Christmas Day. Night was falling, and it was quiet.

Before we reached the blacktop road we heard the burp gun the hillbilly had left leaning against the tree being used in short, crisp bursts. I hoped the wounded Germans had enough ammo to go around.

The rest of the walk back to the barn was quiet. No one talked. No one gave orders. We just walked along in a tired, strung-out group. It was dark, it was snowing, and it was cold.

Last man standing. Colonel Robert "Bob" Sink, left, commander of the 506th Parachute Regiment, with Maj. Gen. Maxwell D. Taylor, commander of the 101st Airborne Division, in Germany after VE day. Colonel Sink was the only regimental commander in the 101st to survive the war still in that job. (courtesy Donald Straith)

Last photo of Noville church. We blew up this church with explosives when we pulled out of Noville to prevent the Germans from using the tower for artillery observation against us. (courtesy Capt. Richard Winters)

Cold and lonely outpost on west perimeter (temperature was 10 degrees below 0), manned by a paratrooper equipped with a 1919 A-6 light machine gun. (courtesy Albert Krochka)

At a foxhole on the east perimeter near Bizory, trooper Harry Mole of E/501 strikes a pose with his Tommy gun, December 1944. (courtesy Harry Mole)

Troopers walking past the water tower of Bastogne, just north of what is now General McAuliffe Square. The water tower no longer exists. (courtesy Albert Krochka)

Wary civilians, wary trooper. Belgian civilians on road N34 to Longchamps suddenly see a trooper rise from the ground and are hesitant. The trooper knows that many Germans dressed as civilians to get close enough to kill. (U.S. Army photo)

*Happy Salamander* was the name of this MKIV German tank knocked out on Christmas day, 1944, in Champs, Belgium. An old country folklore belief held that salamanders can walk through fire unharmed. Although the crew died, the tank did not burn.

On Christmas morning, the Germans came calling. They attacked, but did not survive the battle. Photo possibly taken near Flamierge in the 401/327th Glider section. (courtesy Albert Krochka)

Self propelled gun and other German armor knocked out by 101st paratroopers in the Christmas morning attack. (courtesy Joseph Pangerl)

More German armor knocked out during the Christmas morning attack.
(courtesy Joseph Pangerl)

This Panther MKV was the largest German vehicle knocked out on Christmas morning on the western perimeter. (courtesy Albert Krochka)

Schulyer "Sky" Jackson knocked out this MKIV German tank Christmas morning on a narrow road at Rolle, Belgium, with a bazooka and guts as it approached the 502 C.P. The turret blew off when it exploded and sits up on edge on its own chassis. Jackson received the Silver Star for his actions. (courtesy Albert Krochka)

On December 28, 1944, paratroopers unloading a landed glider between Savy and Longchamps. The three men to the left who are aiding paratroopers are members of the VII Corps 969th Field Artillery Battalion (155mm). A Company 506 left this position the day before this landing. (courtesy Albert Krochka)

Ed Benecke's 75mm howitzer crew of A/377th PFA Bn. posing with captured Nazi flag near Savy, December 1944. Benecke was the gunnery sergeant. (courtesy Ed Benecke)

Armor from Patton's Third Army joins the battle in a counterattack after breaking through a German encirclement, late December, 1944. (courtesy Ed Benecke)

More of Patton's Third Army in the counterattack, late December, 1944.

All out attack. Noville liberated on 16 January 1945. Officers from the 101st plan final attack north from Noville to the German border. Colonel Bob Sink is one among these officers. (Signal Corps photo)

German POWs being herded toward Bastogne from the north perimeter as a result of our attacks. Late January, 1945. (courtesy Mark Bando)

Sergeant Don Brininstool one of the fine soldiers that I knew in the paratroops. Brininstool was my squad leader for the most part of World War II.

Sherwood Trotter was another fine combat soldier with whom I served. (author's collection)

General George Patton awards the Distinguished Service Cross to Brig. Gen. Anthony McAuliffe for his heroic leadership of the 101st Airborne Division during the siege of Bastogne. (courtesy Albert Krochka)

# 5 Sunshine and Friendly People

It was dark when we entered the farmyard. Fresh snow had obliterated our old footprints. It was as though we had never been there. Inside the barn our K rations were still lying on the floor where we had left them. The fire we'd left burning had long since burned out. Our coffee was cold in the canteen cups we'd left sitting on the dirt floor.

Sitting down in the same place where I'd been eating my rations when we got the word to move out that morning, I helped start the fire and then pushed my canteen cup closer to reheat what was left of the coffee. Speer's cup and breakfast were next to mine. Without thinking, I turned to tell him he'd better put his coffee closer to the fire. Then it hit me: I would never see him again.

I hurt every time one of our men in the company was killed, but never before had anything hit me as hard as the realization that Speer was really dead. We had become very close friends.

I thought of Bielski and the bullet that had narrowly missed going through his foot a couple of days before. "That could cripple a man for life," he'd said. It would be better to limp for the rest of one's life than to be dead. And Horn and Alvarado. They were dead, too, along with all the others. They were all dead, and that night their bodies lay frozen amidst the carnage we'd left in the dark Bois Jacques.

I mechanically went through the motions of eating and then moved away from the fire to the hay to get some sleep. That was when I discovered the bullet in my hip. I could see the butt of the bullet flush with the skin and was able to dig it out with my trench knife.

• • •

Speer's food and mess gear were still on the floor where he had left them when I awoke on the morning of 22 December. No one had moved them out of respect for our dead comrade.

Most of the men were already up and had left the barn. I brushed the straw off my jumpsuit, picked up my rifle, and walked outside. Chmiliewski and several other troopers were squatting around a pot that was bubbling over a small fire just outside the barn doors.

"Wat'cha got in the pot?" I asked.

"Chicken," Chmiliewski replied with a broad smile, stirring the contents with his trench knife.

"Don't stir it too much," another trooper said. "Remember, I got some eggs boiling in the bottom."

"Yeah, and don't forget my potatoes," said a third.

"Yeah, yeah, I know," said Chmiliewski. "Everyone's got something in my pot. Anyone want the water to make coffee with?"

A farmer wearing knee-length rubber boots came trudging around the corner of the barn following a trail of chicken feathers and blood that led right to the pot.

"Haf you got my chicken?" he asked in broken English.

"Chicken?" asked Chmiliewski innocently. "No, we don't have any chicken."

"Then how come all the feathers and blood?" the farmer asked suspiciously.

Several men looked down at the snow and began shuffling their feet to get rid of the evidence.

"What feathers and blood?" someone asked.

"Let me look in the pot," said the farmer.

"You look in there," Chmiliewski growled as he rose to his feet, "and I'll break your arm."

Chmiliewski's large, bulky body looked formidable as he stood there in front of the thin, frail-looking farmer. The farmer looked him up and down then stamped away, grumbling to himself. Later he returned with Capt. Roy Kessler, our new company commander. I didn't even know we'd lost the captain who led us into Noville. As I mentioned earlier, the turnover in company commanders was steady. Kessler had been our CO for a while in Normandy. I believe

Lieutenant Borrelli was our CO for a while back in garrison, and he acted like he was in charge when we pulled out of Noville. I wasn't really paying any attention at the time. There had been too many other things to worry about. Now it was Captain Kessler's turn again.

"This farmer tells me you men have one of his chickens," the captain croaked in his gravelly voice. "Is that true?"

"No, sir," the men chorused, rolling their eyes and looking away in different directions. "We wouldn't do nothing like that, sir."

Captain Kessler turned to the farmer and said, "You must be mistaken, sir; these men have no chicken."

The farmer sniffed the air and tried to move closer to the pot but his way was blocked by a couple of troopers who had slipped nonchalantly between him and the pot.

"I can smell it! I can smell my chicken cooking in the pot. Don't you smell it, Captain?"

"No, sir, I don't. Now get out of here and leave my men alone. They need some rest after all they've been through."

Captain Kessler's thin, hawk-like face looked haggard, yet knowing. He was fast moving and athletic in spite of his gangly appearance. Rumor had it that he came from a wealthy family. He could have held out for a rear-echelon desk job. Instead he chose to become a paratrooper so he could get into the real fighting. Of course that was just a latrine rumor, and 90 percent of the time those had no basis in fact. Whenever he wasn't within earshot, we affectionately called him "Frog" because of his voice, which had the quality of a handful of gravel being swished around the bottom of an old, empty lard pail.

The captain placed a hand on the man's shoulder as though they were old buddies and guided him gently but firmly away. As soon as they were out of sight, the contents of the pot disappeared. There wasn't enough for a full meal, but everyone at least got a little something to eat.

Captain Kessler returned later and called us together, complimenting us on our attack in the Bois Jacques. Fifty-eight of us, plus the remnants of C Company, had destroyed an enemy battalion and taken eighty prisoners, eliminating the threat of having an enemy force entrenched in our midst. Men from the 501st PIR captured eighty-five more Germans as they fled our onslaught, running helter-skelter into the 501st's lines. I don't know how many more men the 501st killed as they tried to escape, nor do I recall seeing any German prisoners with us after the fight. Maybe C Company rounded them up.

We lost eight troopers in the assault: four old men and four replacements. I didn't know the names of any of the replacements. I didn't know how many men C Company lost, either. They probably suffered about as many casualties as we did.

The fog was heavy but we could see that it was still overcast through small clear spots in it here and there. As long as the sky remained overcast we knew there would be no support from our Air Corps.

A Company, 506th PIR, now numbered just fifty men. We had suffered nearly 75 percent casualties in just three days of fighting. Now, we were ordered to occupy foxholes in the center of the line manned by the rest of the regiment, with 2d Battalion on the left flank, then our 1st Battalion, and 3d Battalion on the right. Fifty men in our company meant three platoons of approximately fifteen men each, plus a small company headquarters. A platoon with fifteen men broke down into three squads with only four or five men each, plus the platoon leader and the platoon sergeant.

Phillips, Liddle, Benson, and I were assigned to pull guard with our machine gun at the railroad tracks again. When a company is down to fifty men, duties come around pretty often. In fact, in order to stay alive, we were on duty twenty-four hours a day, seven days a week. Still, we rotated getting sleep as best we could.

We made our way through knee-deep snow to the hole atop the railroad bank. We relieved the crew that was there and slid down into it, trying to get as comfortable as possible for the night. We didn't set a particular length of time for each man to stay awake. It's a fact that some men can stay awake longer than others. However, we agreed that two men would stay awake as long as possible. When one man became sleepy he would awaken another to take his place so he could get some rest.

Having two men on watch together helps them keep each other from dozing and reduces nervousness. Many times before and after Bastogne I heard or saw something suspicious while pulling guard, nudged my buddy and indicated by sign what I thought might be the source of danger, and had him take a look. The two judgments together many times kept our imaginations from getting out of hand and kept the outpost on even keel.

My companions were good men. They were battle experienced and cool. I knew I could rest while they were on guard. Even so, a combat man still sleeps in catnaps. Only Phillips tended to be a problem. Every time he slept he snored so loud it sounded as though he were going to tear the roof of his mouth out. We had to keep placing our hands over his nose and mouth until he stopped snoring, opened his eyes, turned his head, and fell asleep again. We passed the entire night like that, shivering in freezing cold, until the sky lightened the horizon at dawn on 23 December.

The morning was relatively quiet. Artillery fire landed randomly within our perimeter and the Luftwaffe managed a small bombing raid, but it was nothing even close to what we'd been through. We knew the enemy had something up his sleeve and figured it to be a large-scale attack, for we could hear the sound of tanks and trucks constantly moving and shifting positions all through the night and into the morning. Then, around noon, it became unnaturally quiet. The sound of small-arms and artillery fire gradually petered out and we sat anxiously at the edge of our hole waiting, watching, and listening. What the hell were they up to?

The hours dragged by. The four of us remained there in our foxhole on the railroad throughout the rest of that day. Benson produced a bottle of five-star cognac from his jacket and shared it with the rest of us. Three of us passed the bottle around time after time, taking short swigs from it to keep warm, or so we thought. Being a Mormon, Liddle didn't drink. Instead, he poured his share of the whiskey on a flat rock in the bottom of our hole and lit it with a match. The almost invisible flame from the alcohol supplied a surprising amount of heat in the foxhole.

The day wore on. Finally, at dark, our relief came and the four of us hobbled back to the barn. Several troopers standing at the large, double barn doors told us to go to the farmhouse where several A Company GIs had a fire going in the wood-burning kitchen stove.

We were standing there warming our hands over the stove when General McAuliffe walked in.

Several troopers yelled "Attention!" at the same time, and the general said "As you were" with a grim smile and a wave of his hand. Then he stood there looking at us for a moment. We were all a mess. But this wasn't exactly garrison life, either. The general briefly explained our situation. He told us we were completely surrounded and outnumbered—close to nine to one was how he put it. Then he told us of the German surrender demand.

Four Germans—two officers and two enlisted men carrying a large, white flag—had walked up the road from the direction of Remoifosse into the 327th Glider Infantry Regiment's lines just before noon the day before with a formal demand for our surrender. If we didn't surrender, they said they had orders to annihilate us. No prisoners would be taken.

General McAuliffe then asked us as a group how we felt about it. The men present replied in unison, albeit in slightly different words:

"Tell them to go to hell, sir!"

"We'll never surrender, sir."

"Tell them to go fuck themselves, sir."

General McAuliffe burst out laughing. "Okay, okay," he said. "That's just what I did tell them. I knew what your answer would be before I asked, but I wanted to hear it for myself. I'm sorry I can't get around to see each and every man in the division, but I'm visiting as many as I can out here on the perimeter."

He told us about one of the men he had just talked to in a makeshift hospital back in Bastogne.

The wounded trooper, who was lying on the floor with other wounded GIs, called to the general when he saw him, saying, "Sir, I have coined a new name for the division. We're the "Battle-Battered Bastards of the Bastion of Bastogne."

The phrase stuck. To this day we are referred to as the "Battered Bastards of Bastogne," "Battered Bastards," "Battled Bastards," or just plain (with no offense intended) "Bastards."

When General McAuliffe and his aide left the kitchen it was dark outside. All of us followed them out into the yard. They strode unhurried to the jeep parked there, climbed in, and the general waved to us as they drove away.

General McAuliffe was neither a tall nor a large man. But he was a general, a commander of men, and his carriage and demeanor reflected that fact.

We reentered the kitchen and stood talking as we warmed ourselves close to the wood stove. That short visit by our general left us with the feeling that we would die to the last man if necessary rather than surrender. Who the hell did those Germans think they were, anyway? Fewer than sixty of us had just destroyed one of their battalions in the Bois Jacques fight and *they* wanted *us* to surrender? We were beating their asses off and they knew it. They were bluffing; they were trying to get us to quit before we kicked the hell out of the rest of them.

As the young hillbilly had said, we had the advantage—we could shoot in any direction and hit them.

The enemy shelling continued, but not in the devastating volleys the Germans seeking our surrender had promised. Bastogne and its surrounding areas were shelled and bombed and attacked by German armor and infantry during the next four days, but the Germans always came out on the short end of those attacks. A lot of them never returned to their lines. Americans in general, unlike soldiers in most other armies of the world, tend to take aim and shoot at individuals, even when they are massed, rather than firing volleys into large groups. This one shot–one man, "meat-on-the-table" type of shooting killed more enemy than did laying down a blanket of fire.

After we finished warming up and eating in the farmhouse we returned to the barn to sleep. I slept heavily in the hay, oblivious to everything until somebody shook me awake early on 24 December.

As we sat around eating our K-ration breakfasts that morning, we had time to listen to and pass on more latrine rumors. Someone had started a rumor that the Germans with the white flag wanted to surrender *their* divisions to us. We knew differently, but that's the way latrine rumors get distorted as they're passed around. If they had really wanted to surrender, General McAuliffe would have gladly accepted the offer and we wouldn't have had to fight them anymore.

Our supplies were getting desperately low at that point. Our tanks and tank destroyers had to sit with engines off until they were really needed. Then they would clank off to meet the enemy with cold engines and crews. All the vehicles in Bastogne sat with empty gas tanks until they were needed. Then they were fueled from five-gallon cans carried up from protective storage in basements just before they were started. After returning, the fuel tanks were drained of the remaining gas and it was carried back to storage in the basements. This was a necessary precaution to prevent the loss of fuel if a vehicle was destroyed by a bomb or artillery fire. The division had less than five hundred gallons of fuel for all of its vehicles—from jeeps and ambulances to half-tracks and tanks.

Our field artillery had played an important part in breaking up most of the German attacks during the opening phases of the battle, but now their ammunition supply was so low that General McAuliffe rationed the guns to no more than ten rounds per gun per day. They were not to fire unless a German breakthrough seemed imminent. Every round had to count.

The same was true for our tanks and TDs. They too were almost out of ammo, on top of being hampered by the fuel shortage. They had to make each yard traveled and every shot fired count. Every time one of their gunners pulled the trigger there had to be meat on the table.

We took stock of ourselves, our ammo, and our food, and then spent the rest of the day cleaning weapons, making what repairs we could, and sharpening our trench knives. The day was uneventful for us aside from pulling our turn on watch out on the perimeter. Our biggest worry was trying to keep from freezing to death.

Fog and mist still blanketed the countryside. Our Air Corps could not do anything to help in that weather. Night came on again and men pulled more hay down from the loft and stacked it along the outer walls of the barn before burrowing into it to get what sleep they could. Phillips, Benson, Liddle, and I were among those who had this time off. Someone else was out in our hole with the machine gun, freezing on the railroad bank. I burrowed into the straw and tried to get what sleep I could. I knew tomorrow would be another day. Maybe the fog would clear off and we'd see the sun again. Sunshine would bring our fighter-bombers. Then Hans and Fritz would *really* get what was coming to them.

I don't know what time it was when I was finally shaken out of the hay, but it was still dark when one of the noncoms called out. "Okay, let's go. We're moving out. Let's hubba-hubba, one time."

We were being pulled off the line to be replaced by elements of the 501st PIR that had been in reserve. We formed up in the farmyard in rough platoon formations, hefted our machine guns, mortars, base plates, ammo, bazookas, and other gear to our shoulders, and headed out toward the Bastogne–Noville road. It was 8:45 A.M. on Christmas Day.

We waded in single file through snow that had drifted to well over our knees. The first man had the rough job of breaking trail. When he became fatigued and sweat-soaked he would fall out to one side, wait for the column to pass, and then fall in at the rear, where the trampled snow made for easier walking. The man who had been behind him would then break trail until he too became tired and fell in at the rear. And so it went, each man taking a turn breaking trail for the others.

After moving a short distance on the Bastogne–Noville road we picked up a secondary east-west road running between Luzery and Savy. We followed it westward, coming out just south of Savy.

Many of us had wrapped our feet in pieces of blankets, rags, or old burlap bags found in and around farmhouses, barns, and other buildings in an effort to keep our feet from freezing. Some had wrapped sheets of newspaper and other paper around their bodies under their shirts to keep in their body heat. This worked well while sitting for hours in foxholes or lying in the fields or woods, but when trudging through deep snow on a forced march the body soon began to pour out sweat. Then, whenever we came to a halt, our sweat-soaked bodies and clothing began to freeze. We would open the fronts of our jackets and shirts to let out the body heat. Once we had cooled down enough, we buttoned up our shirts and jackets and tried to keep warm.

It had been more than a week since we'd had a bath or change of clothing, and we smelled of heavy, dank, oily body odor. I felt sorry for those who had died in this condition. It didn't seem proper, not

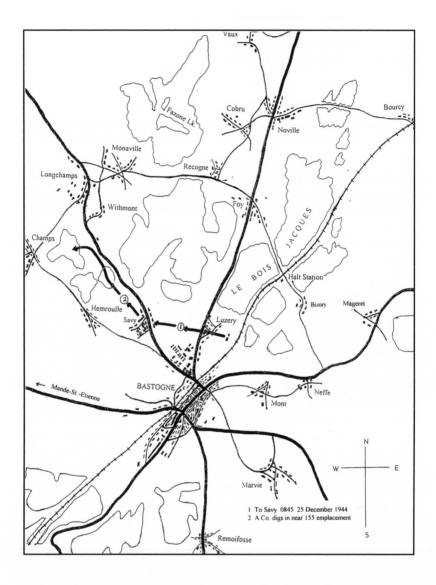

1 To Savy 0845 25 December 1944
2 A Co. digs in near 155 emplacement

being able to clean up a little bit before being killed. But once a man is dead, it really doesn't make any difference, does it?

We entered Savy and came to what would be the main street in that small village. There, forming a barricade across the road, was a makeshift counter of planks laid across barrels that were standing on end. Cooks were serving up hotcakes and hot black coffee in the subzero weather to troops that were billeted in town. The cooks told us to get our mess gear and get in line.

"Come on, come on," one of them shouted; "we've got plenty, and we can always make some more."

We rushed forward, pulling our mess kits from musette bags and pants pockets as we ran to join the line at the makeshift counter.

The cooks and their helpers stood behind the counter, which had several large, insulated mermite cans filled with pancakes and one filled with hot, black coffee. Behind the cooks were portable GI stoves where some of the cooks were frying up pancakes and putting them into more mermite cans, from which they were then served to the passing troops.

The sky began to lighten as we shuffled through the chow line. We each received two pancakes, some jam, and a canteen cup full of coffee—*real* coffee, not the ersatz K-ration stuff. We spread out around the square, hunkered down with our backs to the walls of surrounding buildings, and ate. Some of the men wolfed down their food like animals, in case there were any seconds to be had.

The cooks made the pancakes with flour that had been commandeered from a civilian warehouse along with the jam and coffee. We learned from the cooks that the troops in Bastogne had been getting pancakes and jam all along, while we on the perimeter got nothing but K rations or hunger pains. It was probably for the best, though. It would have been difficult to attack with full bellies, running through the deep snow and ducking underneath low-hanging, snow-laden tree limbs.

We talked with the troopers in Savy, hoping to learn how our positions were laid out around Bastogne and how the rest of the division was holding up. We found out that Bastogne had received its worst bombing of the siege during the previous night. We knew the city had been bombed; we could see and hear it from where we were, but we didn't know how bad it was. Incendiary bombs hit one of our aid stations, setting it ablaze. It took everyone available two hours to get the wounded out. Despite the rescuers' best efforts more than half of the litter patients were burned alive. More than a hundred of them died, plus a young Belgian nurse, Renée Lemaire, who voluntarily stayed in the city to help care for our wounded. She died trying to save American wounded. Most of those rescued had to be treated for burns.

We were told to make ourselves at home but not to get too comfortable, for we might have to move out again at a moment's notice. We moved by squads and platoons into houses, sheds, and cellars vacated by the civilians living there. My squad moved into a small, cavelike place built of rough fieldstone wedged tightly between two larger buildings made of the same material. The entrance was small. A man had to step over a high threshold and duck his head at the same time to get to the dark, windowless interior. Straw was piled mattress high around the four walls and the center of the floor was kept clear for small fires.

Phillips and I kicked the lumpiness out of a pile of straw near the door and settled down for a rest, leaving our musette bags on and keeping our rifles close at hand. At that moment someone stuck his head inside and yelled that we had to form up outside because we were moving out again. We fell out on the double, the order of march was given, and we moved out to the north across snow-covered fields and along little-traveled roads. Our battalion CP would remain in Savy, so we knew we wouldn't be traveling too far.

Near the end of this march we came to a wide expanse of farm fields to the west of the north-south road we were on. A lone farmhouse stood near the north end of the fields on the east side of the road, and evergreen forests grew thick and deep to the west, then spread around to the northernmost part of the open ground. We crossed the fields, passing through a couple of barbed-wire farm fences that had been cut through at different spots to allow our passage, and entered the dark woods on the other side.

The land dropped off sharply where the fields and woods met, forming a bank about three or four feet high that ran parallel to the road we had just left. The woods were thick with low-hanging limbs that were heavy with snow. A small creek ran from north to south about a hundred yards inside the trees. We dug in along the bank overlooking the wide-open fields. The position offered us the advantage of concealment in the trees and the protective cover of the bank, plus a clear field of fire across the level farmland to the road.

We dug our holes large enough for two or three men to huddle to-gether inside for warmth. The temperature was still well below zero and more snow had fallen.

We did not particularly like being in the woods. Incoming artillery or mortar shells hitting treetops explode high above the ground like giant shotguns, driving shell fragments down into foxholes. Tree bursts are terribly effective against ground troops. People instinc-tively seek the shelter of trees during a thunderstorm. They have the same tendency when threatened by an attacking enemy force. Light-ning and artillery fire both will kill you, and trees enhance their ef-fectiveness. You should stay clear of trees if possible whenever ar-tillery may be used.

We dug in so that we could bring our mortars and machine guns to bear in any direction. In addition to digging foxholes for ourselves and primary positions for our machine guns, we dug alternate po-sitions for the machine guns so they could be moved quickly to cover the deepest part of the woods in case the enemy circled to the west and came at us from that direction. The mortars, which had to fire upward, were limited to those spots where there were openings among the trees. The woods might slow German armor but it would not hinder their infantry. We had to be ready at all times in all di-rections.

There we built small, smokeless fires. By small, I mean a fire small enough to hold in your two cupped hands. These fires weren't meant to warm the whole body; they were for melting snow for drinking wa-ter, warming fingers and toes, or simply to stare into and dream about being warm. Men set about trying to get enough water to drink or to make K-ration coffee. We didn't have iodine tablets for purify-ing the creek water, so we hesitated to use it for drinking.

The skies were still shrouded by thick, gray clouds and there was little wind. In the distance we could make out the sounds of shelling punctuated by occasional bursts of small-arms fire. It was fairly quiet for a war.

Men set about cleaning their weapons, straightening out their gear, checking ammo, and sharpening knives. Two men stood guard on each machine gun so the rest of us could get a little badly needed sleep after our weapons were cleaned and ready. Our weapons always came first—before eating, a trip to the straddle trench, or anything else. Care of our weapons came first because our lives depended on them. A malfunction in battle meant death.

I looked at the men around me and wondered if I looked as horrible as they did. Their faces were gaunt, with dark shadows around sunken eyes. Their jumpsuits were caked with filth and grease, and their faces were blackened by dirt and burnt powder. Some of them were sitting around the fires on their haunches, scraping the crud out of their beards with their fingernails, and then cleaning the accumulated dirt from under their nails. Others were sharpening their knives or cleaning their weapons again. We had an oddball collection of weapons that had been gathered from our own dead and wounded, the enemy, or abandoned by other outfits when they fled. We had everything from Lugers to burp guns and M1s to Mausers. Some troopers were reluctant to use German weapons because combat men can tell the difference in the sounds they make. But in close, heavy combat it doesn't really matter.

I sat with several others near a small fire. I had packed my steel helmet full of snow and set it close to the heat to melt for my canteen. Then I took off my boots and socks and hung the socks on the end of a forked stick leaning toward the fire so they would dry. Sitting on the snow I extended my bare feet toward the welcome warmth. I kept my boots back a little way from the fire, turning them frequently so that they would dry more slowly. I had ruined a pair of high-topped leather boots by drying them too fast when I was a kid during the Depression. They had curled up and gotten hard as wood and, because they were my only pair of shoes for the year, I had to wear them that way.

Some of us were scraping and shaving the crud from our jumpsuits with razor-sharp trench knives. Most of the dirt and grease on our jumpsuits was on the front of the upper thigh. We would take hold of the cloth below the knee with one hand and then scrape upward with a trench knife, shaving the dirt, grease, and other crud off the pants leg. After repeating the process on the other leg, we'd do the same thing on any other part of our clothing we could reach and shave. It wasn't as good as getting clean laundry but it was the best we could do.

The 969th Field Artillery Battalion, a 155mm-towed-howitzer outfit, was dug in along the edge of the woods to our east. It was made up of Negro troops. They had been on their way out of Bastogne along with everyone else trying to get away from the German juggernaut roaring through the Ardennes. General McAuliffe, being an artillery commander, well knew the value of their big guns, which were much heavier than our lighter airborne artillery. Seeing them go by, heading west with the other troops fleeing the advancing Germans, the general sent a detail after them and brought them and their big guns back to this area. And here they had stayed.

When receiving fire missions they would sing in rhythmic cadence, loading and firing in death-dealing precision. Their accurate and heavy barrages had helped to break up nearly every major German attack in the 101st's first two crucial days at Bastogne. However, since then they were completely out of ammo and spent their time fussing about their guns and emplacements. Their sleeping and living dugouts were elaborate affairs built of logs that were large enough to sleep several men at a time and high enough to stand upright in. They even had coffeepots. Hell, we never had it that good back in garrison.

Most of our men had finished cleaning themselves as best they could and were busying themselves with other odd jobs, improving their foxholes, cleaning weapons again, and so on, when the miracle happened. I had just finished cleaning my forty-five and had put my socks and boots back on when suddenly we were bathed in sunlight. It was like a storybook fantasy: the fog melted, the clouds parted, and the sun broke through.

Bright sunlight reflected off the crisp, white snow, accentuating the dark shadows in the woods. The sun's rays lanced down through the pines at sharp angles, forming bright, golden shafts that gave the forest around us a cathedral-like appearance. We weren't in a worshipful mood, however. The sun would soon be followed by fighter-bombers, and soon the sky would fill with transport aircraft that would parachute ammo, food, and fuel to us. Soon we would be able to avenge our dead.

We laughed and joked with each other, standing there in the sunlight and gazing upward into the clear, blue sky. Some of the men farther back in the woods put their hands into the sunbeams, turning them over and over as if they were bathing them, staring at them as though they could feel the light itself. Others held their weapons over their heads and danced fancy little jigs in and out of bright, sunlit clearings. Most of us frolicked and gamboled about like kids, with much backslapping. A few sat hunched over, staring silently into the small fires with grim smiles on their lips.

Yes, Hans and Fritz were going to get theirs. They had come down on us with tanks, self-propelled guns, artillery, and waves of infantry. Soon it would be payback time. They had ridden us down in their huge metal monsters, driving into and over our positions, crushing the life out of many of our comrades. We wanted revenge.

When we finally tired of gamboling around we sat or stood and listened for the drone of aircraft engines that would herald the coming of our flyboys. At last we were able to make out the vibrant, deep-throated engines of C-47s. The sluggish old "Gooneybirds" came over in a low formation to the south of us, releasing their payloads over the Bastogne area. The Gooneybirds were fat, slow, and coated from nose to tail with dull, olive drab military paint but they were beautiful—just plain beautiful.

We watched as multitudes of colored parachutes blossomed in the clear air and settled earthward. We knew that thousands of hostile eyes deep in the shadowy woods and wrecked villages surrounding Bastogne also watched the sky fill with 'chutes. What were their thoughts? Their numerically superior armor, artillery, weapons, and manpower couldn't beat us when we were down, so how could they hope to beat us when we were up? Surely they must have known they had lost. Surely they knew we would make them pay for the atrocities and crimes they had committed.

Some bundles without 'chutes were kicked out of the planes and plummeted straight down. The sky was full of incoming supplies and we cheered as the C-47s continued to roar overhead. The air was also black with bursts of flak, and tracers lanced upward, crisscrossing and following the sluggish, unarmed C-47s, occasionally converging on a crippled plane trailing smoke. We later learned that our C-47s had run a gauntlet of antiaircraft spanning the entire Bulge area before they reached Bastogne. Many were hit and several went down in flames, their crews either killed or captured by the enemy. The pilots and crews didn't waver in the face of this onslaught; they stayed in formation, maintaining their course at a highly vulnerable altitude. Courage was the norm for the day.

The flights continued throughout the rest of the day, with supplies coming in by the ton. We watched, fascinated, as the sky filled again and again with hundreds upon hundreds of colored 'chutes. We watched until evening came and the sky began to darken.

Flights of P-47 "Thunderbolt" fighter-bombers also roared overhead. The first flight to arrive on the scene circled in low and began strafing and bombing the German tanks and troops that ringed Bastogne. After their bombs and ammo were used up they would climb to a higher altitude and circle our perimeter looking for and locating new enemy targets. They radioed this information to an air-ground liaison officer who accompanied the division into Bastogne. The liaison officer would then radio the target information to fresh flights of fighter-bombers en route to the area. The previous flight would then head back to its forward airfield in France to rearm and refuel so they could return to the fray.

Thanks to these tactics, the newly arrived fighter-bombers did not have to search for targets. They knew exactly what and where their targets were before they arrived on the scene. We cheered as our fly-boys pounded the Germans with a vengeance.

The fighter-bombers kept up their attacks all day. Columns of black smoke mushroomed up from countless spots from the woods around the 101st's perimeter as our airmen blasted enemy tanks, self-propelled guns, trucks, ammo and fuel dumps, and artillery emplacements. At last the flights ceased and the air became quiet. Off in the distance we could still hear the sounds of battle. The Germans wanted Bastogne bad. They knew they didn't have much time left. If they were to conquer Bastogne, it would have to be soon, very soon. What could they try that they hadn't already tried? The only thing left was to mass their forces and mount an all-out attack at what they figured to be the weakest point in our perimeter.

• • •

It was getting dark fast. We set our guards out for the first watch and the rest of us settled into our holes. Few of us were able to sleep. We were like kids on Christmas Eve: excited and full of anticipation. Excited because the weather had at last broken. Filled with anticipation at the prospect of putting the weapons, ammo, fuel, and food dropped to us to good use.

We also heard that several doctors had been flown in by glider. That meant our wounded would be able to get the treatment they so badly needed. Word also filtered through the ranks that General Patton's spearhead 4th Armored Division was on its way to give us a hand and would reach Bastogne either that night or the next morning at the latest. We may have been as excited as little kids, but we knew that no battle was ever won until after the last shot was fired. We still had a long way to go. We were pleased and proud that we had held the city of Bastogne as ordered, allowing the Allies time to get their feet back under them, regroup, and give us a hand. We had stayed when nearly all others had fled, and we had held.

We stood in our foxholes, leaning our elbows on the edge and surveying everything around us as it grew darker and darker. It is always a good practice to familiarize yourself with the surroundings and what they look like in the growing dark as well as in daylight before the sun goes down. That way, if you spotted a shadow that wasn't there before it became dark, you knew it had to be something that had moved in after it became dark. Several of us watched as the Negro troops in the 155mm howitzer emplacements got ready to call it a night.

"They sure have it made," Phillips said. "They don't pull any guard duty, no patrols, and they are usually so far behind the lines that they don't even use a challenge or password."

Later that night, while Jack Thomas and another man were pulling guard duty on the machine gun, one of the Negro artillerymen crept down through our lines, heading for the straddle trenches in the woods. We all heard and saw the man, but we knew who it was and didn't say anything. Thomas allowed him to pass a few feet in front of his position without challenge. After a short while the man was coming back through the woods and when he was just a few feet in front of Thomas, Jack challenged him in a loud clear voice so we could all hear.

"Halt, who's there? Give me the password," he intoned.

"Man, I don't know any password," said the startled Negro.

"Come on," said Jack. "Give me the password or I'll cut you in half with this machine gun."

The man's response was quick, loud, and clear: "Don't shoot man; you knows they ain't no nigger Nazis."

Everyone burst out laughing. We laughed until most of us lay weak in the bottom of our foxholes.

"That sure was quick thinking on his part," Liddle said, wiping tears from his eyes.

The next day the artilleryman Thomas had challenged forgave us when we went to visit him and his crew in their elaborate dugout. They offered us coffee and treated us with great hospitality, explaining the workings of their big guns and how they worked as a team when fire missions came in. We in turn explained about challenges and passwords, and promised to let them in on the daily password as soon as we received it. They in turn promised to use the system we had taught them from that day on. We developed a deep respect for and friendship with these gunners in the very short time that we spent together.

We spent the rest of the night without any major incident but we remained awake and alert through most of it. We knew the twenty-sixth would be clear and that our Air Corps would be on the job and the Germans would get another pasting. We wanted to be there to watch.

Half of our company was always awake at any given time, while the other half rested or dozed. Combat men really don't sleep. The men on guard with the machine gun were relieved every two hours. Any longer than that and a man becomes drowsy—especially after so many days of strenuous action with little food and sleep.

The sun rose in all its fiery splendor, casting a red glare and long shadows across white snow. By then we had small fires going and were heating K-ration coffee. I took stock of my ammo. I had three rounds left for my M1 rifle and two full magazines for my forty-five, plus what was in the pistol, making a total of twenty-one rounds of .45-caliber ammo.

We thought the previous day's resupply drop was the first since the division had been surrounded, but we later learned the first drop was made at noon on 23 December. Several C-47s came in low over Bastogne and our pathfinders parachuted in and set up radar and guidance systems to direct the following aircraft to the drop zone. Within thirty minutes, eleven gliders followed them in, delivering surgeons and 32,900 pounds of medical supplies. Three of the doctors were killed by flak just before their glider landed. Many more airdrops followed over the next several days.

The day after Christmas began no differently than had the previous couple of days. A fresh snow blanketed the countryside. Not long after sunrise, enemy planes bombed and strafed our lines. They came in low from the east, out of the sun, their engines drumming loud and low, sounding almost like washing machines. They opened fire with their machine guns and bullets ricocheting off the frozen ground, then skipped through the woods, causing pine needles, limbs, and tree bark to fall all around us. Then there was a rush of air as five-hundred-pound bombs hurtled downward and exploded all around the area. We suffered no casualties and I did not hear of any damage caused by this air attack.

Antiaircraft gunners blasted away at the enemy fliers but I didn't see any hits or any of the fighter-bombers trailing smoke. Our own Air Corps had yet to arrive. They were busy at other, more important, places in the Bulge, wreaking havoc on German armor and ground troops. Their tactics may have kept the enemy from mounting the full-scale attack we all were anticipating.

Our fighter-bombers finally appeared overhead shortly before noon and began delivering belated presents to Adolf's boys. Hans and Fritz had gotten their stockings filled on Christmas Day, and now they had to endure a repeat performance as our P-47s swooped out of the skies and plastered the enemy tanks and infantry ringing our perimeter. We could see columns of black, oily smoke rising from burning vehicles all along our lines. The Luftwaffe withdrew after its early-morning raid, leaving our own fighter-bombers to romp unopposed all over the skies. They came in so low at times that the bellies of their aircraft struck the tops of pine trees. None appeared to be damaged by the near misses as they hosed the German lines with their machine guns and dropped bombs on targets scattered through the woods to our front. They cut the enemy to ribbons.

Some Signal Corps troops drove up in a jeep in front of the 969th Field Artillery Battalion's positions and began laying marker panels out in the flat, snow-covered field. When they finished, they ran to the safety of our tree line and stood and watched. Several of us walked over and talked to them. They told us there would be an equipment drop in just a few minutes. Several different DZs were being used because the Germans would bring in extra antiaircraft guns and machine guns close to a previously used drop zone and lie in wait, hoping to shoot down more of our transports the next time around. Moving the drop zones to different fields for each drop helped prevent our planes from running into a heavy concentration of flak when they did come in.

The C-47s appeared on schedule. They flew in low, homed in on the panels, and began to drop supplies. Red, yellow, and white 'chutes drifted down not far from where we stood. Red 'chutes were employed for ammo and explosives, yellow 'chutes were used for food and clothing, and white 'chutes indicated the cargo was medical or other equipment. Nearly all of it landed in the flat, snow-covered fields to our front. All the while German antiaircraft gunners filled the air with flak bursts, and machine-gun tracers snaked through the air. Our C-47s held right on course, even when a couple of them went down.

A C-47 trailing black smoke came in low, striking the pine tops behind us, skimmed over our positions, and slid across the snow-covered fields to our left front. It came to rest after tearing a path through several barbed-wire fences. The crew piled out in a hurry and ran to our positions in the woods. Troopers ran out to the plane, retrieved a fire extinguisher from it, put out the fire, and unloaded the aircraft's cargo.

The drop continued. What seemed to be hundreds of C-47s roared in low over our lines and dropped what must have been thousands of parachutes. We went out into the DZ in front of us and dragged the goodies to the protection of our lines.

Tons of supplies rained down on the 101st Division troops scattered around Bastogne. Troopers were frolicking like kids, running out of foxholes and woods to where 'chutes lay on the ground, then dragging back all kinds of goodies: ammo, food, grenades, bazooka rockets, mortar and artillery shells, medical supplies, and communications equipment. But there wasn't even a single canteen cup of water. We were dying of thirst. In combat a man needs water, lots of water. It seemed to take an acre of snow to melt a single quart. No one thought to drop us any water. In Holland, L-5s dropped water to us in five-gallon plastic bags. Not this time.

One trooper walked laughing through our company area holding high above his head a fruitcake in a colorful round tin.

"Help yourself," he said. "Compliments of the Air Corps."

A card attached to the cake read, "Merry Christmas, from the men of the 53d Wing, IX Troop Carrier Command." I held the card and reread it. I'll never forget it.

Several more fruitcakes and other small, thoughtful gifts turned up in the supplies dropped on our DZ. One small package my squad picked up contained a toothbrush and a tube of toothpaste. After all the 'chutes and supplies had been gathered and piled safely inside the concealment of our tree line, several troopers went to the creek, broke a hole through the ice, and took turns brushing their teeth, passing the lone toothbrush from man to man. I passed on that one, preferring to use a small spruce twig I had chewed into brush form.

Back at the fire, men were frying bacon from the ten-in-one rations in their mess kits. The odor drifting through the trees in the crisp, below-zero air was enough to drive a man out of his mind. I pulled my mess kit from my musette bag, found a can of bacon in one of the boxes, opened the can with my trench knife, cooked all that was in the can, and shared it with the rest of the men in my squad. We pulled other food from the box, but the bacon was first.

At last we were ready. The Germans were going to be sorry they'd ever heard of Hitler, and even sorrier that they'd ever heard of the 101st Airborne Division, the Screaming Eagles.

Trucks and jeeps pulled into our area to retrieve the supplies we had gathered from the drop zone. These were then taken back to a

central location in Bastogne, inventoried, and parceled out to where
they were most needed.

News traveled quickly at Bastogne. Couriers and word of mouth
ensured that the latest scuttlebutt was passed from unit to unit. So
it was that we learned of the 23 December attack near Marvie in
which a large force of German tanks and armored infantry overran
and captured a hundred men from the 327th Glider Infantry Regiment. The enemy managed to breach our lines there and two enemy tanks broke through and entered Bastogne. They were quickly
destroyed.

American tanks and TDs backed by artillery were rushed to the
breach in our lines and, after a bitter struggle, the gap was closed.

The 327th's roadblock at Flamierge was also overrun on the
twenty-third. The glidermen pulled back to high ground overlooking the position, set up a strong defense, and held there throughout the rest of the battle for Bastogne.

The 327th was catching hell from all around. Not only were they
being attacked in force by German armor and infantry, but P-47s
bombed and strafed them in their positions in and around Marvie
on the twenty-fourth. Later that day the P-47s returned and hit the
327th again in spite of the large ID panels laid out in the snow so
the airmen would know they were friendly troops.

During this time men from our battalion were sent out on patrols
through the deep snow and dark woods to make contact with the
Germans and find their locations, strength, and probable intentions.
Our command wanted to know what good ol' Hans and Fritz were
up to. Somehow I was not chosen to go on any of those patrols.

In the middle of the afternoon on 26 December we heard German artillery moaning in. Not in large concentrations, but inter-
mittent and spread out, as though the German gunners were
searching for us. Shells landed in the open field in front of the
969th's positions, scattering small papers to the wind. I walked out
with several other troopers to retrieve some of them and discovered
they were propaganda leaflets, one of which looked like a Christmas card.

The Christmas card leaflet showed a picture of a sad-faced little girl with big, sad eyes and long hair. A tear showed on one of her cheeks, and she held a bit of holly in one hand while a burning candle illuminated her features. A gaunt, bearded paratrooper's face showed ghostlike above and behind the little girl. The caption below the picture read, "Daddy, I'm so afraid." Sketches of Christmas objects surrounded the following propaganda message on the back of the leaflet:

> Hark . . .
> The herald angels sing!
> Well soldier, here you are in "no-mans-land" just before Christmas far away from home and your loved ones. Your sweetheart or wife, your little girl or perhaps your little boy, don't you feel them worrying about you, praying for you? Yes, old boy, praying and hoping you'll come home again soon. Will you come back? Are you sure to see those dear ones again?
> This is Christmas time, Yule time. . . . The Yule log, the mistletoe, the Christmas tree, whatever it is, it's home and all that you think fine to celebrate the day of our Savior. Man, have you thought about it? What if you don't come back? . . . What of those dear ones?
> Well soldier, "PEACE ON EARTH GOOD WILL TOWARDS MEN." For where there's a will there's a way . . . only 300 yards and . . . MERRY CHRISTMAS!*

I dropped that leaflet and picked up another one. There's no record of its exact wording that I'm aware of but, as I recall, the gist of it was that the Germans knew they had lost the war but wanted us to know they were going to fight on until the very end as a matter of honor. The leaflet said the war would last only a couple of months, so they wondered why any of us Americans would want to become one of the war's last casualties. To avoid that fate, all we had to do was

---

*Rapport and Northwood, *Rendezvous with Destiny,* p. 544.

bring this leaflet to the nearest German position and we would be taken prisoner and treated better than the Geneva Convention called for. We would sit out the war comfortably and be assured of being alive when it ended. It concluded with an exhortation not to risk being one of the last men killed at the very end of the war.

The Germans had propaganda for every personality type. What they hadn't counted on was that we were angry and stubborn enough to stay in Bastogne and fight to the last man.

As I bent over to retrieve several more of the propaganda leaflets to take back to my buddies to read, another trooper held up a handful and asked, "What the hell do you think of these?"

"They're junk," I replied. "There's no way I would take one of these leaflets and walk up to the German lines waving it and ask to be taken prisoner. We're winning this war. I'll take my chances."

"Me either," he said. "They'd probably wait until you were right in front of them, then shoot you full of holes with a machine gun. Or if they did take you prisoner, they'd probably treat you worse than a dog."

I looked at the handful of leaflets he held in his hand and noticed he had even more in his side jacket pocket. "What are you going to do with all those leaflets?" I asked.

"There's a shortage of toilet paper around here; I figured these might come in handy."

That sounded pretty logical to me. I gathered up a handful and stuffed them into one of my pockets. The leaflets did come in handy. Most of us used them for toilet paper or for starting small fires to melt snow. Melting snow was a never-ending process. It takes two or more helmets packed with snow to get a canteen cupful of water—and getting water was one of our priorities.

It was late in the afternoon when the last of our C-47s dropped its load and disappeared from sight. They were brave men who dared the heavy antiaircraft fire to bring us supplies and ammunition. The 50th, 52d, and 53d Wings of the IX Troop Carrier Command were the units that supported us in Bastogne. They lost a hundred men wounded, killed, or missing during this operation. Nineteen of their planes were destroyed by flak and 211 were damaged. The 50th and

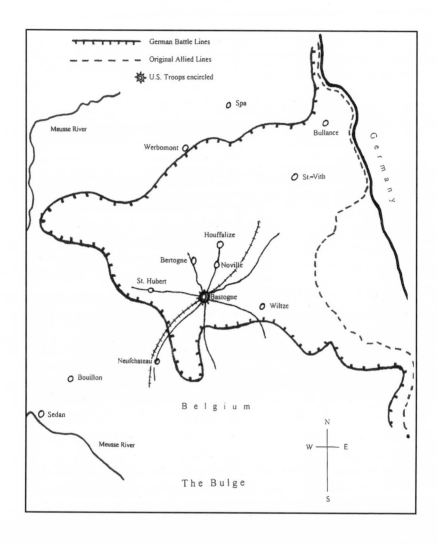

53d Wings were the outfits that carried us into Normandy and Holland. They suffered a lot in support of us but we knew they were returning to safety, a hot shower, hot chow in a mess hall, a cold beer, and a good night's sleep between sheets in a warm barracks. Such luxuries were memories to us, available only in our dreams.

• • •

We squatted around small, smokeless fires scattered around our campsite and stared into the flames, each man deep in his own thoughts. I thought of home. It seemed so far away, so long ago. A picture came to mind: America as a large island on a distant horizon, covered with flowers and trees, bathed in sunlight, a bright rainbow bridging overhead. People could stand upright and walk freely wherever and whenever they wished, and they all had clean, warm beds to sleep in at night.

We existed in an alien world of constant horror, misery, and death. There was no escape. We could be dead the next minute, and we had to live with that threat twenty-four hours a day. The airmen who had just delivered our supplies took grave risks every time they made a run through heavy flak and machine-gun fire, but then they went back to their base in France. They did their share, for which we were grateful, but there was simply no letup for us. Sudden, violent death was our constant companion. If my luck held, I figured I might make it to my twentieth birthday. That would be on 5 April 1945.

Men were taking care of their feet and other matters of personal hygiene as best they could under those conditions when a truck and a jeep pulled in close to our area next to the trees. The truck was loaded with all kinds of ammunition: bandoliers of rifle ammo, belts of machine-gun ammo, mortar shells, bazooka rockets, .45-caliber rounds, and grenades. They had all the ammo we could carry.

We went to the truck in small groups to get our share and then returned to our fires, leaving the machine guns and mortars well tended. The jeep driver walked over with a stack of papers in his hands and began passing them around. I took one and read it. It was a mimeographed message from General McAuliffe. The message read more or less as follows:

24 December 1944
Merry Christmas!
Headquarters, 101st Airborne Division
Office of the Division Commander

What's merry about all this, you ask? We're fighting, it's cold, and we aren't at home. All true. But what has the proud Eagle Division accomplished with its worthy comrades of the 10th Armored Division, the 705th Tank Destroyer Battalion, and all the rest? Just this: We have stopped cold everything that has been thrown at us from the North, East, South, and West. We have identified four German panzer divisions, two German infantry divisions, and one German parachute division. These units, spearheading the last desperate German lunge, were headed straight west for key points when the Eagle Division was hurriedly ordered to stem the advance. How effectively this was done will be written in history. Not just in our Division's glorious history but in world history.

The Germans actually demanded our surrender in the following impudent arrogance:

> December 22, 1944
> To the U.S.A. Commander of the encircled town of Bastogne:
>
> The fortunes of war are changing. This time the U.S.A. forces in and near Bastogne have been encircled by strong German armored units. More German units have crossed the River Ourthe near Ourtheuville, have taken Marche, and reached Saint-Hubert by passing through Hompré–Sibret–Tillet. Libramont is in German hands.
> There is only one possibility to save the encircled U.S.A. troops from total annihilation: that is the honorable surrender of the encircled town. In order to think it over a term of two hours will be granted beginning with the presentation of this note.
> If this proposal should be rejected, one German Artillery Corps and six heavy A.A. Battalions are ready to annihilate the U.S.A. troops in and near Bastogne. The order for firing will be given immediately after this two-hour term.
> All serious civilian losses caused by this artillery fire

would not correspond with the well-known American humanity.

The German Commander

The German Commander received the following reply:

> To the German Commander:
> NUTS!
> The American Commander

Allied troops are counterattacking in force. We continue to hold Bastogne. By holding Bastogne we assure the success of the Allied Armies. We know that our Division Commander, General Taylor, will say, "Well done!"

We are giving our country and our loved ones at home a worthy Christmas present, and we who are privileged to take part in this gallant feat of arms are truly making for ourselves a MERRY Christmas.

C. McAuliffe Commanding[*]

We later learned the details of how the surrender demand was delivered and how General McAuliffe's famous reply came about.

A German major, a first lieutenant who spoke English, and two enlisted men delivered the formal surrender note. The two German enlisted men were left under guard in the cellar of a house that was being used as an outpost by the 327th Glider Infantry Regiment. The officers were then blindfolded and taken to the F Company, 327th CP, where they handed the note over to the company commander, Capt. James F. Adams, who promptly notified regimental headquarters. Major Alvin Jones, the 327th's operations officer, took the call and went forward to get the surrender note and deliver it to General McAuliffe.

After hearing the German demands, General McAuliffe laughed and said, "Aw, nuts." The whole thing seemed pretty funny to him, for we were beating the Germans' asses off and everyone knew it.

---

*See Rapport and Northwood, *Rendezvous with Destiny,* p. 545.

Later, when his staff asked what reply he was going to make, the general said, "I don't think I'll bother."

"That first crack you made would be hard to beat," said Lieutenant Colonel Kinnard, the division G3.

"What was that?" asked the general.

"You said 'Nuts!'" replied Kinnard.

"That sounds okay to me," McAuliffe said, then picked up a pen and wrote his short, defiant answer to the German commander.

Colonel Joseph H. Harper, the 327th's commander, asked for and received permission to deliver the note to the Germans waiting for McAuliffe's reply. He went by jeep to the F Company, 327th CP and ordered the officers brought to him. The enemy lieutenant, acting as interpreter, told Colonel Harper they were authorized to negotiate surrender terms and politely asked for the commanding general's reply.

Harper handed the German major the note.

"But what does that mean?" asked the perplexed German interpreter.

All this time the Germans had been acting aloof and arrogant. Colonel Harper, who was losing his temper, snapped, "If you don't know what nuts means, in plain English it is the same as 'Go to hell!' And I'll tell you something else: if you continue to attack we'll kill every goddamned German that tries to break into this city."

The two German officers stiffened in the face of the colonel's outburst and saluted. The major, after hearing the lieutenant's translation, snapped a sharp, indignant look at Colonel Harper, and asked that they be returned to their lines.

The Germans, who had been driven blindfolded to the CP, were again blindfolded and escorted back to the outpost where the two enlisted men were being held. There their blindfolds were removed and the four of them returned unharmed.

Heavy shelling continued throughout the day on the twenty-sixth. Some of our men were picked for patrol duty and set out, tracking through heavy snow in fields and woods to check on enemy positions and movements. The rest of us sat around cleaning weapons, sharpening knives, and checking the distribution of ammo. Whenever a trooper could find nothing at all to do, he would sharpen his trench knife. There were competitions to see who had the sharpest knife. Paratroopers and Rangers were the only ones issued them. No other American unit I know of received them, so they became quite a status symbol. The way some men continued sharpening their knives it was a wonder they had a blade left at all. Still, it was better than sitting there drumming your fingers, tapping your feet, or getting into a fight with your best buddy.

There were times when having a sharp knife was a lifesaver in combat, but most of the time we just used them for opening K- and C-ration cans, scraping the crud from our beards and jumpsuits, and cutting branches with which to reinforce the walls of our foxholes, make covers for the openings, or to line the bottoms.

The pine boughs we placed in the bottoms of our holes served two purposes. First, they served as mattresses. Second, a good, thick layer assured us of a dry place to sleep. The heat from our bodies in a completely closed hole was enough to cause a thaw, even in sub-zero weather. We learned that the hard way when we first moved into our position outside Bastogne. We would crawl into our covered holes in twos and threes to keep from freezing to death and awaken in the morning with several inches of water accumulated in the bottom and our clothing soaked to the skin. Then, when we went on patrols in the daytime with the temperature below zero, our clothing would freeze stiff with ice. After that we made sure to put a thick bedding of pine boughs in the bottom of our holes.

We stayed close to our fires that afternoon, reading and rereading General McAuliffe's Christmas message.

I had taken one of the yellow cargo 'chutes from the DZ, cut the suspension lines from it, and kept the canopy. Now Liddle and I set the canopy up as a tent near the center of our bivouac area. We were tired of sitting in our foxholes or out in the open, and this was the nearest thing we had to a house. There we were able to sit out of the wind, cook our food, clean our weapons, and dry our boots and socks.

Before dark we carefully put out our fires and headed for our foxholes. Phillips and I had a bottle of cognac and went to visit Benson and Liddle, who had dug their hole into the bank. Our hole was dug in the flat ground and covered with pine boughs and frozen dirt.

Benson produced another bottle from his jump jacket and three of us drank from one and then the other, until they were empty. Liddle sat in the cramped confines with us but didn't drink. He had become accustomed to the fact that we liked our beer and whiskey. He'd gone out with us a couple of times back in garrison but he stuck to apple cider. That was how we celebrated a belated Christmas in Bastogne on 26 December 1944.

Later that night we again heard the familiar drone of a lone enemy bomber and someone laughingly asked, "Is that Hank the Yank or Herman the German?"

Sure enough it was "Herman the German," or "Bedcheck Charlie" as most of us called him. He usually arrived shortly after dark, just when we'd gotten scrunched down in the bottoms of our holes to try and get a little sleep. Soon there was a heavy rush of air as large bombs hurtled toward us. They exploded in and around our positions. One of the Negroes from the 969th Field Artillery Battalion was killed. A bomb splinter decapitated him, and his head, with the helmet still on, was lying about fifty feet from his body.

Several of us walked over to console the rest of the man's gun crew. They had never had one of their own killed before. While the rest were talking, I wandered over and looked first at the man's body, then strode over and looked at his head. No one seemed to want to move the body or fetch the head and put it with the body. I was going to do it, but then I figured that perhaps it might be better if one of his buddies did it.

Elsewhere around the perimeter the action was hot and heavy on 26 December. German infantry backed by tanks attacked the 327th Glider Infantry Regiment's lines west of Bastogne. They drove on through the glidermen's positions, overrunning them. Then with German infantrymen piled high on their backs, eighteen enemy tanks attacked toward the 502d PIR's lines. The paratroopers opened fire on the German infantry with small arms, killing many of them. The German tanks then wheeled left in an attempt to protect the men riding on their back decks. That placed them in a neat line, nose to tail like ducks in a shooting gallery, running broadside in front of several of our tank destroyers hidden in a woods on a ridge backing the 502d's lines. The TDs opened up with their heavy 90mm guns, destroying all of the German tanks. None escaped.

German bodies lay scattered in the blood-spattered snow, and the tanks they'd been riding on sat in fire-blackened circles melted in the snow. Men from A Company, 502d PIR, counted ninety-eight German dead and rounded up eighty-one survivors. The tank crews were incinerated in their vehicles and could not properly be counted. The fight was over by 3 P.M. and the 327th's lines were restored.

At about the same time the 327th was recovering from the penetration in its sector, lead elements of General Patton's 4th Armored Division, which had fought their way to within four miles south of Bastogne, watched as several flights of C-47s flew toward Bastogne to drop supplies. Their commander, Lt. Col. Creighton Abrams, decided after watching the flak concentrations that instead of attacking Sibret, he would lead his tanks directly into Bastogne through Assenois, which lay between heavily armed Sibret and Remoifosse.

Lieutenant Colonel Abrams ordered his 37th Tank Battalion forward. They were followed by Lt. Col. George L. Jacques and his 53d Armored Infantry Battalion. After extremely heavy fighting, these elements of the 4th Armored Division crashed through Assenois with 1st Lt. Charles P. Boggess, the commanding officer of C Company, 37th Tank Battalion, leading.

As darkness fell Lieutenant Boggess and his other two tanks cautiously approached an outpost manned by men from the 326th Airborne Engineer Battalion. They had broken through the German lines and entered our perimeter. It was 4:50 P.M. The siege of Bastogne was officially broken. Not lifted but broken. The enemy counterattacked and, after heavy fighting, closed the road again. We were still completely surrounded.

As the lead tank approached the 326th Engineers outpost, troopers in foxholes alongside the road alerted the rest of their outfit. Many times before the enemy had tried to enter our lines with captured Shermans. It became a cat-and-mouse game of who was friend and who was foe.

Lieutenant Boggess saw the foxholes and called out. The troopers challenged him. The tanker stuck his bandaged head out of the turret and gave the right password. Word of the 4th Armored Division's arrival spread like wildfire in our tight little circle. Victory yells and shouts of joy could be heard from woods, fields, and nearby villages.

The sun came up bright and clear on 27 December. The 4th Armored Division's tanks hammered at the Germans from inside and outside our perimeter in a running tank duel that punched the daylights out of the German armor. The 4th Armored Division won, but not without cost to themselves. Exploding and burning hulks of the once-proud German panzers were left in the wake of the 4th Armored's Shermans and TDs.

The road was open again and more tanks raced into Bastogne followed by supply trucks and infantry that had been waiting in the wings. Replacements would be coming in. We had ammo for all our weapons and food aplenty (both K rations and ten-in-ones). Our wounded were being cared for by the surgeons and doctors airlifted in earlier. The heavy fog, darkness, and shadows had melted away. Bright sunlight shone down and friendly people from outside came to join our fight on the ground and in the air. We had held Bastogne for eight days against overwhelming odds. Now we had it made. We were surrounded by sunshine and friendly people.

# 6 The Long Road Back

Major General Taylor, our commanding general, and his jeep driver rolled into Bastogne with the first units in the 4th Armored's convoy on 27 December to assume command of his division. He had been back in the States when we'd gotten the call to mount up at Camp Mourmelon.

The German encirclement was broken but our fight was not yet finished. We still had to accomplish what we'd been sent to do: drive the Germans back where they'd come from.

Our friends in the dead Negro artilleryman's gun crew got their revenge on the twenty-seventh. A fire mission came down that afternoon and they were able to put some of the ammo delivered to them by air to good use. With plenty of ammo at hand now and more on the way, the gun crews didn't let their barrels cool. They received their orders and then worked in singing, rhythmic precision—loading and firing, loading and firing, and loading and firing again at their distant targets.

Loaders would slam the breeches shut and gunners would hold the lanyards, waiting for the order to fire.

"Battery—fire!" a voice would ring out.

"Now Hitler, count yo' chillun," said the gunner each time he pulled the cord, sending death-laden projectiles toward the enemy.

Those Negro gun crews were efficient. Hordes of Germans were cut down by the devastating power of their guns. Frozen German bodies lay in almost every wood, field, ditch, and house surrounding Bastogne, bearing mute testimony to the 969th's deadly efficiency.

Yes, they got their revenge. They knew it, too. They grinned broadly when we asked them. They knew they had killed and would kill multitudes of Germans in retaliation for their dead comrade. We also got our revenge. The main difference between us was that they could only fantasize about the men they killed. We, on the other hand, killed many Germans at arm's length. We got to see the results of our handiwork up close.

We spent the next four days in static positions. When we weren't out on patrols probing the German lines, we took stock of ourselves and our weapons and kidded around with the men on the 155s. As it happened, I never was picked to go on any patrols at this time— but I didn't cry over it. Any old-timer will tell you: never volunteer for anything.

The twenty-eighth was misty. There was a little action along the front line, nothing big, just some small German probing attacks around the perimeter. Another truck convoy entered Bastogne and with it came the graves registration unit. The men in that outfit had the grim task of gathering up our dead, identifying them, and getting them buried properly. The first thing they did when they entered Bastogne was to round up a group of German prisoners, march them to the cemetery, and put them to work digging graves. The Germans at first thought they were being made to dig their own graves. Some of them went limp with fear and were almost unable to work. It took a while to convince them their labors were for American dead.

The IX Troop Carrier Command towed in gliders loaded with ten tons of medical supplies that same day. It was their last delivery to Bastogne. After that, ground convoys brought in all of our supplies.

The next day, 29 December, was clear and bright with good visibility. Trucks and jeeps pulled into our area again, this time with an issue of overcoats and overshoes, K rations, and some ten-in-one rations. We went over to the trucks in small groups and pawed through the clothing until we found overcoats and overshoes that fit us. I always had a rough time finding boots that fit me. I wore a size six and a half at that time. The drivers told us the troops billeted in Bastogne were served a belated Christmas turkey dinner. Those of us on the line had to settle for good ol' K rats again.

A new type of shell was delivered to the men on the 155s. They were the new POZIT (proximity-fused) shells. Instructors taught the men on the big guns how to use the new shells. They learned fast and were soon ready. Proximity shells could be set to explode at predetermined heights above the ground. Instead of burrowing into the dirt, they acted like giant shotguns, blasting the men below with shell fragments. It was a devastating weapon.

Our patrols discovered the Germans were concentrating troops and armor northwest of Bastogne. It was evident they meant to mount an all-out attack from that direction soon. The question was, when?

On the thirtieth our intelligence section got word from the U.S. First Army, holding the northern shoulder of the Bulge, that the Germans had ceased their attacks and seemed intent on digging in and holding the ground they'd gained. Meanwhile, Field Marshal Gerd von Rundstedt had shifted his finest troops, the 1st SS Panzer "Adolf Hitler" Division and the 12th SS Panzer "Hitler Youth" Division, both part of the Sixth Panzer Army, south, to attack Bastogne. He realized he had to take Bastogne immediately or fail.

General Patton entered our city on the thirtieth, took one look at the situation, and decided to launch an attack immediately, with whatever troops he had on hand. He ordered two new divisions that had never been in combat before, the 87th Infantry and 11th Armored Divisions, to conduct the operation. The 101st Airborne Division was to give support.

Patton's two green divisions moved out and immediately ran head-on into the large German force attacking southward at the same time in an attempt to reencircle Bastogne. Patton's attack smashed the German thrust.

That night Bastogne received its worst bombing of the battle. The following morning, 31 December, the Germans attacked in force in the 502d PIR's sector. The 502d's 1st Battalion launched a counterattack, killing fifty-five Germans and capturing five more; they also recovered one of their own squads that had been overrun and captured earlier.

The 101st now had the 11th Armored Division on its left flank and the 6th Armored Division on its right. Elements of the 10th Armored

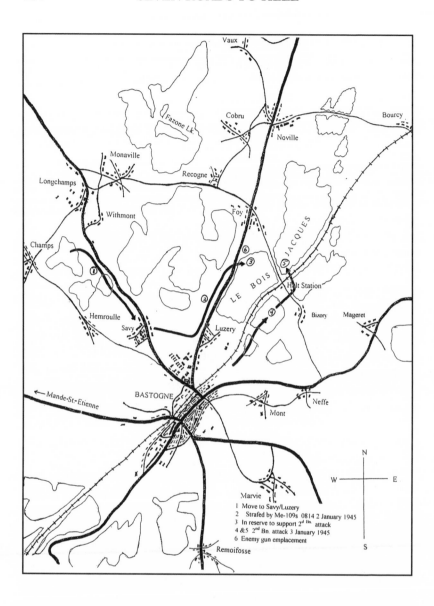

Vaux

Fazone Lk.

Cobru

Bourcy

Monaville

Noville

Recogne

Longchamps

Foy

Withmont

LE BOIS JACQUES

Champs

Halt Station

Hemroulle

Savy

Luzery

Bizory

Mageret

Mande-St-Etienne

BASTOGNE

Neffe

Mont

N

W —— E

Marvie

1  Move to Savy/Luzery
2  Strafed by Me-109s 0814 2 January 1945
3  In reserve to support 2$^{d Bn.}$ attack
4 &5  2$^{nd}$ Bn. attack 3 January 1945
6  Enemy gun emplacement

S

Remoifosse

Division were still with us, and the 4th Armored Division was in reserve. We were ready to attack. It was time for payback. If we could
slice north through the German bulge and link up with our First
Army, which was attacking south to meet us, we could cut the Germans off just as we had been in Bastogne.

The Germans realized this and poured more of their finest troops into the fight against us in the Bastogne area. Their grand plan was a shambles. Now, the best they could hope for was to stall us and hold open a corridor through which they could withdraw their troops and armor back into Germany for a last stand in their homeland.

We got the order to move out early in the morning on 2 January. I rolled up the parachute canopy I had been using as a tent and used it for my seaborne roll. Many nights after that I rolled up in it like a sleeping bag and stayed quite comfortable in the subzero weather.

It was still dark when we said our farewells to the men on the 155s. They had been busy the last couple of days and nights firing their big guns in response to requests radioed in from all around our perimeter. German bodies littered fields, ditches, and villages around Bastogne in grisly tribute to those Negro gunners.

We quickly finished packing up our meager belongings in small seaborne rolls and slung them over our shoulders after distributing the food and heavy weapons amongst us. Less than twenty minutes after getting the word, we moved out in long, strung-out columns of twos, maintaining a distance of no less than twenty feet between men and staggering the lines so as not to have several men lined up behind one another. Men bunched up close together or lined up made inviting targets for artillery and machine guns. A single shell or a short burst could take out several men at once.

We struck out through the woods, over fields, and onto the snow-covered blacktop roads. We were heading back into the Bois Jacques. Our 2d Battalion was to attack northward through the woods and clear out all of the Germans from east of the railroad to the Mageret–Bizory area and along the Foy–Bizory road.

My battalion was to move into the Bois Jacques, slip through the woods to the north end, dig in there, and remain ready to support the 2d Battalion. We were ordered to make every effort to conceal our presence. Our being in that spot would ensure that the enemy did not swing around the west flank and come back in behind the 2d Battalion.

We moved cross-country from Savy back to Luzery. There we turned north toward Foy on the Bastogne–Noville road. The 2d Battalion's attack was to run parallel and east of the railroad tracks, clearing the woods of enemy east and north of the Foy–Bizory road. In addition to protecting the 2d Battalion's left flank, we were to take prisoner or kill any Germans attempting to withdraw through our sector. If that had happened, our presence would have been discovered anyway.

A fresh snow blanketed the countryside, hanging in great clumps from the trees and bushes. It reminded me of a beautiful postcard setting but the beauty was lost in the grim business at hand.

As we walked north on the road, tiny specks in the sky to our left caught our attention. They grew rapidly in size, streaking west to east toward us. O'Neal had attended aircraft identification school. Sergeant Vetland, leading up front, turned in a half-joking manner and asked, "Hey, O'Neal, whose are they, theirs or ours?"

"If they're Mustangs they're ours," replied O'Neal. He squinted his eyes and stared for an instant, then blurted out, "They're not Mustangs!"

Sergeant Vetland had sort of grinned when he'd asked the question because we all believed the remnants of the Luftwaffe wouldn't dare to show themselves on such a clear, bright morning. It had taken months of hard fighting and heavy losses, but our airmen now ruled the air. They had all but swept the Nazis from the skies of Europe.

O'Neal's warning came too late; they were on us. We were as much of a surprise to the German pilots as they were to us. They dipped their wings and fired their machine guns and sent five-hundred-pound bombs screaming toward us. Men were diving for the ditches amid flying dirt, snow, tree limbs, bullets, and exploding bombs.

Bullets and bomb fragments whistled through the air. We had been walking with our weapons at sling arms, and as I dove for the ditch on my right, a bullet from one of the planes caught the barrel of my rifle. The impact caused me to somersault through the air and land on my back. The bullet narrowly missed my head and chopped off the barrel and gas cylinder just in front of the sling swivel. The weapon was useless.

We had one six-by-six truck with us at the front of the column. The trooper manning the vehicle's .50-caliber machine gun managed to get off a burst but evidently didn't do any damage to the aircraft. The

Me-109s flashed by too fast. One of the bombs landed close to the truck and the explosion knocked our battalion commander, Major Harwick, over the ditch and into the field. His map case went sailing through the trees, scattering his maps and papers to the wind.

One of our men, Joe Wycstand, jumped from atop the truck and broke his leg. Wycstand's leg, the major's map case, and my rifle were the only casualties. No one else was hit. It was lucky for us the Me-109s had crossed us at right angles. If they had made their run down the length of our column the casualty toll would have been great.

Troopers ran through the fields and climbed trees to retrieve the major's maps and papers. When they finished gathering them up, we reformed on the road and continued our march toward the woods where we waged the grim, hand-to-hand struggle on 21 December. All around us were mounds in the snow—the bodies of the enemy we had slain. Occasionally we could see a snow-capped knee, or an arm, leg, or shoulder of a dead German protruding from the white blanket of snow. I wondered if Speer, Alvarado, Bielski, Horn, and the others were still lying out there. We brought the bodies of our officers back to be buried in the cemetery in Bastogne; the bodies of enlisted men lay where they fell, to be recovered later when it was convenient. I like to think that all of the men were later located and given a decent burial.

It was deathly quiet, the calm before the storm. We were now well armed, well fed, and properly clothed. There weren't as many of us as there had been when we'd left Camp Mourmelon on 18 December. What we lacked in numbers, we more than made up for with anger. We wanted revenge and the new men who had survived their baptism by fire were now veterans. Our mission here was to move in close to the enemy's west flank and lie quietly in wait. These were the same Germans who had been encamped on the east side of the railroad line on 21 December, just outside our perimeter, while we attacked and killed their comrades in the woods. The 3d Battalion, 506th PIR, and the 3d Battalion, 501st PIR, had pushed them back a ways but they'd stayed right here during the siege, attacking us from time to time at their convenience and when they had the advantage. Now that we were on the comeback trail these Germans had to go.

We moved quietly into position and began digging in, taking advantage of some old foxholes that remained in the area. Across a field to our front we could see German 88mm gun crews working around their emplacements. They were so close that I could tell which ones had gloves and which ones didn't. It would have been no problem killing them with rifle fire, but our orders were to do nothing but watch.

A little later, about midmorning, the 2d Battalion went into action. We lay in our holes listening to the growing din of battle. A few shots, then the rattle of machine-gun fire, then more rifle fire, mortar rounds striking, grenades going off. The firing grew until it became a terrible, ragged din that was deafening in the cold winter air.

Gradually the firing moved away toward Foy. Troopers charged forward laying waste around them. The surviving Germans fell back grudgingly, many more dying in the process. Americans also died. It was not a free ride. But, as was the case in our woods fight, the 2d Battalion's casualties were light in comparison to the Germans'. What made the fighting so difficult for them was the fact that the snow was waist deep, even in the woods. Snow hung heavy on the pine boughs, bending them down until they touched the snow on the ground. Men carrying weapons, ammo, supplies, packs, and seaborne rolls had to mush through this deep snow and at the same time force their bent bodies under and through the low-hanging, snow-covered tree limbs.

Visibility was such that men could not keep contact with each other on the move. They strayed, became separated, and some even lost their sense of direction. Troopers plowing through the snow-covered trees often found themselves face-to-face with heavily armed, well dug-in Germans. Much of the fighting was hand to hand, and both men and snow quickly became blood spattered in that desperate fight.

We wanted to join the fight to help our comrades but all we could do was sit there and watch. If we had been allowed to join in with our 2d Battalion, I don't think there's any doubt we could have killed every goddamned German in Belgium. At least that's how we felt at the time.

The enemy eighty-eights in front of us went into action, firing their big guns in support of their troops who were being pounded by our 2d Battalion. Brininstool had been ordered to another platoon for a while and I was in charge of the 2d Squad at this time. I told Benson to call regimental headquarters on the walkie-talkie and ask for artillery fire on the eighty-eights. For once the damned thing was in working order. Benson made contact and relayed my request. It was denied.

I grabbed the handset from Benson. "They're killing our men," I argued. "We need that fire mission."

The answer was still no. We were not to let the enemy know in any way we were in this position.

"How in the hell would artillery shells landing on an enemy position let the enemy know there were Americans hidden nearby?" I shouted into the mouthpiece. "There are shells falling all over goddamned Belgium."

The answer was still no.

I wished I could have taken that indifferent son-of-a-bitch and dragged his butt up to where the 2d Battalion was being hammered by the eighty-eights and seen how long it would have taken to get artillery support.

A German medic left the eighty-eight emplacements and strolled toward us. He didn't seem to have anything particular in mind; he was just strolling. Gradually he worked his way toward us until he was not more than fifty feet in front of our position. He was wearing a white, poncho-type smock emblazoned with a Crusades-style red cross that ran from neck to waist and from shoulder to shoulder in front and in back.

"Let me kill him," Benson said.

"No," I replied. "That would give us away to his buddies. We can't even take him prisoner. Don't do anything unless he sees us. If he does, we'll have to kill him with a knife as quick as possible and get his body out of sight without the other Krauts seeing us."

The enemy medic came closer still. We lay there not daring to breathe. We knew we would be difficult to see with the bright sunlight reflecting off the snow and us in foxholes in the deep shadows of the pines.

Benson and a couple of others drew their knives. Benson was up front, ready to be first out of the pines, his knife at the ready, his right foot dug in for leverage. Two other troopers leaned forward behind him in the same manner, just in case Benson missed or stumbled.

During the time it would take to run the German down, kill him, and drag his body back into the cover of the woods, our men would be out in the open. We could only hope that none of the enemy gunners looked in our direction.

Long moments dragged by. We didn't move. Our eyes followed the German medic's every step and facial expression. If his eyes flickered or a facial twitch suggested the slightest hint that he had seen us, he would have to die. He turned to his left, following the edge of the woods. Gradually he sauntered back in the direction of the guns, all the while toying with some small object, flipping it back and forth from hand to hand. Evidently he hadn't seen us, for none of his gun crew looked our way when he returned to them.

The fighting to the east slowed. It had been going on most of the day. Finally, late in the afternoon, German resistance collapsed. The 2d Battalion had cleared the woods and the Foy–Bizory–Mageret road of enemy. Darkness came on and we settled in our holes to wait for dawn. No one slept.

January third was another clear day. Our fighter-bombers showed up bright and early. They wasted no time setting about the task of pounding every German they saw. Three P-47s circled our positions, strafing hell out of everything. I took my binoculars, searched the area where the eighty-eights had been, and could find no sign of them. They had moved out quietly during the night.

Our attention was drawn back to the P-47s. The lead plane's engine cowling and tail were painted bright red. His buddies followed close behind him. Their maneuvers and hedge-hopping tactics were enough to make us stand up in our holes just to watch them.

Enemy armored vehicles scuttled from one patch of woods to another, frantically trying to hide, but the hawklike planes followed their every move by the tracks they left in the deep snow.

The red-trimmed fighter led his group in low, tight circles, skimmed the treetops, dipped low across a field, and dropped a bomb that headed straight toward the side of a huge Tiger. At the last instant the pilot pulled sharply up and to his left and the second plane, which had been following close behind, fired several machine-gun bursts into the tank's side. At that same moment the bomb exploded, showering the tank and the ground around it with a spray of flaming jellied gasoline. Black smoke boiled up and the tank and crew were incinerated on the spot. We cheered. We learned later that the bomb contained napalm. Napalm was another new weapon and this was the first we had ever seen or heard of it.

The second plane took up the lead position. They made another tight circle overhead, and the plane that had been third in their formation slid into the second slot. They followed the same procedure as before and soon there were two tanks burning in the field. The snow melted around the flaming hulks, making them look like blackened bull's-eyes.

The flames soon reached the ammo stored inside the tanks and they exploded, one after the other, with such force that they bounced a couple of feet into the air, seeming to expand and contract before they slammed back to the ground. We could feel the concussion from where we stood outside our holes, flushed with excitement.

The three P-47s made one more circuit of the area, leaving a third tank burning in the field.

"Give 'em hell! Give 'em hell! Kill every goddamned one of them!" we were yelling, cheering our flyboys on.

A lone tank fled across the field, a cloud of snow flowering behind it in twin rooster tails as it raced eastward.

The P-47s circled 180 degrees to the left, climbing a little before dipping their noses down and coming in low, head-on at the racing tank, firing bursts of machine-gun fire at it. The path of their flight now was from east to west, straight at us. Bullets lanced through the trees all around us. Others ricocheted off the frozen ground, whining overhead and showering us with torn limbs, bark, pine needles, and dirt. We hit our holes and hugged the bottoms.

"Watch where the hell you're shooting," someone yelled, then laughed.

One of our men was wounded, not seriously but badly enough that he would have to be evacuated to the aid station. I acquired his rifle to replace the one that had been shot from my shoulder when the Me-109s strafed us. I had been armed with nothing but my forty-five since that time.

The red-trimmed fighter-bombers left the scene but others soon took their place. All that day our Air Corps kept up their deadly pace around Bastogne's fourteen-mile perimeter. The enemy was being torn to ribbons. Enemy vehicles scuttled like gigantic, frightened iron mice, racing from woodlot to woodlot. It did them little good. Our flyboys simply followed their tracks to wherever they tried to hide. When their tracks entered a woodlot but did not leave, our pilots knew they had to be in there and strafed and bombed the trees mercilessly. More often than not they were rewarded with an explosion and an oily black cloud of smoke rising skyward. Scores of German tanks, trucks, self-propelled guns, half-tracks, staff cars, and antiaircraft guns fell prey to our marauding airmen.

We didn't want to leave the shelter of our woods for fear our fighter pilots would mistake us for the enemy and strafe us. We had been mistakenly strafed and shelled before in Normandy and Holland, and the 327th Glider Infantry Regiment had been strafed and bombed by our own planes almost every day since the fog had lifted.

Later that evening, after our airmen were clear of the area, we felt free to stand up and walk wherever we pleased. Sergeant Vetland gathered our platoon into a fairly close group in the woods but left us spread far enough apart that we were still in battle form. Other platoons were gathered in much the same manner. Then we were briefed on the next day's plan. There was to be another attack, and this time our tanks and armored infantry would be involved. We were to make a big push deep into enemy territory, into some of their most heavily fortified positions.

At noon on 3 January the 2d and 3d Battalions of the 501st PIR began attacking through the Bois Jacques while our 2d Battalion was attacking on their left (western) flank. The 6th Armored Division's 50th Armored Infantry Battalion was to attack along with them on their right flank. The 501st immediately ran into stubborn resistance. The troopers pushed forward, fighting the enemy and the deep snow with every step. The 50th Armored Infantry met enemy forces backed by armor headed south along the railroad line. The armored infantrymen fell back on the double through the woods to their holes. This left a wide-open gap on the 501st's right flank through which the Germans poured infantry and armor into the regiment's rear. The advancing troopers swung to meet the enemy moving up behind them and cut down their lead elements with small-arms fire.

The Germans swung farther south with men, tanks, and half-tracks and opened up on the paratroopers with heavy concentrations of small-arms, mortar, and tank fire. Their mortar fire was especially deadly, exploding in the treetops and driving shrapnel downward on men who had no time to dig into the frozen ground. This reportedly was the heaviest concentration of mortar fire on one spot anywhere in World War II. It is estimated that one round per second fell on the 501st for well over an hour.

Responding to radio calls for help, Colonel Ewell sent tanks from the 10th Armored Division's Team O'Hara to aid his embattled battalions. These tanks knocked out one Mark IV and broke up the German armored attack. The 501st troopers took care of the rest of the German infantry, tanks, and half-tracks with small arms and bazookas.

The 501st now had its neck stuck out with heavy German counterattacks against their forward positions and no one covering their exposed right flank. Just before dark they received orders to pull back to their original positions. As we had learned at Noville, it is one hell of a job trying to execute an orderly withdrawal in the face of an attacking enemy. The 501st accomplished the task by pulling one company at a time out of the line and moving it back through the company behind it. The two assault battalions leapfrogged backward in this manner until they were back in their original positions at 3 A.M. on the fourth.

At the same time the 506th and 501st Regiments were attacking on the third, more than thirty German tanks slammed into the 502d PIR's lines. Some of the paratroopers were gassed in their holes by the exhaust from German tanks squatting over their holes and gunning their engines. Others were crushed and ground into the frozen dirt under the tanks' tracks.

The 502d took a hell of a beating in this attack but the troopers held their lines. They picked off supporting German infantry with their rifles and machine guns and knocked out several tanks with bazookas. General Taylor ordered every available artillery piece to fire into the attacking Germans, and several TDs from the 10th Armored Division's Team Cherry rushed to help the troopers out. That was enough to break up the enemy attack.

A critique conducted by unit commanders on the fourth determined that if the 50th Armored Infantry had continued its attack alongside the 501st, the objectives would have been reached and the attack would have been successful.

For the moment we had little to do but stay in our foxholes, every man alert for a possible enemy counterattack—something for which the Germans were notorious.

Speer and I used to dig in together but now that he was gone I preferred to be alone. I tried to stay awake but fatigue made me doze and raw nerves and chills kept waking me up. I don't know how long I napped or how many times I awakened in this fitful manner. All I know is that it was cold and uncomfortable and it looked to be another long, miserable night. Later, just after dark, word was passed down that we were moving out. Squad leaders were to form up their men in the woods.

Once we were sorted out, the 2d Platoon moved out with 1st Squad in the lead, my squad next in line, and 3d Squad bringing up the rear.

As we were moving along I bumped into someone. I don't know how I knew it in the dark, but somehow I just knew he was a stranger.

"Who the hell are you?" I asked.

"Carl Angelly."

"What outfit are you with?"

"A Company, 506th," came the reply.

"What platoon?"

I had my rifle pointed at his belly, and now I released the safety.

"Second Platoon, Second Squad."

"That's *my* platoon and *my* squad and *I* don't know you," I said. Instinctively I went into a half-crouch.

In the split second I spent deciding whether to pull the trigger or take him prisoner he blurted out, "I'm a new replacement. They brought several of us up here in the dark."

"That's right," a familiar voice said, "they came in while you were sleeping. We're getting replacements now."

Guides had brought several replacements into our positions and I had slept right through it. What if they had been Germans? I could

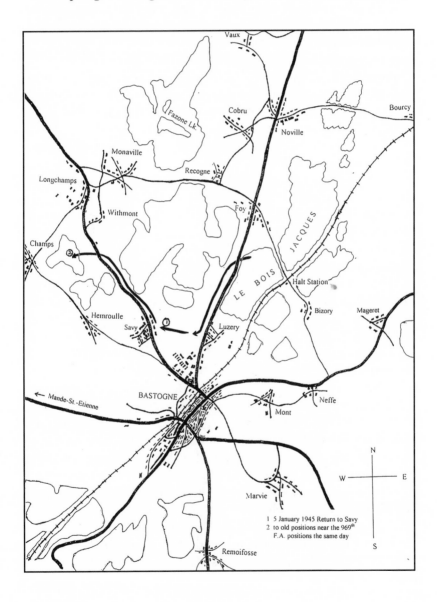

1  5 January 1945 Return to Savy
2  to old positions near the 969th
   F.A. positions the same day

have had my throat cut or been shot through the top of my head. I was worn out and tired and needed sleep, but I didn't need it that bad. That is one good reason to keep two men in each foxhole.

"Come on, follow me," I said. I started off behind the other men and felt the mound of dirt outside a foxhole with my foot. Without thinking about it I felt my way around it as I walked, without breaking stride. Many small actions such as that become second nature with men who have to live without lights for months in combat.

Carl Angelly followed me. However, when he came to the hole he walked straight ahead and fell into it. I waited for him to climb out but he groveled around in the bottom cursing and swearing half aloud.

"Come on! What's taking you so long?" I asked.

"I had a mortar shell in my shirt and I lost it down here somewhere. I've got to find it."

"To hell with that," I snapped. "We've got plenty of 'em now. Come on before we're left behind in the dark."

He climbed out of the hole, fell in close behind me, and we hurried through the pitch-black night, brushing between the trees and through the branches as fast as we could to catch up with the rest of the men moving out ahead.

"I've been carrying that shell for a week now," he muttered. "Damn! I sure hate to lose it now. I was hoping to use it against the Krauts."

Carl complained about losing the 60mm shell all the way through the woods until we reached the Houffalize–Bastogne road. There we formed up in our usual spread-out battle formation. Our company was about the size of a normal platoon now, even counting the new men. It made us feel good. The war was finally turning our way.

We moved out in the dark of night back toward Savy. There we did little more than send patrols into the German lines. We had to keep in touch with them, to know what they were doing and what they might be up to. During this time Carl Angelly and I became friends; it was good to have a foxhole buddy again. Carl was about my height and build. He was a few years older than my nineteen years, and he had dark, curly hair, brown eyes, and had been in the army since before Pearl Harbor. He'd spent nearly all of his time in Alaska, and he told me that he was going nuts up there.

Carl was home on leave in Illinois when the call went out for volunteers for the paratroops. After his furlough ended he signed up so he wouldn't have to go back to Alaska. They shipped him to Fort Benning, Georgia, for his three jumps in one day and then shipped him and a boatload of other replacements to Europe. Now, here he was a member of the 101st "Screaming Eagle" Airborne Division in the battle for Bastogne. Considering his chances of survival, going back to Alaska would have been the better choice.

Carl and I dug our hole the same way everyone else did. Ordinarily each man would dig a circular hole big enough to get into and deep enough to cover him to about his armpits when standing in it. This afforded maximum protection under the circumstances. But we were in a static defensive position now, so we dug them large enough for two men to lie side by side. We lined the bottoms with pine boughs and used more pine boughs and the excavated dirt to cover the top, leaving a hole large enough for two men to stand upright in and fire at the same time. We covered that opening with a door made of woven pine branches to help retain our body heat during the night. The dirt on top would then freeze, offering us bunker-like protection. This type of foxhole afforded protection from both shell fragments and bullets. It almost took a direct hit to get at the men inside.

The ground was frozen to nearly two feet deep and it was like chipping concrete when dug in. Once we got past this frozen layer, the rest of the dirt was normal and could be dug out easily with an entrenching tool. Some men, after chipping through the frozen crust, would tunnel back underneath, forming a cavelike hole in which to take shelter when the shelling became heavy.

On 5 January our battlion was alerted that we would be taking over the 501st PIR's positions in the woods between Savy and Recogne. Brininstool had returned to take command of 2d Squad and I was once again a rifleman. We moved out just after nightfall. It was dark as hell and sweat soaked our bodies as we trudged through the deep snow. After several hours we made it to our assigned positions in the woods and settled into the holes that were already there.

Shortly after 9 P.M. we again received orders to move out, this time to take over positions held by the 3d Battalion, 502d PIR, between

Monaville and Recogne. We hadn't been in our new positions long enough to cool off yet. Knowing there would be no rest for us that night, we all exercised our GI rights. We bitched.

When we moved out it was as dark as the inside of a whale. I still don't know how whoever was in the lead was able to tell where we were going. The snow on the roads was a hard-packed glaze of ice. To add to this misery, a light, freezing rain had been drizzling all day and into the night, forming a sheet of wet, slippery ice over the entire area. It made walking very difficult, more like sliding around on a frozen pond.

The route to the 502d's positions was up a gradually sloping, rutted back road that looped through the woods. Men kept slipping and sliding around. It was difficult to balance machine guns, mortars, and ammo on our shoulders and keep our footing at the same time. Slips and hard falls were common, especially for those carrying the machine guns and mortars. Time and again men fell hard with their heavy tools of war. One man carrying a machine gun fell especially hard, badly injuring his shoulder. He had no choice but to stay with us and suffer his pain in silence. We divided his personal equipment amongst ourselves to carry for him. At long last the torturous journey ended. We had finally made it to a ridge overlooking the enemy. I glanced at my watch. It was twenty-five minutes after midnight on the morning of 6 January.

The 502d had just pulled out, so we settled into their holes. Our command was jockeying us all around, getting us lined up in proper company, battalion, and regimental order for a big push deep into German territory.

Two days later, Carl and I were sent to man an outpost on the extreme edge of our ridge overlooking enemy-held ground. It was bitter cold. Our machine gun kept freezing up and every once in a while we had to sit beside it on the ground, grab hold of the barrel, and kick the bolt open. We had to keep the gun in operating order in case it was suddenly needed. The telephone in the hole also froze up from moisture that formed on the diaphragm when a person talked into it, rendering it useless.

We could hear German armor and other vehicles moving about in the woods below the ridge and to our right. Carl used the phone, holding it cupped tight in his hands and breathing into it to defrost

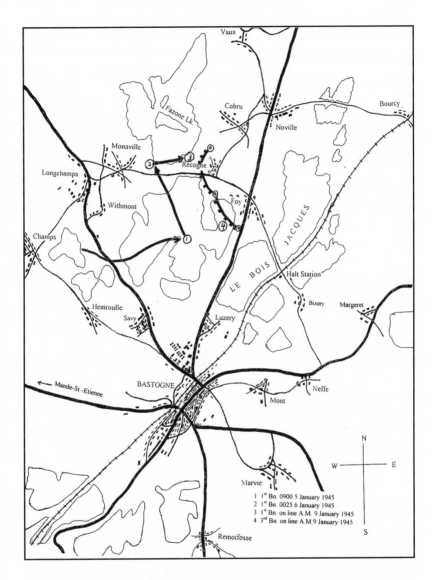

the mechanism with his warm breath. We contacted our company CP, which was located in an old farmhouse about a mile to our left rear. Carl reported the tank movement and was told that we were to keep our eyes and ears open and not to do anything unless the unfriendly people started moving toward our lines. Hell, we already knew that.

Just before daybreak we heard what we thought was an enemy tank moving in the woods just to our right rear. Again Carl freed the phone and contacted the company CP. The thought of enemy armor on top of the ridge with us and to our right flank made somebody there edgy. Calls and messages went out and were relayed up and down the line. Finally word came back to us that we'd heard some of our own tanks moving into our positions and not to worry about them. They were friendly people. We appreciated having tanks to back us up, but they should have at least alerted us in advance.

After daybreak Carl and I were relieved from the outpost and walked half-frozen back to where the platoon had a small, smoke-less fire going behind a screen of pine boughs. We squatted down, opened a box of K rations each, and boiled some coffee.

Chmiliewski had built an elaborate latrine over a straddle trench, complete with a one-hole bench. It was formed with limbs wired together with communication wire and walled over and around with the full-needled pine boughs that were so plentiful in this area. Chmiliewski was proud of his construction and would gaze fondly at it for long minutes at a time, then walk around to view it from a different angle. At times he would ask troopers who had just used it if it was comfortable, how it looked to them, and how did they like having a seat for a change instead of squatting over a straddle trench in the deep snow.

Carl went to use Chmiliewski's wonderful work of art and found he had to wait in line. I stayed in our foxhole reading the remnants of an old comic book someone had found in the snow. We must have all been preoccupied, because no one noticed that a thin trail of smoke was drifting up from our untended fire.

Suddenly three artillery shells screamed in. One hit the fire smack in the middle, scattering burning embers all over the area. The other two hit farther toward the edge of the woods and the ridge. Men hit the ground and then leaped for their holes. While I was reading I was in another world and didn't fully realize what had happened until I heard the sound of incoming artillery. I looked up just in time to see the shells explode. I saw the one that hit the fire, which was about fifty feet away, send up an orange ball of fire and black smoke when it exploded. Shell fragments churned through the air, cutting limbs and thudding into tree trunks. I felt shrapnel slash by on either side of me. It was too late but I ducked down into the hole anyway, figuring there might be more on the way. But no more shells followed, and life quickly returned to usual in our camp. No one was hit.

We spent the next couple of days running patrols into enemy territory to determine their positions, strength, and how they were equipped. Our patrols reached clear to Fazone Lake, west of Cobru and Noville, and ran into very little real opposition.

The 506th PIR held a line from a point between Monaville and Fazone Lake, running east from that point to just south of Recogne and Foy, then following the perimeter around northeast of the Halt railroad station and on east of Bizory. The 502d PIR held the perimeter from our left flank near Monaville down through Longchamps and southeast of Champs. The 501st PIR held positions from our right flank east of Bizory southward through Neffe and Marvie. The 327th Glider Infantry held nearly the entire southern half of the perimeter. Our command had rightly guessed that the ground south of Bastogne was not suitable for tanks and would not face the heavy tank and infantry attacks that we encountered in the northern half of the perimeter. The entire perimeter measured a little over fourteen miles in circumference and was only about three and a half miles in diameter. Most of the artillery used in the battle had a range of at least eight miles.

On 9 January the 2d and 3d Battalions of the 506th attacked through our positions and drove forward between Fazone Lake and Cobru. We remained in reserve and followed the 2d Battalion. However, as it turned out, we ran into our own private little war.

We moved down a small, narrow road that wandered through thick, tall pines that stood next to a wide, snow-covered field. Enemy artillery rounds exploded intermittently among us over a wide area. Either the Germans were low on ammo and were trying to cover our entire front or they didn't know for sure our exact location and were searching for us.

Our own artillery screamed overhead, then pounded the enemy positions to our front for several minutes. Jerry Janes had recently discarded his .50-caliber machine gun. He had run out of ammo for it with little prospects of getting more and it was really too heavy and cumbersome for dismounted infantry combat anyway. He had simply thrown it away in a roadside ditch on one of our marches.

We waited there, spread out in the woods and snow, for our artillery's second barrage to lift so we could move in on the enemy. Some of our men discovered an American half-track parked behind some low, thick trees. It sported four .50-caliber machine guns mounted in a turret-like affair in the bed of the half-track. The gunner sat on a small seat while operating the unit. With a fire rate of 450 rounds per minute, per gun, the four of them together made a hell of an antiaircraft weapon, which is what it was designed for. Used against ground troops, it was devastating.

Someone had evidently abandoned it there when they withdrew from that sector in the early part of the fight. We all thought it had been rendered useless, but Janes fooled around with it and got it started. He then backed it down the road under cover of our artillery to our jump-off point along the edge of the woods next to the wide-open field.

When the shelling stopped, we rose up and started forward. Janes swung the quad fifties to the left, pressed the electric trigger, and traversed the turret to the right. He burned up every round those guns carried. The results of our artillery and the quad fifties were terrible. The woods on the other side of the field were turned to a ragged shambles. Shredded tree trunks stood with broken limbs hanging on all sides, as though they were some terrible things drooped in mourning. Other trees were reduced to splintered stumps. Debris, pine needles, and shattered boughs littered the snow.

We were up, yelling and screaming, running low and zigzagging through deep snow toward the enemy positions in the deep, dark woods on the other side of the field. Overcoat tails flapped around our legs as we plowed our way through the snow. Sweat soaked our bodies, running freely down our faces as we raced forward. It seemed impossible, but there were still survivors in that torn section of woods.

They opened up on us with rifle and machine-gun fire. Bullets cracked as they passed close by, at times nipping clothing, at times thudding into a trooper's body. I always got a sick feeling in the pit of my stomach when I started a running attack into frontal fire, knowing that at any moment an enemy bullet might tear through my body, face, or limbs, severing arteries and ripping away organs. But once we started, there was no turning back. There was only one option as far as I was concerned: run forward and kill. Once the enemy was dead there was time to rest my mind and body, secure in the knowledge that I had survived once more.

Phillips was to my right, Benson to my left, and Carl Angelly followed close to my left rear. Then we were in the woods. We were in the enemy's front yard. German dead lay all around the area, some in the open, others half in and half out of holes. In the swirl of fighting I lost contact with some of my buddies but I kept a watchful eye on Carl. Liddle was close by, and I glanced at Phillips.

A grenade-like explosion went off just to my left front. A trooper with his helmet smashed flat sideways on his head went stumbling through the trees. It was Benson; something had exploded close to him, smashing his helmet flat on his head. He had lost his senses and dropped his carbine. He ran into trees and stumbled over fallen branches. Phillips and Liddle finally tackled him, throwing him to the ground. Carl and I ran over to them. Normally we would not stop for a wounded comrade, but Benson was running amok and was at risk of running into the enemy and getting himself killed. We tried to straighten him out on the snow. He thrashed wildly. Carl and I pried his helmet off with great difficulty while Liddle and Phillips held him down. There were traces of white froth around the corners of his mouth. The way he acted, his skull must have been cracked. We found communication wire, which was always lying around a battle scene, and tied him securely. We left him trussed on the ground for our medics, who were always right there with us. The medics would see that he was properly cared for. We had to continue the attack.

This all took place during heavy firing, the main body of our men still moving forward into the enemy positions.

Phillips, Liddle, Carl, and I went running forward into the melee. As we spread out, an enemy bullet smashed against my rifle. It spun out of my hands and clattered against a tree. The gas cylinder and front stock were destroyed; it was useless. The rifle left my hands so violently that I thought every bone in my fingers had been broken. I stood for a moment shaking my hands. It felt as though all my fingers had been hit with a hammer at the same time. Again I was forced to use my forty-five as I pressed forward in the attack with the others.

The relatively few Germans still alive were deep in their covered holes and bunkers. We used a lot of grenades. I fired round after round at the fleeing enemy with my pistol but doubt if I even came close to any of them. A forty-five is mostly good only for morale and as a last-ditch defense weapon. It is accurate up to about ten feet or so. After that it's mostly just a noisemaker. I did grenade two bunkers that had Germans inside. We yelled for them to come out but they refused, yelling back at us in German. I don't recall any prisoners being taken during or after this fight.

Again the attack ended and we found ourselves standing in the center of broken and torn equipment and bodies. And again I was among the survivors. The dead had been pulled from their holes and dumped unceremoniously on the ground. They lay scattered about in uncomfortable-looking positions. The carnage and the smells are impossible to describe with mere words on paper.

I stood with the others in the middle of this battlefield. I suddenly felt exhausted. My arms hung loosely at my sides, my hand still clutching my pistol. How was it possible for one to survive the battles and frontal assaults I had survived? The battles through Normandy, Holland, the bayonet attacks, the hand-to-hand fighting, the door-to-door fighting, the street fighting? Yet each time I found myself standing there tired and feeling all alone with just a few others in the center of so much death and destruction. Why was I always among the few survivors? I don't know.

The familiar smells came to me: the odor of burnt gunpowder, the taste and smell of iron and steel, the smell of human blood and torn flesh, and the sweet, sickly smell of death.

I gazed absently at the broken, green-uniformed bodies. Slowly realization returned when several Sherman tanks and TDs moved into our positions. A truck loaded with K rations followed them in. Men in the back passed out boxes of K rats and five-gallon cans of water from which we were able to fill our canteens. Someone had finally thought to bring water. Then we dug in, covered our holes with pine boughs and dirt, settled down to eat, and waited for a German counterattack.

The expected attack never came but heavy shelling did. We spent that afternoon and night under constant artillery pounding, the shells exploding in the treetops and driving shrapnel down on us. The tankers thought the Germans were getting a fix on their radios and moved nearly a mile out of the woods in an attempt to draw the artillery away from us, but it didn't help. We stayed put, moving out of our holes only when we absolutely had to.

Colonel Ewell, the 501st PIR commander, was badly wounded in the foot and was never able to go into combat again. Many troopers were wounded and several were killed in this attack. Carl and I found the remains of an American trooper who had been killed in the attack. During the dark of night the tanks had run in single file over his body. Just by chance, while going to the truck to refill our canteens with water I noticed a dog tag protruding from the remains, which had been ground into the snow and dirt. I probed with my trench knife and fished out a crumpled pack of Lucky Strike cigarettes from among the flesh and splintered bone. I hung one of the dog tags on a limb near the body in hopes the medics would find it. I don't know if they ever did.

I acquired another rifle from a trooper who had been killed. This attack had been a diversionary one, to make the enemy think we were driving straight through their center and cause them to shift their armor and troops away from the place our command really wanted to attack. Our purpose had been fulfilled, the enemy shifted in response to our feint, our main attack was accomplished, and we were ordered back to our original positions.

Benson had been picked up by our medics and transported back to Bastogne, where our wounded were sent for safekeeping and made as comfortable as possible until they could be evacuated to hospitals in France. The doctors and surgeons who had been airlifted to Bastogne were swamped with work. Time and effort could not be wasted on those they believed would not make it. Many men needed amputations or other major surgery. They had to wait their turn or die. It was the best our overworked medical folks could do under the circumstances.

Benson regained consciousness while there, knew we were still in combat, and simply got up and left, walking out of Bastogne to be with us. He caught up with us two days later, walking into our position without helmet or weapon. It didn't take long to scrounge up a carbine and helmet for him, and he took back his walkie-talkie radio. Benson refused to listen to our pleas for him to return to the aid station for examination and possible treatment. Neither he nor any of the rest of us really knew just how badly he might have been injured. He was adamant about not letting us go into combat without him. He remembered nothing of being wounded in the head, and since he had left Bastogne without being treated, there would be no record of him ever having been wounded.

Our command started moving our units around again, feeding the stronger ones into the line and pulling weaker ones back into reserve. We were getting ready for another attack.

On 10 January our division was ordered to seize Noville. The 4th Armored Division was to move through the 6th Armored Division's area in the east and strike north, taking Bourcy. The 501st PIR was given the mission of leading off the 101st Airborne Division's attack through the same area it had attacked through on the third and then had been forced to withdraw when the 50th Armored Infantry Battalion failed to keep up with them. The 320th Infantry Regiment, which had been attached to the 6th Armored Division, was assigned to cover the 501st's right flank. The 501st struck out over the same ground it had fought over before—north through the Bois Jacques, west of the railroad track running toward Bourcy. The regiment battled its way through heavy fire coming from well-prepared German positions to their front and from the direction of the railroad tracks on their right flank. Still, they were able to seize their objective.

The 320th Infantry Regiment failed to keep up with the 501st's advance, again leaving the 501st's right flank exposed along the railroad line. Our high command was determined to use that railroad as a boundary, with one outfit on one side and another outfit on the other side. Even General Patton was opposed to requests from our leaders that the paratroopers of the 501st be allowed to cover both sides of this railroad. Patton maintained that it was the only clearly visible line through the Bois Jacques, and he ordered that it continue to serve as a boundary between his armored forces to the east of it and the 101st Airborne on the west side.

Lieutenant Colonel Robert A. Ballard, who had succeeded Colonel Ewell as commander of the 501st, sent out a patrol to find out why the 320th Infantry wasn't attacking. The regimental commander told the officer in charge of the patrol that he had orders to hold in place. He refused to move.

The whole attack was in jeopardy again and fizzled out. The 501st was again ordered to withdraw to its original positions, leaving only outposts at the farthest point of their advance.

Then came an order that no one understood. The 506th and 502d PIRs were also ordered back to their original jump-off lines, giving up all the ground we had fought so hard and died for. As soon as we pulled out, the Germans returned.

Whoever issued those orders probably had good reasons, but to the fighting men who suffered, bled, and died in response to them, it seemed incomprehensible. It sounded just like one of Monty's "tidy up the lines" orders while we were under his command in Holland. Perhaps if we could have put some of those rear-echelon commanders out front as scouts for our next attack they might have thought twice before making us give back ground we'd paid such a high price to gain.

That night, Lieutenant Colonels Kinnard and Ballard and Brigadier General Higgins met to formulate a plan that would resolve the problems along the 501st's right flank.

We sat in the frozen woods for the next two days, sending out patrols and licking our wounds while the Germans improved the strong defensive positions they had established in the woods we had been ordered to vacate. They knew we would be attacking there again and they intended to be ready and waiting.

The thermometer was hovering around zero on the morning of 12 January when the 101st Airborne Division was again ordered to attack. One of the objectives was to recapture Foy. Our artillery laid down a heavy barrage and we moved out as soon as it lifted. The 502d and 506th PIRs led off the attack heading north, followed by the 501st PIR on the right flank. The 501st had shifted over the railroad line in the Bois Jacques against Patton's orders in order to cover ground on both sides of it and thus protect their own right flank. This time their attack was successful even though the 320th Infantry Regiment again remained in place.

The 327th Glider Infantry Regiment's attack got off to a slow start. Its A and C Companies had lost so many men that they had to be combined into one company, dubbed "Ace" Company, under the command of Capt. Walter Miller. Ace Company fought hard, advancing quickly and taking a patch of woods in the Bois Jacques before being cut off by Germans who had circled in behind them. Ace Company had to dig in there.

After dark, Captain Miller ordered his company to withdraw to where the rest of the battalion had halted for the night. In an unhurried, orderly fashion Captain Miller sent a few men at a time back about a hundred yards and had them set up a hasty defensive position. The men who had been left up front to cover their withdrawal then slipped quietly back through the new line and set up another hasty defensive position. Ace Company spent the entire night leapfrogging rearward in this manner until Captain Miller had extracted all of his men from their exposed position forward of the rest of the battalion's line of advance. Captain Miller was a good company commander, cool under fire, able to make sound decisions under stress, and in full command at all times.

Our E and I Companies led the 506th PIR's attack on the morning of 13 January, heading straight up the road toward Foy. After about an hour of heavy fighting they had taken that town, capturing twenty-three Germans in the process. Heavy fighting continued until late that afternoon, when E and I Companies established a line just north of Foy.

That night the enemy shelled the town and surrounding area with everything they had, but the troopers held their ground.

The 1st Battalion, 506th PIR, moved along a road that ran through a thick wood. When we entered a large expanse of open fields surrounded by tall, dark forests, we were called to a halt right out in the open.

"Set up your machine guns here," someone shouted.

One was placed near the road and another was set up near the center of the field on our right flank. Those were not the most effective places to site the machine guns.

In spots the snow reached to the bottom of my shirt pockets, approximately forty-four inches deep. In other spots it was boot-top high. We did not have time to begin digging into the frozen ground before artillery fire suddenly screamed in on us.

A lot of us dove into the ditches alongside the road; others were caught in the center of the flat, open fields and could do nothing but lie there in the snow amidst the explosions as shrapnel slashed through them. A large piece of paper about the size of a newspaper was blowing across the field at this time. Dobrich caught it and pulled it over his prone body and head like a bedsheet and peeked out from under it like a turtle.

"Hey Dobrich," Trotter yelled. "That paper ain't going to stop no shrapnel."

"I know that, but it sure as hell makes me feel better," Dobrich shouted back from under the paper.

We had to laugh in spite of the pounding we were taking. Men were being killed and wounded but still we laughed.

Paul Devitte was the gunner on the machine gun set up in the field when a shell struck just in front of his weapon and exploded. The blast sent shell fragments slicing forward in a fan shape over the frozen ground. The assistant gunner and two others were killed outright. Devitte had his left arm torn off above the elbow, his right leg above the knee, and his left leg below the knee.

Several men carried Devitte to the road after the shelling stopped. Dave Clark, our medic, gave him a shot of morphine, stuck the needle through his lapel, and bent the needle to affix it there.

Devitte never lost consciousness. A jeep arrived and he was strapped onto a litter that was then fastened on the jeep. Just as the jeep started out, Devitte asked the driver to wait.

"Would someone get my watch for me?" he called out. "It was on my left arm; it was a graduation gift from my parents. They would feel bad if I lost it."

We went to the spot where he had been wounded and kicked around in the deep snow but could not find his arm. The jeep pulled out while Dave Clark tended to the wounds of other troopers. Clark was crawling from a foxhole occupied by a man who had found and crawled into it during the shelling and who only thought he was wounded when Clark's hand brushed against something in the deep snow. He pulled it up and discovered it was Devitte's arm.

Clark took the watch from it and, after returning to civilian life after the war, had it repaired and sent it on to Devitte, who somehow survived his ordeal.

When the shelling ceased we were again ordered into formation. New men took over as machine gunner and ammo carriers to replace those we had just lost. Weapons and ammo were taken from the dead and wounded. We formed up again to continue our attack, which had carried us across deep, snow-covered fields and through woods to a point between Fazone Lake and Cobru. We were able to consolidate our positions on the objective by midafternoon that same day.

Our 2d Battalion, which had been attacking since noon, entered and secured Cobru just as night fell. We spent the night on the newly established lines, once again using foxholes that had been dug by the enemy.

The next morning, 14 January, the Germans counterattacked at 9:30 in the vicinity of Foy with infantry and eight tanks. The 2d Battalion moved in behind H and I Companies for support, but I Company (with only twenty-one men left out of their original two hundred plus) was forced to withdraw into the village. The troopers continued taking a heavy beating there but held their ground throughout that night.

We jumped off early that same morning in a continuation of our attack. We had the enemy on the run and we weren't going to let him sit in one place long enough to reorganize or dig in.

The enemy pulled out before we got moving, leaving a few young zealots to hamper our progress with small arms. As a result, we didn't meet with too much opposition but we were harassed constantly by long-range artillery while we were in the open. We drove across open farmland, crossed barbed-wire fences, and searched houses and barns we encountered along the way. The enemy had cleared most of their dead from the preceding battles. The only dead Germans we saw were the ones we killed during our advance.

We headed for the high ground north of Noville while the 2d Battalion left the 3d Battalion companies in Foy to deal with the enemy there and struck out straight up the road from Cobru toward the center of Noville itself.

Captain Kessler led A Company to the base of the hills northwest of Noville and began following a narrow footpath that angled northeast across the face of the hills leading to the crest. All the while German guns concentrated their fire on the town. Random shells exploded indiscriminately in the village, gutting the hulks of what had once been homes and shops.

Strung out in a long, scattered single file, our battalion made its way up the hills, moving at a steady pace. Captain Kessler knelt with his subordinate leaders and studied his maps for a moment, waving the rest of the company on.

"Keep moving," he said in his gravelly voice. "Keep moving."

He was about twenty feet ahead of me to the left of the narrow path we were following. Suddenly he grunted and rolled over on his left side just as Don Brininstool started past him. One of the men who had been kneeling there with him looked at his eyes. He was dead. A tiny piece of shrapnel from one of the enemy shells exploding in the valley below had struck him in the right side of his head, just under the rim of his helmet. It was almost identical to the wound that killed Ollie Barrington in Noville when we pulled out on 20 December. It was a one-in-a-million chance that a piece of shrapnel would travel that distance but it had, and a good company commander was dead as a result of it.

The enemy was still in command of the far eastern rim of the horseshoe-shaped hills ringing Noville. That was the end that Phillips and I were scouting toward when our battalion first entered Noville on 19 December.

We slowed our forward movement and waited for the 2d Battalion to advance through the center of Noville and come abreast of us. We stopped, looking down into town as troopers made their way from house to house. Germans were escaping from the far end of town, heading for the safety of the eastern hills.

What a view from up here, I thought. It's no wonder the enemy could blast us so well when we were in town. If it hadn't been for the fog, they could have seen our every move.

This was unique, sitting high on the side of an amphitheater watching a real-life drama unfolding on the stage below. The troopers were making their way through the rubbled streets toward the Germans, who in turn grudgingly gave way, moving from ruin to ruin as they retreated toward the open ground behind them.

"How the hell do you like it?" someone yelled. "Now *we're* up here and *you're* down there."

Suddenly it became clear to us just where we were. We had come back. We had driven the Germans back to the point of our first meeting north of Noville. It was a bittersweet homecoming. This was the true turning point for us. From here on we'd be on their turf, beating them back to where they had come from. Outnumbered and outgunned we had beaten Hitler's finest. Now we would be taking the fight to them on their own ground.

Scattered stands of pines grew in between cultivated woodlots on the hills. Our men stood for long moments in complete silence among the trees and woods, staring at the valley below with its tiny, ruined village. I knew what they were thinking; they were reliving every moment of the fiery hell of those first two days.

Enemy soldiers raced toward the hills in front of the advancing 2d Battalion. Even though we could see the enemy clearly, they were too far away for our small-arms fire to be accurate. Besides, the 2d Battalion would be between them and us in just a few minutes. They would take care of them. We didn't want to run the risk of endangering our own troops.

Once they were into the fields on the far end of Noville the 2d Battalion troopers could see the enemy running up the hillside in front of them. The troopers opened up and mowed them down. Few of the retreating Germans made it to the top of the hills.

A Sherman tank was sitting halfway down the hill we were standing on, its back toward us. Seeing it there, we remembered that no tanks had been with us in this attack. The tank's engine was idling, for we could see the exhaust vapors. A small fire burned next to its port side and there was mess gear close by.

"I'll bet that's one of them Shermans the Krauts captured and were using," Dobrich said. "Let's go down and check."

Several 88mm shells exploded around us as we started down the hill but no one was hurt. Dobrich started forward again and a lone shell hit the frozen ground just in front of him. It didn't explode. Instead the round bounced in a spinning arc over his shoulder. The way it was spinning end over end it actually rolled over his left shoulder. The timing was perfect. Any deviation in either the shell's spinning or Dobrich's position and it would have passed clear through his body.

The projectile hit the ground in back of us, high on the hillside, spun around like a bottle in a spin the bottle game, then tobogganed back down the slope point first between us. It melted a path in the snow, leaving a trail of steam behind it. Troopers were scattering in all directions. We didn't know if it had a time fuse or if it was a dud. One thing was sure, none of us wanted to be around it if it did go off. The damned thing skidded down the hill past the idling Sherman and disappeared between the remains of two small, ruined buildings on the edge of town. It never did explode.

"Did you see that? That damned shell rolled right over my shoulder and didn't even touch me!" Dobrich exclaimed. He was grinning from ear to ear.

Dobrich and several other troopers made it to the tank and looked inside.

"No one's here," they yelled back up to us. The mess equipment near the fire was German and the tank had black swastikas painted on its sides. Gerald Day, who was a heavy equipment operator back in civilian life, volunteered to operate the tank. Day, Dobrich, and a couple of others climbed in and drove it back up the hill to where we stood waiting. We scraped the black swastikas off. The Sherman was a new one. It had the new 76mm cannon with a muzzle brake on the end. It also had the new, large bogie wheels instead of the little ones of the older model. Every round was in place. Its main gun had never been fired.

"Why in hell would the crew run off and leave something like this for those goddamned Krauts?" Day asked.

"You can never tell," Dobrich replied. "Maybe they were killed when the Germans broke through and never even had a chance to get to the tank to use it."

"That's right," Day mused. "They might've been killed in their beds that first morning and never even knew there was a breakthrough."

Night wasn't far off, so we moved past the hillcrest into a wooded area and dug in. The night was cold, as always, but there wasn't much action. We positioned our machine guns, posted guards, and then we settled into our holes for the night.

The following morning, 15 January, we formed up in battle formations and moved out. All of the divisions at Bastogne—airborne, infantry, and armored—moved out in the attack together. Our advance carried us over farmlands, through woods, and past a scattering of farmhouses, always bearing northeast toward Wilcourt and Rachamps. We occasionally passed a dead German. Usually the bodies were alone and in the most unlikely places. Several bodies in a farm field had been looted.

A Company didn't engage in any firefights worth speaking of during this advance. We just kept moving forward with the others. We moved most of the day without stopping to eat or rest. The only time we halted was when the units ahead of us stopped for whatever reason. When we finally did get a lengthy break, I found a German foxhole near a barn and crawled into it. A German body lay about fifteen feet away. I could see he had no rifle and that he had already been looted, so I didn't bother going over to where he lay. I didn't usually loot the dead but I did take a cheap pocket watch from a German prisoner in Holland once.

A short time later we moved out again. We made our way to open farmland interspersed with trees and pine woods. We were assigned areas and dug in on line. Our lines ran along the back side of a sloping bank that leveled off into a wide stretch of open field in front of a dark wood occupied by the enemy. Tanks from the 11th Armored Division moved slowly between our foxholes and gradually worked their way to the crest of the ridge. They lined up with fifty yards or so between them, their bows pointing toward the enemy but positioned so that none of them showed above the bank.

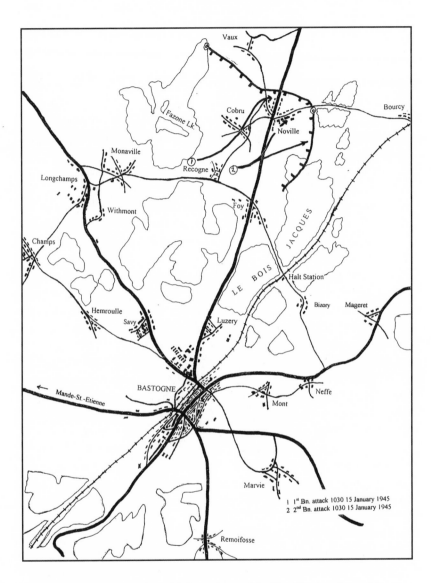

We pulled the tank we'd found outside Noville in alongside our positions and started preparing K rations. Then we heard some of the tank commanders talking, wondering what the enemy's strength was or if they had any tanks or *Panzerfausts*.

"Hell, let's find out for them," Day said.

A bunch of us piled into our tank, gunned the engine, plowed out over the crest of the ridge, and headed toward the woods. As we approached the tree line, three high-explosive shells slammed into the side of our Sherman. Day spun the tank first to the left, then to the right, but we kept bearing toward the woods.

Our radio crackled and a voice screamed, "Who the hell are you?"

"This is Kidnap's own personal armor. We're reconnoitering for you," Day replied.

"Get your asses back here before we blow you all over that field. We've got four guns trained on you right now."

Day spun us in a quick 180-degree turn to the left and headed back for our lines. More shells struck us and mortar shells burst in the field around us. We made our way back over the ridge and came to a halt back at our position.

A mob of tank commanders and several of our own officers met us as we crawled from our vehicle. All of them were hollering and yelling at the same time. Standing on top of the turret with all those officers and noncoms down below barking up at us, I knew just what a treed coon must feel like. When it was all over we had been well chewed.

"These crazy paratroopers," one of the tank officers muttered as he walked away. "They come out of nowhere with a tank and play games with it in enemy territory. They're crazy. I can't understand it. They're crazy."

The next morning, 16 January, before we resumed our attack, a delegation from the 11th Armored unit approached our new company commander with a demand that our tank be turned over to them.

"Go to hell," he said. "These men captured that tank from the enemy, and by God they're going to keep it."

"But we're armored and you're paratroopers; we should have the tank," one of the tank officers said.

"If you wanted that tank so bad, you shouldn't have let the Krauts have it in the first place," our commander replied. "We've got it now and we're going to keep it."

"We'll settle it later," the ranking tanker said. He motioned to the others and they left. The attack was about to start.

About an hour after daybreak on the sixteenth we again moved out as part of a massive attack that carried us northeast of Noville in a wide swinging movement. We ran into little opposition, saw few enemy. It was as if they all had picked up their toys and had gone home.

The enemy kept pulling out ahead of us, leaving only small delaying forces to hamper our advance. They no longer wanted to stay and fight. Evidence of their food situation showed in the trees. They would fashion a small hoop out of twigs, place a cord noose in the center of it, and hang bright red berries underneath the hoop. They hung these small traps within arm's reach from the limbs of almost every tree in the woods. Birds would land on the hoops, swing underneath to get at the berries, and hang themselves in the process. The Germans would then gather the small birds to eat and reset the nooses. Our K rations had begun to seem pretty raunchy, but after seeing this, they suddenly looked like a banquet.

Those Germans were good woodsmen. They were survivors. Many of them had been in combat since 1939. The last couple of years they had been taking a pounding both in the air and on the ground, living off the land, and fighting an organized war. Even here in the Battle of the Bulge they had kept an escape corridor back into Germany open and were conducting an orderly withdrawal. We would have to face them again, sometime, somewhere.

At one point during the attack we crossed an open field to clear a woods of possible enemy. The snow was chest deep and plowing through it with a .30-caliber machine gun on my shoulder brought out a sweat that soaked my body. We had started out in lines of skirmishers but now as I looked around I saw that most of the troopers had fallen in behind a few who were breaking trail through the heavy snow. Then I looked behind me and discovered my whole squad following me in single file.

"That takes the cake," I said. "Not only am I carrying the machine gun but I have to break the trail for the rest of you. Somebody take this gun for a while and someone else take the lead."

Phillips volunteered to take point and went ahead breaking trail, followed by Angelly and the rest of the squad. I fell in at the tail end of the squad. Steam rose from my sweat-soaked body and I knew I would just about freeze to death if we were ordered to halt now. The man I'd given the machine gun to was directly in front of me. We headed into a dark wood in single file and the thought occurred to me that this was a bad way to approach the enemy.

This wood had less snow on the floor because much of it had been caught up overhead in the thick upper limbs. It was dark there amidst the trees, with plenty of places to hide an entire battalion of enemy troops. There were signs that the Germans had been there in force but had recently moved out. We pressed on quickly, trying to keep abreast of the other attacking units.

Fortunately the retreating Germans had left no one behind to delay us.

Our attack finally came to a halt. Exhausted by the long march, we began digging in at nightfall. This time our lines were established well north of Noville. The terrain was rolling, raggedly spaced with open fields, and dotted with large and small stands of trees and cultivated woodlots.

As we started digging in, the enemy began throwing a wide spread of time-fused artillery fire at us. Their time fuses weren't as accurate as ours. The result was that some shells exploded too high, others burrowed into the frozen ground before exploding, and still others exploded on contact. Shells were hitting all around, over, and among us. The Germans were no longer firing in heavy salvos as they had when we'd first arrived in Noville. Instead the shells steadily rained down all along the front.

In order to survive we had to get below ground level in a hurry. The frozen dirt was like concrete. Dropping to my knees and adjusting the blade of my shovel to a ninety-degree angle, I used it as a pick. Frozen dirt flaked off with each stroke like chips of flint. It would take too long to get through the frost line like this. An exploding shell or shell fragment would get me first. Then I looked to one side and noticed a spot where a shell had struck close by just a couple of minutes before. It had burrowed into the ground before exploding. The earth had absorbed much of the blast and fragments or I might not have lived to tell you about it; it was that close. The ground there had ruptured into fairly large loose chunks. I went over to it and began prying the pieces of hard dirt out, stacking them around the small crater. The dirt beneath was soft and easy to dig in. I was well on my way to having a foxhole.

Phillips yelled at me for digging where a shell had landed, saying another shell could hit in the same spot. He refused to dig where artillery had struck and kept chipping away at the frozen ground, sweat running freely on his face. He had begun digging very fast when we halted; his pace slowed as he tired. When more shells landed close by, his pace picked up again. We all did the same thing, but I was now down about waist deep and Phillips still had not penetrated the frost line. There was no way, I thought, that the enemy gunners could hit the same spot on purpose—not even by chance.

A few of the other men had found shell craters as I had and were by now equally well along. Others like Phillips were still chipping at the frozen ground, fully exposed.

Later that evening the shelling stopped, the medics took care of the wounded, and we rested in our holes, waiting for daybreak.

Word filtered down that elements of the 11th Armored Division from Patton's Third Army had made contact with First Army's 2d Armored Division in Houffalize to the north of us. The Germans west of that point were cut off. Now it was their turn to be surrounded.

Several days earlier, the Germans, upon realizing their battle in the Ardennes was lost, positioned their best combat troops and armor to form a corridor leading from the Bulge back into their homeland. These troops were able to beat back any and all attacks made by the Allies to cut through this corridor. It remained open long enough for the Germans to extract the bulk of their troops and equipment back into the "Fatherland" for a last stand. They left behind a motley crew to fight a rear-guard action, holding the pursuing Allies at bay while the cream was extracted. Those battle-weary troops were all that was left of the powerful force that had launched the German offensive on 16 December 1944 and plowed deep into Belgium.

Later that night, as we rested in our holes, Lieutenant Dunham, our present platoon leader, who came to us as a green replacement with Carl Angelly's group, called me to him and told me to pick a patrol and make contact with the 3d Battalion, which was supposed to be on our left flank.

Lieutenant Dunham and I did not get along too well. We had had a difference come up between us that pitted my combat experience against his rank. His authority prevailed but later I was proved right. He now had me memorize our positions on a map and instructed me to point them out to the 3d Battalion commander as soon as I could find him.

I chose Carl Angelly and Liddle to accompany me and we struck out into the night. Liddle and I each carried M1 rifles, while Carl carried an M3 .45-caliber "grease gun" he had picked up somewhere. I didn't like the damned things. They were a cheap, toylike piece of junk made of pressed metal. They were good to a range of only about fifty feet or so.

We made our way across the open field, then along low spots growing thick with brush and small trees. After moving about half a mile or so and finding no one at all, we realized we were out there alone.

"Maybe they're more to our right," Carl suggested. "They might have gone a little farther than we did in the attack."

"Maybe," I said. " I don't think they would be behind us."

We struck out to our right, heading due east. The ground sloped gradually downward. As we made our way through a wood we came to a small river. We could look through holes dotted here and there in the ice and see swift water running underneath. We crossed it very carefully, made our way up the far bank, then moved along a narrow dirt road that cut back to our right. It was dark but up ahead we could make out a small clearing faintly outlined against the slightly lighter skyline. With me in the lead we made our way quietly toward the clearing. We were able to peer into the clearing from the road and see what appeared to be trucks and tanks parked there, with men sleeping on the ground inside a semicircle formed by the vehicles.

"Well, it looks like we finally found them," I whispered to the others.

We approached the vehicles slowly and quietly, expecting to hear the challenge with each step. We didn't want to startle a spooky GI on guard and have a misunderstanding. With each step I mentally rehearsed the challenge and password. Forgetting or even stammering could get you killed. Slowly, quietly we entered the camp. Nobody challenged us; the guard must have been asleep. Then we were in the center of camp. As I reached down to wake one of the sleeping men so I could ask him where the battalion commander was, I felt a hand touch my arm.

"Those don't look like our tanks," I heard Carl whisper.

Liddle and I looked around. I squatted down so I could get a better look at the outline of the tanks' silhouettes against the lighter sky. I could feel the hair crawling up the back of my neck. The tanks were Panthers, with one large Tiger in the group. We were in the center of an enemy camp.

"What do you want to do now, Donny boy?" Liddle whispered, flashing a large, toothsome grin.

*Why does he do that? Why the hell does he have to grin like that now?* I thought. *Does he think it's funny?*

"Let's get the hell out of here," I whispered back. "There's too many of them. Remember this spot so you can locate it on a map if only one of us gets back. Then they can direct artillery fire on it."

The three of us tiptoed over and around sleeping Germans. One of the bodies I stepped over was that of a huge man wrapped in a blanket, snoring lightly. I stepped ever so lightly, thinking, God, what if he wakes up now, with me straddling him?

We cut back on a right angle and headed toward the river. Every second we expected to be challenged by an enemy, but we made it without incident. We didn't see anyone on guard at all.

We came across our own footprints and backtracked on them to our own camp, seeing no one on the way. Just as we came to our holes we saw three men walking toward us, just to the left of our machine gun. They came abreast of us, looked as though they were going to speak, changed their minds, and continued on.

"Who are you?" Liddle asked.

They looked our way. The one out front looked like Jack Bram. He mumbled something to the other two and they kept on walking. I squatted down to get a better look at them against the skyline. They were wearing long-billed forage caps! They were Germans!

In one fluid movement I pulled my rifle from my shoulder, aimed it at the leader, and flipped the safety off. We had been walking at sling arms when we entered our own area.

"Hands up! They're Krauts!" I yelled, loud enough to wake up every trooper in the company. The leader spun toward me, threw up his hands, and yelled *"Kamerad!"* His companions followed suit.

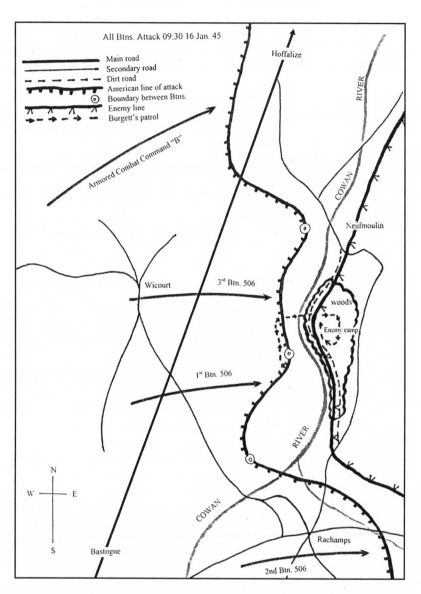

All Btns. Attack 09:30 16 Jan. 45

Main road
Secondary road
Dirt road
American line of attack
Boundary between Btns.
Enemy line
Burgett's patrol

Hoffalize

RIVER

COWAN

Neufmoulin

Armored Combat Command "B"

Wicourt

3rd Btn. 506

woods

Enemy camp

1st Btn. 506

RIVER

N

W — E

S

COWAN

Rachamps

Bastogne

2nd Btn. 506

Everyone in camp came to life. Brininstool, who was on guard,
picked up the machine gun, tripod and all, pivoted, and set the gun
down aiming straight at the enemy patrol. The Germans, their
hands above their heads, turned toward us and all yelled together,
"*Kamerad! Kamerad! Kamerad!*"

"I thought it was Jack Bram and his squad," said Brininstool. "It looked just like him walking along our front. That's why I let them go by."

The enemy soldier did have an amazing resemblance to Jack Bram—his build and even his walk. In fact, Carl, Liddle, and I thought it was Jack with two new replacements, until Liddle questioned them and they didn't answer.

Each one carried a Schmeisser burp gun, a knapsack filled with extra magazines, a pistol, and a bag filled with grenades. I took a Beretta pistol from the leader but gave it away. I was already carrying my forty-five and a Walther P-38 besides my rifle.

Carl looked through their knapsacks and found a piece of sausage and some black bread in one of them. After biting into the sausage he threw it down and said, "A dog wouldn't eat that stuff." Then he ground it under his heel into the snow.

The German noncom begged Carl not to destroy the food because it was all they had. Now they would go hungry. The other two stood staring at the ground. I noticed that they had tears in their eyes.

*"Nicht essen,"* one of them murmured half under his breath. *"Nicht essen."*

Lieutenant Dunham had his radioman call regimental headquarters. Within minutes a jeep from our intelligence section came to pick up the prisoners for questioning. I believe they were the last enemy soldiers to be taken prisoner by the 506th PIR in the battle for Bastogne.

"Did you make contact with the 3d Battalion?" asked Lieutenant Dunham.

"No, sir," I replied.

"Then go back and find them," he snapped.

"Yes, sir," I said. Then I told him about the enemy camp we had passed through and suggested he call regimental headquarters and request artillery on it.

Lieutenant Dunham eyed me for a few moments, then said, "I think those Germans just wanted to surrender. Don't you?"

"Yes, sir. I could tell by the large white flag they were carrying," I replied. With that I turned and left.

The three of us retraced our steps back toward the river. This time we found the 3d Battalion where it was supposed to be and had been all the time. The men, mostly new replacements, were well camouflaged, and in the dark of night it was impossible for us to see clearly ahead unless an object or person happened to be outlined just right against the snow or skyline. Therefore we had walked straight through their lines without seeing them. They, of course, saw us, knew who we were, and didn't bother challenging us.

After reporting to the battalion commander and telling him where we were located, I told him of our capturing the three Germans behind our lines. He sent out word to challenge everyone, whether the men on guard knew who it was or not. On our way back we were challenged four times in the same area where we had seen no one the first time through.

The night was fairly quiet now when we returned to our position. I reported to Lieutenant Dunham's hole but he was asleep, so I didn't awaken him.

Liddle, Angelly, and I slept well the rest of the night. The morning of the seventeenth I reported to Lieutenant Dunham and asked if he had notified headquarters of the German encampment and called for artillery.

He said he hadn't bothered.

A short time later a truck pulled into our area carrying the barracks bags we had left behind in Mourmelon-le-Grand. Some Services of Supply (SOS) troops riding in back dumped our bags on the ground and we sorted through them to find our own. The bags had been slit down the side with knives and looted again. Our personal things—cameras, pistols, money, souvenirs, boots, clothing, et cetera—were gone. Pictures of families and loved ones were torn from their frames and the frames stolen. The only thing most of us had left was our dirty laundry. Some bags were completely empty. Some of our troopers didn't even get an empty bag.

The war seemed to have moved on without us. We could hardly hear the artillery now. We knew we must be far behind the lines, for the SOS men had driven their trucks right into our camp.

We built large warming fires and men began pulling off their boots—some of them for the first time in weeks—to see what was left of their feet. I sat on the cold ground and unlaced my boots. They finally came off with some difficulty. My socks, what was left of them, looked like crud-encrusted spats. My feet had turned white as snow.

Large cracks laced around them and my toes were swollen. Many of the men's feet were in bad shape. Later, some men's toes and feet had to be amputated.

We were sitting around the fires massaging our feet and scraping the crud from our beards and clothes when the 17th Airborne Division came marching up the road. The troopers were fresh-faced, well fed, clean shaven, and had neat, clean jumpsuits.

Then we looked at ourselves. We were dirty, ragged, gaunt, and hollow-eyed. But we were full of spirit, and we started yelling friendly jibes at the newcomers, as is the custom with men from brother outfits.

Some of the 17th Airborne troopers called back that they were there to relieve us and that we'd better not get too damned smart or they wouldn't do it. We couldn't believe it. We were going to be relieved!

Late that afternoon our officers formed us up on the road to move out. The order of march was 3d Battalion, 1st Battalion, and 2d Battalion. The last of the 2d Battalion was relieved after 9 P.M. that night.

We were supposed to ride back to France in the same style trucks that had transported us to the front. However, for some reason the motor transport division would not come up where we were. We wound up having to walk eight miles back to a monastery where they were waiting for us.

The night was cold and dark as we shouldered our weapons and ammo and moved down the road. It had all begun for us at 2:30 in the morning on 17 December 1944. The end came at 9:10 P.M. on 17 January 1945.

We could no longer hear the big guns booming in the distance. Our mission had been accomplished. We had defeated and beaten the Germans back to where they had come from. It had taken a lot more than the couple of days we had boasted it would—and a hell of a lot more fighting, suffering, and lives.

We marched in strung-out battle formation carrying our light and heavy weapons and newly acquired seaborne rolls. The Sherman we'd found on the ridge overlooking Noville chugged along behind us like a huge, faithful mascot bearing men on her back deck who were suffering too much pain to walk. They had done all the walking that was necessary. They walked, ran, and carried their loads without complaint. Only now, when the battle was all over, did they give in and allow themselves the luxury of a short ride on the deck of a tank.

I looked at my buddies as we strode along. Their torn and ragged jumpsuits were caked with grease. Sunken eyes stared out of gaunt, bearded, grubby faces. These men were soldiers? These men were paratroopers? These men were the elite "devils in baggy pants" that the Germans feared so much? Damn right they were.

I realized I looked no different than they. Strange, I hadn't really thought about it. I looked just as bad as the rest of them and I was damned proud of it.

It hurt to march tall and proud on cracked and swollen feet, but we did. We marched proud with frozen feet on frozen roads.

Again I heard the familiar sounds of creaking of weapons straps and shoulder harnesses, the shuffling of jump boots on the snow-covered roads, and the muted clanks of machine guns and mortar tubes as they were shifted from shoulder to shoulder. No one talked. Each of us was deep in his own thoughts. I thought of the truck ride from Camp Mourmelon, of the many men who were no longer with us—of Speer, Alvarado, Bielski, Horn, Chief, Barrington, and all the others. I had survived another operation. My seniority as an old man was growing. I was nineteen years old and now I had three major campaigns under my belt. I had been wounded three times and was one of the oldest of the old men. I had survived another one.

Our columns were shorter now, even with our replacements. It was only about eight miles back to the monastery where the trucks were waiting for us. We had walked into Bastogne on a dark, cold, quiet night, and now we were walking out. Eight miles through another dark, cold, quiet night. The distance didn't seem so far now. Hell, we had it made!

# Epilogue

The 101st Airborne Division paratroopers who participated in the Normandy, Holland, and Ardennes campaigns were the hard core of the U.S. Army's elite airborne forces. These veterans of a new and controversial organization had to prove themselves from the very beginning, from first training to combat, by physically and problematically outdoing any other unit or force that had preceded them. They were volunteers, from the very first to the present day. No one has ever been drafted into the paratroops. Still, despite the high demands and standards required of paratroopers, there are more than enough volunteers. The airborne force can be choosy about whom it accepts.

Paratroopers are a special breed. They have an inborn instinct to work as a well-organized group or to go it alone when necessary. In 1942 the men of the 506th PIR—with full equipment and carrying all their crew-served and personal weapons—marched 115 miles in three days in a freezing rain without a single man dropping out. That performance broke the world's record for a forced march, then held by the Japanese Imperial Marines. I believe that record still stands.

It was paratroopers who held Bastogne with that certain pride and unbreakable spirit during the winter siege of 1944–45, turning the Nazis's last great offensive into a total failure for Germany. They fought with insufficient arms, ammunition, food, and winter clothing in temperatures that reached ten degrees below zero. Many later suffered amputations because of severe frostbite.

But Bastogne wasn't the end for us. We performed other missions with equal success. Our presence in Alsace helped thwart yet another

threatened Nazi breakthrough during the German Nordwind offensive in the Vosges Mountains. Later there were battles in Hage-
nau and the Rhine River crossings into the Ruhr Valley, diverting the
German armor reserves and clearing the way for General Patton to
attack and cut the valley in half, eliminating the Krupp arms empire.
More than a million German soldiers surrendered in that operation.
Then we rushed across Germany to liberate four concentration
camps, where German guards were still stoking the furnaces with human bodies as we tore through the barbed-wire enclosures. We witnessed atrocities there that were beyond human comprehension.

We fought battles through the Black Forest, Bavaria, and into Austria and Hitler's home in Berchtesgaden. Finally the Eagle came to
rest in the Eagle's Nest and Zell Am Zee, Austria, just up the road
from world-famous Innsbruck. Our war in Europe had come to an
end.

Before long we learned we were scheduled to spearhead the invasion of the Japanese homeland. We moved to Joigny, France, to
prepare ourselves for the long trip to our last battle. It was estimated
that as many as a million men might become casualties in that operation.

I was in the hospital being treated for recurring trench mouth
when we got the word that Japan had surrendered unconditionally.
Our Air Corps had dropped some kind of a bomb that had wiped out
an entire Japanese city. We couldn't believe it. Not a single bomb. But
it was true. Not one but two cities were destroyed by atomic bombs
before the Japanese finally saw the light. It was over. Thank God. We
could all finally go home. Too many of our buddies had been killed
and maimed. There were eleven of us left in A Company who had
jumped into Normandy with that outfit. All eleven of us had been
wounded at least three times each. Sergeant Vetland had been
wounded twice that many times and was still with us when we returned
home to our families. The four of us who had lived in Stable 13 in
England before the invasion had made it through: Donald B. Liddle,
Leonard Benson, Harold Phillips, and me, Donald R. Burgett.

Prior to D day, A Company was billeted in horse stables in the
small town of Auldbourne. The four of us had been assigned to Stable 13. The number thirteen had a special significance to me. My

father had worked in the Detroit Police Department's Precinct 13. For twenty-five years he drove Car 13. In jump school I was usually the first man in the second stick. There were twelve men in a stick, so I was the thirteenth man out the door. In Normandy I was wounded in "The Battle of Bloody Gulch," which was fought on 13 June 1944.

After our missions in Normandy, Holland, Belgium, the Rhineland, Bavaria, Germany, and Austria, Stable 13 was the only stable that had all of its men, although wounded, return for each campaign. All the other stables that housed A Company had men killed, severely wounded, or missing. The four of us from Stable 13 made it home. I was twenty years old. It had been a long war.